THE
MAN
WHO
SHOUTS

THE
MAN
WHO
SHOUTS

SIMON MICHAELSON

For April

First published 2023 by DB Publishing, an imprint of JMD Media Ltd, Nottingham, United Kingdom.

ISBN 9781780916491

Printed in the UK

PREFACE

Let me tell you, if I may, how I ended up working at the old Wembley stadium for the London radio station Capital Gold Sport on 31 May 1999 at the Division One play-off final between Watford and Bolton Wanderers, sitting in the press box alongside Jonathan Pearce, Billy Bonds and others as the 'Watford reporter'. It was a privileged position to be in; the press box was not far from the Royal Box and you can be sure that the royals were located somewhere with a good view of the pitch.

1

The world began again after the Second World War. People wanted to put the conflict behind them and have a good time and one way of doing that was through football, whether by playing or spectating. If you take a look at the history of the English Football League you will see that in season 1938/39 a full programme of matches was completed and Everton finished top of Division One, four points ahead of Wolves. In the following season, 1939/40, the league programme was abandoned in September after three matches with Blackpool at the top of Division One with a 100 per cent record, a point ahead of Sheffield United. The Football League did not begin again until 1946/47 with Liverpool pipping Manchester United by one point in Division One at the end of the season.

Similarly, there was an FA Cup final, Portsmouth beating Wolves 4-1 at Wembley in 1939, but the next final didn't take place until 1946 when Derby County beat Charlton Athletic after extra time by the same score.

I arrived on the planet shortly after, midway through the 1950s, a formative decade for English football. I began to get into the sport in the early 1960s and was fascinated to learn about what had happened in the decade in which I was born. I had a good teacher in my grandfather, Neville, who was a big football fan and a keen observer of the game. He was born in 1899 and followed football for his whole life until he passed away in 1973, the year I left school. He told me about how football had developed in postwar Britain and entertained me by recounting the feats in the decade of my birth of the great players who were around at the time. Grandpa Neville lived in the Potteries and we didn't see him that often but from an early age I used to look forward to family gatherings at which he would be present.

For a start Grandpa Neville told me about the 1953 FA Cup final, in which Blackpool beat Bolton Wanderers 4-3 after being 3-1 down, when Stan Mortensen scored a hat-trick for the Tangerines. The game is still known as the 'Matthews Final' after Bobby Charlton's hero, Stanley Matthews, whose selfless wing play inspired his side to victory. Three years later Matthews, who played in Division One for Stoke City as a 50-year-old, became the first European Footballer of the Year.

On the losing side in the Matthews Final had been Nat Lofthouse, who the previous year had gained legendary status himself and acquired the moniker the 'Lion of Vienna' when, in a 3-2 England win in Austria, he scored two goals and put in a heroic performance.

The 1950s was the decade English football grudgingly opened up to the wider world. Birds are used as nicknames for some Football League clubs – Crystal Palace are the Eagles, Norwich City are the Canaries and Sheffield Wednesday the Owls. Grandpa Neville's nickname for the England football team up until the 1950s was 'the Ostriches' due to the English football establishment's propensity to stick its head in the sand and its elitist attitude which led to an unwillingness to engage with foreigners who attempted to play the game 'we invented and gave to the world'.

I listened to Grandpa Neville as he told me that there had been three World Cups before the Second World War – 1930, played in and won by Uruguay; 1934, played in and won by Italy; and 1938, played in France and won by Italy – in which England had not taken part. After that the World Cup wasn't held again until after the Second World War, in 1950. By then the prize for the victors had been renamed the Jules Rimet Trophy after one of the two Frenchmen who had conceived the competition (the other being Henri Delaunay). In 1950 England became the first home nation to participate in the competition. The tournament was a disaster for England, one of the favourites to win it, and whose squad included players such as Billy Wright, Alf Ramsey, Tom Finney, Stan Mortensen, Wilf Mannion and Stanley Matthews. England beat Chile 2-0 in their opening match but then lost 1-0 to both Spain and, in one of the most shocking results in the country's history, the USA to be eliminated at the group stage.

Grandpa Neville told me that he believed that generally speaking English football had a superiority, rather than inferiority, complex at the time and that instead of an acknowledgement that the national team had fallen behind other countries in terms of fitness and tactics and there being an analysis of how it might learn from others and improve, lame excuses were made for the poor performance.

After the 1950 World Cup England fell back on their record of never having been beaten at home by a side from outside the British Isles. In 1953 the myth of invincibility on home soil was shattered by what Grandpa Neville told me was a brilliantly inventive Hungary side who won 6-3 at Wembley, with Nándor Hidegkuti scoring a hat-trick, Ferenc Puskás hitting two and József Bozsik one. Hungary were vastly superior to England, both individually and technically as a team. Similar to the Dutch in the 1970s, the 'Magnificent Magyars' thrilled the football world in the 1950s but never won the World Cup. Like the Dutch 20 years later, in 1954 Hungary reached the World Cup final only to be beaten by West Germany. But just to prove that the win at Wembley wasn't a fluke, Hungary beat England 7-1 in Budapest in 1954.

English football got its act together later in the 1950s and when it did the dividends were spectacular and led to the World Cup win in 1966.

Grandpa Neville was a Port Vale supporter but he had a good appreciation of other clubs and he delighted in telling me of the achievements of Wolverhampton Wanderers in the 1950s. Stan Cullis managed Wolves between 1948 and 1964 and helped to produce the most successful period in the club's history. In each of the seven seasons between 1952/53 and 1958/59 they finished in the top six, winning the title on three occasions – in 1953/54 (their first championship win), 1957/58 and 1958/59. They won the FA Cup in 1949 and 1960 and had Billy Wright, a one-club player who became the first man to win 100 England caps. He ended up with 105 caps, 90 of which were as captain, and was the forerunner of the modern-day David Beckham-style celebrity footballer through his marriage to Joy Beverley, a member of the all-girl popular combo the Beverley Sisters.

When I became a football reporter, I once turned up to do a game at Molineux in a taxi. As the driver slowed to a halt outside the ground he said 'hello, Billy' out of his open window. I initially thought that he must have been acknowledging one of his mates but there was no one nearby. I then realised that we were close to the statue of Billy Wright and he was paying his respects to the man, which, he told me, he always did when he arrived at the ground.

Grandpa Neville explained that unwittingly Wolves were instrumental in the birth of the European Cup. Floodlights had been installed at Molineux and Wolves played several high-profile friendlies against teams from around the globe. In 1954 they took on and beat Hungarian champions Budapest Honvéd 3-2. The Honvéd side included six members of the Hungary team that had won at Wembley the previous year, including Sándor Kocsis and Puskás. Reacting to the idea which had been posited in England that victories such as this meant that Wolves were somehow 'champions of the world', former France international Gabriel Hanot ran a piece in L'Équipe proposing a European club championship. UEFA accepted the suggestion and in 1955/56 the European Cup was born. Chelsea won the Division One title in 1954/55 and applied for permission to take part in the inaugural competition. Games against continental opposition had clearly caught the public imagination in England, with 60,000 people having been at Molineux to watch Wolves v Honvéd. Grandpa Neville was often scathing about those in positions of authority and he criticised the Football League's secretary at the time, Alan Hardaker, for lacking foresight and vision and persuading the league chairmen to oppose Chelsea's application.

Thus, the first European Cup, won by Real Madrid, took place without English representation. Real Madrid went on to also win the next four European Cups. When they won the trophy for the fifth time, in 1960, beating Eintracht Frankfurt 7-3 at Hampden Park in one of the most celebrated games ever played in the competition. Puskás was in their side, scoring four goals in that final.

Grandpa Neville was full of admiration for Manchester United for being the trailblazing first English club to enter the competition when they took part in the 1956/57 season under the enlightened leadership of Matt Busby, a pioneering manager, the first – Grandpa Neville told me – to have control over transfers, team selection and training. The board's decision to allow Busby the freedom he wanted was well rewarded. Busby became manager of Manchester United in October 1945, prior to the resumption of the Football League in 1946/47, and in 1948 they beat a Blackpool side that included Stanley Matthews 4-2 in the FA Cup final. It was United's first FA Cup win for 39 years and only the second in their history. At that time United were still playing home matches at Manchester City's Maine Road stadium as in 1941 Old Trafford had been hit by a bomb meant for the industrial complex at Trafford Park. United didn't move back to Old Trafford until 1949.

According to Grandpa Neville, in the early 1950s Busby showed courage by breaking up an ageing side and instead of buying expensive, already established players he introduced youngsters. In 1951/52 the Busby Babes won Manchester United's first title for 41 years. They followed that up by winning the championship again in 1955/56 and 1956/57, and on 4 May 1957 they were one game away from becoming the first team in the 20th century to win the double of Football League and FA Cup. On that day they lost the FA Cup final to Aston Villa in extraordinary circumstances. The game was played at a time when players were still permitted to barge the goalkeeper and after six minutes, with the score 0-0 Peter McParland crashed into Ray Wood, breaking the United goalkeeper's collarbone and leaving him unconscious. At the time substitutes were not permitted and Wood was replaced in goal by Jackie Blanchflower for all but the final seven minutes of the game when he returned as keeper, having played as best he could as an outfield player. Villa won the game 2-1, McParland scoring both their goals.

In a grave voice which conveyed the enormity of the tragedy, Grandpa Neville told me about the Munich air crash which had a far-reaching and profound impact on English football. On 6 February 1958 Manchester United were making their way home from Yugoslavia where they had drawn 3-3 with Red Star Belgrade in the second leg of their European Cup quarter-final to give them a 5-4 aggregate win and set up a semi-final against AC Milan. On the way back they stopped at Munich airport so that the plane could be refuelled. The runway was covered in ice and slush and the plane made two aborted take-off attempts. A third try was to be the last as the plane careered through a fence and hit a house. Of the 23 people who lost their lives, eight were Manchester United footballers – Roger Byrne (28), Eddie Colman (21), Billy Whelan (22), David Pegg (22), Tommy Taylor (26), Mark Jones (24), Geoff Bent (25) and Duncan Edwards (21). Edwards, at the heart of the Busby Babes, was already established as an all-time great. He had made his United debut as a 16-year-old in 1953 and first played for England in 1955 aged 18 in a 7-2 win over Scotland.

Of the Manchester United XI which had started in the 1957 FA Cup final, six – Byrne, Colman, Whelan, Pegg, Taylor and Edwards – lost their lives through the crash.

At the time of Munich, the Busby Babes were in contention to win a third successive league title, vying with Wolves at the top of the table. Their last Division One game before Munich had been a stunning 5-4 win against Arsenal at Highbury. Inevitably, after Munich they fell out of contention in the league, but on a wave of public sympathy they reached a second successive FA Cup final only to lose again, this time 2-0 to Bolton Wanderers with Nat Lofthouse scoring both goals. The European Cup also proved to be too much for them and they succumbed to AC Milan 5-2 on aggregate in the semi-final.

In Grandpa Neville's view the basis of Manchester United's greatness and legend, which like the flower of hope the snowdrop blossomed at the end of winter, was based on the way in which they responded to Munich, a tragedy of grotesque proportions and traumatic effect, to eventually achieve glory when in 1968 they realised Matt Busby's dream and won the European Cup.

*

When football first entered my consciousness in the early 1960s it was like a ray of early morning sunlight. Just before the time at which the Beatles awoke me to the possibilities of music, in the 1960/61 season Tottenham Hotspur became the first club to win the double in the 20th century. I was five years old at the time and although I wanted to see them, I never got to watch that Spurs side play. Even so the names of players like Danny Blanchflower, Dave Mackay, John White, Bobby Smith and Cliff Jones got inside my head and have stayed there ever since. I was lucky enough to see a great team play later in the 1960s though, Matt Busby's Manchester United.

My desire to watch Spurs play in the early part of the decade having not been fulfilled, the first game of football I attended was at the Jalan Besar Stadium in Singapore after my family moved there for three years in 1965. Every summer two English sides would tour and play against each other and also against a Singapore XI. In 1966 I saw Fulham beat a Singapore XI 6-0 with the 'Maestro'

Johnny Haynes arrowing an array of perfectly weighted passes over the heads of his diminutive opponents. It was a memorable and enthralling experience but the game was a little too one-sided to be completely satisfying.

The following year I went one better and saw the match between the two English touring teams, on this occasion Southampton and Leicester City, which promised to be more competitive. A couple of Saints legends, Ron Davies and Terry Paine, were playing, as was David Webb who became a legend at another club when he scored the winning goal for Chelsea in extra time in their 1970 FA Cup final replay with Leeds United. In the first game at Wembley, Chelsea and Leeds battled each other to a standstill in a 2-2 draw in which Webb had been left on his knees by the trickery of Eddie Gray. It was the way Webb responded to the public humiliation of the first game to ultimately triumph 18 days later which appealed so much to the neutral like me.

The story surrounding Leicester at the time I saw them play Southampton in Singapore was all about the goalkeeping position. In April 1967 the Foxes had sold Gordon Banks to Stoke City for £50,000. Sixteen-year-old Peter Shilton had made his Leicester debut in May 1966 and had played four times the following season. After the departure of Banks, he faced Southampton in Singapore in the summer of 1967 as Leicester's first-choice goalkeeper.

Shilton played his part in an entertaining 2-2 draw. After the game, as we made our way back to the car, we passed the Southampton team coach. The players had all got on board still in their kit. The door was open and in a split second of boldness I climbed on, and I went round the players asking for autographs which they gave willingly. What struck an impressionable 12-year-old was that every other word uttered by the players seemed to be an expletive. Before we'd reached the car the coach drove past, then David Webb took off his sweat drenched short sleeved red-and-white-striped V-neck shirt with a huge number six sewn on the back and threw it to me out of the window.

Those two games gave me a taste for watching live football and by the time we returned to England in 1968 the slow way, by boat with stops in Ceylon, South Africa, Senegal and Portugal, I had decided that when I got back home my priorities were firstly to stuff my face with the glorious sweets you could only find in an English sweet shop like gob stoppers, fruit salad (you have to get your five a day), sherbet lemons and pear drops and secondly to arrange a trip to watch Watford FC. I'd been offered a visit to Vicarage Road before we moved to Singapore but they were in Division Three and to my junior school mind that was virtually non-league and at that time they hadn't featured on my football radar. Then while we were living in Singapore, I had a change of heart and going to watch Watford play when we returned to England moved to the top of my agenda. A big attraction was that living in Leverstock Green, just outside Hemel Hempstead, it was only a bus ride to Watford and I would be able to go with a mate without any adult accompaniment.

Watford, then called Watford Rovers, were founded in 1881. The Football League was founded in 1888 and consisted of one division until 1892 when Division Two was added. In 1920 the Southern League's First Division, which included Watford, became Division Three of the Football League. In 1921 that became Division Three South when a corresponding northern section was added. Watford moved to Vicarage Road in 1922 and competed in Division Three South until 1957/58, never finishing higher than fourth. In 1958 they became founder members of Division Four following a re-organisation of the lower echelons of the Football League.

In 1952/1953 Cliff Holton, a player who spent much of his career on the fringe of the England team, scored 19 goals in 21 games to help Arsenal win the league title. In October 1958 Watford beat off competition from bigger clubs to sign the 29-year-old 6ft striker for £10,000. The move was a resounding success as Holton scored 42 league goals in 45 starts in 1959/60 and Watford finished fourth in Division Four to win their first promotion since joining the Football League.

Watford were still in Division Three when on Saturday, 31 August 1968 Steve and I jumped on the number 347 bus to go and watch them take on Stockport County in their third Division Three home match of the season. Watford had been finishing consistently in the top half of Division Three under manager Ken Furphy, who'd joined in November 1964, but at that time I was unaware of the history of the club and their form in recent seasons; I was just a 13-year-old kid wanting to have a fun day out.

My first impressions of Vicarage Road knocked me out and Watford became the window through which I gazed in wonder at the beautiful game. Watford lost

1-0 to Stockport – Jim Fryatt, a centre-forward with huge butcher's sideboards and a Mexican bandit's moustache which earned him the nickname 'Pancho', scoring the only goal of the game with a header from a corner. Fryatt was a much-travelled player who did the rounds of lower-league clubs mainly in the north of England, scoring goals pretty much wherever he went.

The result didn't matter at all; the whole experience of going to a game and watching football played at that level was wondrous – it was real, the shared experience with 8,500 or so other people roaring in unison when Watford attacked, the ground itself like some Roman amphitheatre with most of it open to the elements, even the urinals which stank of urine exactly like they should and didn't have a roof were mind boggling and like something I had never experienced before, the Watford left-back Johnny Williams kicked the ball further than I'd ever seen a human being kick a football – always down the line – the huge soggy chips smothered in salt and vinegar which we devoured after the game on the way to the bus stop tasted like a fine delicacy. This was all for me and I was immediately taken. At some point during that day a lifelong bond formed between me and Watford Football Club. The decision to follow a particular club is a huge one that is often taken at an early age, without any real deliberation or thought about the consequences, but once you have made your choice that is it. In our society it is generally more acceptable to get divorced than it is to change the football club you support.

The experience had been so enjoyable and uplifting that there was never any question in my mind that I wouldn't start going to games as often as possible. It was a day that had far-reaching consequences and would lead decades later to me reporting on Watford matches on the radio.

I didn't fully appreciate my good fortune at the time but in 1968/69 Watford had their best ever season up to that point in their history as they won the Division Three title. I am sure that it was much easier and more enjoyable to watch a successful, winning team and the players who formed that side became heroes to me.

In the midst of the title-winning season came what is known as 'a plum FA Cup tie'. Watford beat Cheltenham Town, Brentford and Port Vale to reach the fourth round of the competition and were then drawn away to Manchester United. By that time Watford were leading Division Three and they went into the game on a run of one defeat in 20 matches in all competitions. Ken Furphy was determined to make the most of the opportunity. To ensure good weather he took his players to Jersey to train, a move which caught the imagination of the public.

By the time of the match Watford were in the national spotlight and Stewart Scullion, a right-winger whose dribbling skills made an important contribution to the championship side, and after whom I named my pet white mouse, sensationally put them ahead in the second minute. Scullion drifted in from the right past a couple of United players and let fly from 25 yards with a shot which beat Jimmy Rimmer in goal as it sped into the top corner. Watford's defence, which was well organised and that season only conceded 34 goals in 46 league matches, repelled the inevitable United onslaught until the hour mark when, with the noise of the home supporters in the crowd of 63,498 making communication between Watford's defenders difficult, goalkeeper Micky Walker came for a cross and collided with his own centre-half Brian Garvey, spilling the ball to John Fitzpatrick who squared for Denis Law to equalise.

The result was a blessing because it gave the Watford public the chance to experience first-hand the aura surrounding Matt Busby and Manchester United, who on 29 May 1968 had conquered their demons and become the first English side to win the European Cup when they beat Benfica 4-1 after extra time at Wembley. They'd been beaten in European Cup semi-finals in 1957 by Real Madrid, in 1958 by AC Milan and in 1966 by Partizan Belgrade and finally winning the trophy, the pursuit of which had cost lives ten years previously, was an achievement almost too huge and too sweet to comprehend; it was a heroic triumph over tragedy. When considering the significance of a particular victory and how much it means, Manchester United's win over Benfica is off the scale.

I turned up at 6am on a Sunday and queued for a few hours to get the ticket which meant that I was part of Watford's record attendance of 34,099 on the evening of Monday, 3 February 1969 when the replay took place after a postponement the previous week. The iconic prial of aces – George Best, Bobby Charlton and Denis Law – were all playing. The Manchester United supporters were given the Rookery End which was normally the domain of the home fans and before the game they triumphantly celebrated the achievement of the previous May. For a full ten minutes in authentic Mancunian accents, they consistently maintained a chant of 'We are the champions, champions of Europe; we are the champions, champions of Europe.' It went on and on and on; I'd never heard a chant like it. The emotion in their voices reflected the joy which the triumph had brought ten difficult years after the horror of Munich.

On the night United's more skilful players were far better able to cope with the hard, slippery and bumpy pitch and they won comfortably 2-0 without ever having to exert themselves, Law adding to his goal in the first game with two more, the first laid on by an incisive cross from Best which bamboozled the Watford defence.

The defeat didn't do any harm to Watford's league season and promotion was sealed on Tuesday, 15 April 1969, Roy Sinclair striking the goal in a 1-0 win over Plymouth Argyle in front of a crowd of 22,515. I was on a school skiing trip to Austria and was gutted to miss the game and the celebrations on the pitch.

It all meant that in the 1969/70 season Watford would be playing in the second tier for the first time in their history, in a division which included clubs like 1967 League Cup winners Queens Park Rangers, 1969 FA Cup finalists Leicester City and Midlands giants Aston Villa who were actually relegated to Division Three at the end of the season. Watford had a tough start and didn't score in their first five league games. One of those was a 1-0 home defeat to QPR watched by Watford's record home league attendance of 27,968. With QPR being just down the road, they brought a large contingent and there were big rucks in the Rookery End before and during the game between rival supporters. It was the first time I'd seen football violence first-hand.

My main preoccupation during the school holiday in the summer of 1969 was waiting for Watford to score their first league goal of the season. It came on 30 August, at home to Sheffield United, their sixth league game. Watford were awarded a penalty and 'the leader of the team', Keith Eddy, coolly put it away. It had been a long wait but Watford had finally scored a league goal in Division Two and when I got back to school and was asked to write about 'what I'd done in the summer holiday' I wrote about Eddy's goal. I described in great detail how Watford were awarded a penalty, how the crowd went silent to allow Eddy maximum concentration and the ecstatic reaction when the ball hit the net.

My teacher didn't think much of my adolescent attempt at sports journalism and at the end of my carefully crafted piece she wrote, 'This isn't what you did in your school holiday.' Actually, it was; I waited all summer for that goal and when it came, I celebrated like crazy. It made my summer. Watford lost the game 2-1 but the home crowd had seen the team score its first goal in the second tier of English football. The teacher's reaction to my piece showed that not for the first time in the history of the world one human being didn't understand what was going on in another person's life.

That season was a struggle in the league. Watford achieved their objective and did enough to stay up but won only nine games out of 42, finishing fourth from bottom.

Out of nowhere, when no one was expecting it, came a proper FA Cup run. As a Division Two club, for the first time Watford had the luxury of a bye to the third round and were drawn to play away to Bolton Wanderers from the same division. Watford had won 3-2 at Burden Park in the league earlier in the season but part of the magic of the cup is that it pairs teams from different divisions who wouldn't normally play each other. It wasn't a tie to get excited about and I was sceptical about the chances of winning again at Bolton. I was wrong. Barry Endean, who would later achieve legendary status at Watford, scored twice in a 2-1 win on 3 January 1970. Endean was a force of nature. He was spotted by a Watford scout who covered the north-east of England. The season before he signed for Watford, he had played for two pub sides, Pelton Fell on a Saturday and the Black Bull in a Sunday league, and had scored a combined total of 220 goals for the two clubs. He played for Watford reserves at the beginning of the 1968/69 season and having impressed through his application, heading ability and work rate, he was signed on as a professional. Ken Furphy recognised Endean's worth and gave him his first start in the league on 9 November 1968. Just over a month later Endean got his first two goals for Watford in a win over Oldham Athletic and he became a key component of the side that won the Division Three title. He ended that season with 18 league goals from 28 starts.

After the FA Cup win over Bolton, Watford were rewarded with a home game against Stoke City who had finished the previous season in the top half of Division One and had Gordon Banks in goal. England's World Cup winning goalkeeper couldn't have been beaten by a shot from 25 yards out too often but in that fourth round FA Cup tie he was, Colin Franks' goal being the only one of the match. It was ridiculous and I ecstatically hugged a stranger after seeing Watford score.

Watford held their nerve to beat Gillingham 2-0 at home in the fifth round before drawing Bill Shankly's Liverpool at Vicarage Road in the sixth round. A win would take Watford further than they had ever previously been in the FA Cup. Liverpool had yet to become the dominant force in the English game and serial title and European Cup winners but Shankly had already laid the foundations on which the subsequent success was based, establishing an ethos and a belief and setting high standards.

Since Shankly had arrived at Anfield in 1959 they had won the league twice, in 1963/64 and 1965/66, and the FA Cup for the first time in their history in 1965. With Liverpool still in Division Two Shankly had signed two Scots in 1961 who became an integral part of the team that in the 1960s won those three trophies and challenged for more. Ian St John had arrived for a club record £37,500 from Motherwell and scored the extra time winner against Leeds United in the 1965 FA Cup final to give Shankly not only his first major trophy but what he called his greatest day in football. Ron Yeats, a centre-half who was made captain, cost £20,000 from Dundee United and earned the nickname 'Colossus'. Another integral part of the side was Tommy Lawrence, to whom Shankly gave his first-team debut in 1962 as a 22-year-old, and the goalkeeper went on to hold down a place as first choice between the sticks for the remainder of the decade. He was affectionately dubbed the 'Flying Pig' by Liverpool supporters for his propensity to throw around his 14st frame and to come racing out of his goal to snuff out opposition attacks.

Visiting fans arrived in Watford en masse on Saturday, 21 February 1970 and you could tell that they took their club and their football seriously. An apocryphal story circulated that Shankly had watched Watford the previous week and had left at half-time muttering, 'We've got nothing to worry about here.' Whether it was true or not the tale added spice to what was already an intriguing prospect.

Unlike for the visit of Manchester United the previous year, Watford supporters were in the Rookery End and it was from there just after the hour mark that I saw Ray Lugg nutmeg Liverpool left-back Peter Wall and play a diagonal curling cross into the penalty area right in front of where I was standing. Barry Endean anticipated the cross and flung himself at the ball before Geoff Strong could react. Endean landed in the soft mud just as the ball ended up in the net. Endean had a resemblance to one of the popular comedians of the day, Marty Feldman, and as he picked himself up and ran to the Watford supporters his eyes were popping out and the look on his face suggested that he'd just heard one of the funny man's best one-liners. Liverpool were not laughing though; Strong flung his arms around just after the goal went in and after the game Shankly decided that firm, decisive action was required. It was time to break up the first incarnation of his Liverpool side and out of the team went Lawrence, Yeats and St John who had all played at Vicarage Road that day. When Liverpool took to the field for the 1971 FA Cup final against Arsenal none of those three players featured.

Finally, I got to take part in a post-match celebration on the pitch along with hordes of other Watford supporters and from a safe distance of about 60 yards I triumphantly stuck two fingers up at the Kop.

The win over Liverpool was the undoubted highlight of my early years as a Watford supporter, although the FA Cup run came to a shuddering halt in a 5-1 semi-final defeat to Chelsea at White Hart Lane. With the score 1-1 at half-time, Chelsea's talented cup kings Charlie Cooke, Alan Hudson and Peter Osgood tore Watford apart in the second half.

Watford survived three seasons in Division Two before being relegated in 1971/72. By that time Ken Furphy and the nucleus of the side that had won promotion and reached the FA Cup semi-final had left Vicarage Road. Furphy departed in the summer of 1971, to be replaced by George Kirby at the end of whose first season as manager Watford finished bottom of Division Two.

A further relegation followed in 1974/75 and with Watford back in Division Four I had a dilemma. I had left school and started work and was playing as much sport as I could fit in – football on Saturday and Sunday, squash on Monday, football training on Wednesday and squash on Friday. I was playing for Emerald Vale in the West Herts Saturday League and I couldn't decide whether to keep doing that or go and watch Watford. At Vale we had a wise centre-half, Dave Thorpe, who was a bit older than the rest of us ('Old Man Thorpie, he just keeps rollin', he just keeps rollin' along') who was the sort guy you could go to for advice. I asked Thorpie whether he thought I should play on a Saturday or watch Watford. He said, 'You can always watch Watford when you're too old to play,' which I thought was sound reasoning, so I stopped watching Watford on a Saturday to concentrate on playing football. I played for Vale on a Saturday and Longdean Invaders Reserves in the West Herts Sunday League until a couple of years later I stopped playing for both when I decided to go travelling.

2

Morocco has played a part in my life. I've been there three times but my first visit in 1977 made the biggest impression and started a chain of events that led to me becoming a football reporter just over 20 years later. Jimmy and me put on backpacks and hit the road. The big trip at the time was overland to India, through Turkey, Iran, Afghanistan and Pakistan.

I hadn't read any Jack Kerouac at the time I decided to go travelling and I was initially inspired by a couple of mates who'd gone away. Catney and Gannit did the India trip in 1976 and came back bearded, tanned and grinning with exciting and outrageous stories. I thought, 'I want some of that.' Catney was so knocked out by it all that one night down our local, the White Horse, he climbed on to the flat tarpaulin roof about 20ft up and for our entertainment and amusement he jumped off, still grinning as he landed on his feet. It was his way of saying to the assembled gathering, 'Go travelling, I've been and it's good for you.' At the time I'd been out of school a few years and was working in an office in the City of London. In the glorious summer of 1976 I used to gaze wistfully out of the window at the clear blue sky and ask myself whether there was any more to life than working in an office. I decided that the only way to find out was to quit my job so I cashed in my pension and decided to spend it on a trip, trading certainty for the great unknown. I needed to escape and fly a little.

A couple of months before Jimmy and me left England I heard a programme broadcast on BBC Radio 4 called *Kathmandu for Christmas*, which heightened my sense of anticipation and longing even more. The programme was about a girl who in 1966 hitchhiked on her own on the hippie trail from Israel to Kathmandu, receiving unquestioning hospitality from the locals she encountered along the way, the aim being for her to reach Kathmandu by Christmas and meet up there with other travellers.

Jimmy and I decided not to do the India trip but we wanted somewhere exotic so we bought a one-way coach ticket to Alicante in Spain with a rough plan to make our way to Morocco, stay there for about a month before heading to Algeria, then Tunisia and up to Sicily and mainland Italy.

We played as a tennis doubles pair so we knew each other pretty well. Jimmy was good at sport and played football, cricket, tennis, squash and golf to a decent level. He liked sport so much that he used to go around singing, 'I like sport and cheese and biscuits, can I have some more of them please?'

We got to Ceuta, the Spanish possession on the tip of North Africa, spending time in Marbella, Granada and Algeciras on the way. We met people travelling in the opposite direction who had been to Morocco and the consistent message was, 'Take care, you're going to get hassled by the locals in Morocco.'

It's one thing being told something and reading about it in a guidebook, it's another experiencing it directly yourself.

I was 21 years old, Jimmy a year younger, and we were novices. In Ceuta we bought bus tickets to Tétouan with Spanish pesetas and had to disembark at the Spain-Morocco border to go through passport control and customs. Everyone else on the bus was a local and they all got through quickly; it took us ages to get cleared. The driver decided that he couldn't wait for us any longer and he drove off leaving us in Morocco, stranded at the border waiting for the next bus without any Moroccan dirhams to pay for another ticket.

Morocco is only about 30 miles from Europe but it felt like a million miles and we could have been on another planet. The air was thick with the smell of hashish which locals were smoking leaning against a wall, yards from the border crossing. We got talking to a youngster who spoke about four or five languages – all the Moroccans we met seemed to be linguists which gave them the ability to engage with foreigners from a wide range of countries – who when we told him our predicament very kindly lent us some local currency to pay the bus fare. He gave us his address in Tétouan so that we could go and pay him back the following day.

My feeling of remorse remains that we never managed to repay him because of the way events unfolded and the madness we got caught up in.

When we disembarked at Tétouan bus station we lost control of our destiny and we didn't regain it until about 24 hours later. As expected, we were greeted at the bus station by locals chorusing 'welcome to Morocco' and offering to help us. We were able to shake most of them off politely without causing offence but a couple of them who were a bit older were more insistent and wouldn't take 'no, we're OK thanks' for an answer.

It was the start of an elaborate game they played, in which we were the pawns. The prize for the locals was our money but at no point did they use violence or even threaten to use violence to try to get us to part with it. They were far more subtle than that – and subtlety is a trait I admire, so fair play to them. Their game involved applying psychological pressure which was supposed to persuade us to hand over cash. They were detailed in their preparation as well. They spent a long time hatching their plan which played out over the day we arrived and the following morning and involved about half a dozen of them taking coordinated action.

What the locals knew was that for most people who got the bus from Ceuta, Tétouan was their introduction to Morocco. They capitalised on our lack of knowledge by taking control very quickly before we had a chance to realise what was happening and to get used to the ways of the country.

It was late afternoon and the opening gambit was to take us to a shop in the medina and get us each to try on a djellaba, the flowing robe worn by Arabs, which frankly didn't suit us and which we didn't need or want anyway. Having got out of that one without parting with any cash the Moroccan pair, on finding out that we didn't yet have anywhere to stay, offered to fix us up with a room for the night. Except that they didn't so much 'offer' to help us find a room, they insisted on finding us one. We put up about as much resistance as an ice cream being devoured by a schoolkid on a hot day and just went along with it.

We had gone away to travel on a shoestring; Jimmy had to be back in England the following August to start at teacher training college but my plans were open-ended and I didn't know how long I'd be travelling. We were right at the start of our trip and we made it clear that we couldn't afford to give them any money, which didn't make any difference to the Moroccans.

After they had found us a room in a cheap hostel which we shared with a Finnish guy, they announced that they had to go and meet another bus. They weren't going to go without any money at all so we handed over the equivalent of about a quid each, then off they went and we thought that was the end of it. It turned out that it was only the beginning, the opening round of a 12-round contest. We'd only been sparring up until then and it got serious the following day.

One of the main reasons I travel is to experience a culture that is different to my own. Going to Benidorm and drinking 'tea just like mother makes' doesn't do it for me. If I go somewhere, it is for an authentic experience of a different way of life, of being and behaving, otherwise I may as well stay at home. We went to Morocco in 1977 as relatively affluent westerners and in the eyes of the locals we were fair game.

The day after we arrived Jimmy and I got up and left the hostel to walk round town, get some local currency and go and find the guy who had lent us money at the border the previous day so that we could pay him back. We hadn't got very far when a couple of youngsters we'd never seen before came up to us and said, 'Those two guys you were with yesterday, they're friends of ours and they've been arrested for selling you hash.' We didn't know how to respond so we mumbled something back and continued walking. Before long another Moroccan, this time on his own, approached us and told us, 'Those two guys who were just talking to you, don't take any notice of them, they're police informers.' He seemed to be trying to help us so we thanked him and he went off. Then not long afterwards the first two guys reappeared and repeated the same story, 'The two guys you were with yesterday have been arrested for selling you hash.' We weren't sure why they were telling us this because they would make the statement and not follow it up with a demand or anything. Then the other guy who was on his own would emerge from nowhere and tell us not to take any notice of the other two because they were police informers. This was briefly reassuring but the encounters kept being repeated over and over again. We were being watched and followed as we walked round Tétouan and would be approached as these guys, first the pair then the one working on his own, suddenly loomed out of an alleyway in the medina as we passed by. The three were obviously working together and after a while their repeating behaviour had the effect they presumably desired. We became disconcerted and disorientated. At one point as we were talking to the pair whose friends had been 'arrested for selling us hash', Jimmy started to shake. One of them noticed this apparent sign of weakness and asked him why he was shaking. 'Because I'm cold,' replied Jimmy as we stood there bathed in spring sunshine.

After this had gone on for a couple of hours with no sign of it ending, Jimmy and I were unsettled enough to decide that the only solution was to leave Tétouan and Morocco altogether, and we made our way back to the hostel to carry out this plan. It appeared that they expected this reaction from us and it played right into the hands of the Moroccan pair whose friends had 'been arrested'. It was what they wanted us to do and they followed us into the hostel and up to our room. Before we could close the door, they forced their way in. The whole experience had temporarily paralysed us mentally and physically and we didn't even have the wherewithal to close the door quickly enough to keep them out.

Once they were inside our room, they cranked up the pressure. First of all, they repeated the by-now familiar refrain, 'Those two guys you were with yesterday, they're friends of ours and they've been arrested for selling you hash.' This time we responded by saying categorically, 'We don't know what you're talking about, we haven't bought any hash.' On hearing that the one who seemed to be in charge said to the other, 'OK, search the room.' We watched as the guy got down on his hands and knees, crawled under a bed and came up clutching a large plastic bag full of powder, which could have been curry powder, or maybe ground ginger, or maybe it was hash; whatever it was he gave the bag to his accomplice who flourished it in the air as though it was incontrovertible evidence that we had bought hash from his friends who had been arrested, and he asked triumphantly, 'What's this then?' Everything had been leading to this moment. We were stunned by this unexpected turn of events and couldn't come up with a more imaginative response than to tell the truth and lamely say, 'We don't know how that got there.'

The main man wasn't having any of it and he told us that if we didn't each give them the equivalent in dirhams of about 40 quid, they would call the police and we would end up in prison. You hear stories of travellers getting wrongly convicted for drugs offences abroad and the thought flashed through my mind, 'I gave up my safe, secure office job in England to go travelling, I'm going to end up rotting in a Moroccan jail for five years, everyone will forget about me and that will be my life over.'

The guys had delivered what was supposed to have been the *coup de grâce*, the point at which we crumbled, gave them what they wanted and we all went our separate ways and got on with our lives. But we held firm and refused to hand over any cash which infuriated the main man and he smashed the bag on to my knee, splitting it and spilling the contents over the floor. There followed a stand-off, with them insisting that we hand over the money they demanded and us refusing to do so.

At this point fate intervened on our behalf and the situation was resolved in our favour in an instant just as the two guys must have thought that their plan was about to succeed. The Moroccans became increasingly frustrated by our refusal to give them what they wanted and they started to shout at us. Fortuitously for us they made so much noise that the owner of the hostel, a gentle Moroccan lady, came along to see what the fuss was all about and she brought an end to our ordeal. She could see immediately that a couple of her customers were being hassled and she threw the two guys out of our room. It was something she had probably witnessed before and it was not good for the reputation of her hostel. When Jimmy and I later looked back on what had happened, our theory was that a malleable hostel employee had planted the bag of hash or whatever it was in our room in return for a few dirhams. But crucially the owner was not part of the scam and she saved the day.

Suddenly the guys had gone and the game was over; an entertaining score draw, no one had won or lost, no one had been hurt. The Moroccans would go through the charade with another couple of travellers, maybe tweaking their tactics a little, and Jimmy and I could carry on with our travels.

Relieved and grateful we hastily packed our bags, paid for the room and splashed out on a taxi to take us back to Ceuta to avoid having to walk the gauntlet again at Tétouan bus station. When we crossed the border with Spain, I hadn't brushed all the powder off my jeans but thankfully it wasn't picked up by customs. Once back in Ceuta we discussed what to do next. I favoured going back to Morocco, to another town – maybe Tangiers – and giving Tétouan a wide swerve. We had set out with the intention of spending time in Morocco and I'm not easily deflected. I saw what had just happened as a learning experience and the glimpse I'd had of a foreign culture had left me wanting more. I hadn't been put off by what had happened and I was fascinated by Morocco. But Jimmy had been completely freaked out by the whole episode and thought that everywhere in Morocco would be the same as Tétouan. He didn't want to go back. Without consensus the only course of action was to choose the safe, sensible option and return to mainland Spain, which we did.

I've had some lucky breaks in my life and getting out of that predicament in Tétouan unscathed in the way I did ranks right up there.

*

Back in those days people tended to make an assumption when you were travelling with a backpack and you told them that you'd been to Morocco. Hash was cheap and readily available in Morocco and people assumed that your primary reason for visiting the country was to smoke.

After Spain, we crossed into Portugal, travelled the length of the Algarve, made our way up to Lisbon and then to Coimbra. In Coimbra we decided to split up and hitchhike separately to Rome where a cousin of Jimmy's, who he wanted to visit, lived. We had tried to hitchhike in Spain and Portugal but as two blokes hitching together, we found it very difficult to get lifts. We knew it would only be possible to hitch the 1,500 miles from Coimbra to Rome if we did it separately.

One of my lifts was through the Pyrenees in northern Spain. As we got chatting the driver asked me where I'd been and when I told him he made that classic assumption. As soon as I said the word 'Morocco', without saying anything he stopped the car, got out and retrieved a huge lump of hash from the back seat, some of which he crumbled into a little wooden pipe and offered to me. He was already out of his head when he picked me up and was even more stoned after he'd had a smoke of the pipe he'd made up. We set off and he was soon driving at over 100km an hour doing four-wheel skids round the bends with a sheer drop by the side of the road and no barrier. The guy had lived in England and was playing Earth, Wind and Fire loudly on the car stereo as he drove. It seems that was one of the ways he got his kicks. It was like an X-rated fairground ride, exhilarating and scary.

As I got out of the car relieved to still be in one piece, I said to him, 'That's the lift I'll tell people about first.'

3

Just over ten years after I went travelling, I decided to move from St Albans to London. I'd always wanted to live in a certain part of west London. I knew that the heart of the area I liked, All Saints Road, Ladbroke Grove and Portobello Road, would probably be beyond my reach so I concentrated on trying to get somewhere in North Kensington, W10, that was within walking distance of all the magical places. There was a mystique to that part of London. The Notting Hill Gate end of Portobello Road with its quiet row of well-kept, pastel-coloured cottages had the air of a country village. When I walked down Portobello Road towards the Earl of Lonsdale, past the antique shops, I got that liberating feeling of being abroad, maybe in a town in rural France. Flat-shares in that area were highly sought after and finding a good one that was affordable wouldn't be easy.

I didn't know when I started looking that because of my trip to Morocco I was holding a trump card in my back pocket.

I would have to work against character as I am unofficially the third-slowest person in the world. Back in the day a friend we called Turk, because of his liking for baklava, used to get frustrated because he wanted to do everything and go everywhere in a hurry. Three of us, Spiney, Bunit and me, would be sitting around playing backgammon and Turk would be rushing around trying to persuade us to get ready to go down the pub. Exasperated at how long it took us, he decided that we were the three slowest people in the world. Bunit was the slowest, Spiney was next and I was third.

A decent flat-share in London was like gold dust and would be snapped up within hours of being advertised. I knew that I was going to have to act quickly. My chosen method was to use the Capital Radio flat-share list which was a great service. Rooms in flats were advertised on a handwritten list and you had to go to Capital Radio in Warren Street and get a copy as soon as it was released at midday to stand a chance of getting the best available. People would grab the list and run to the nearest phone box as soon as it came out.

After a few weeks of trying without success, I saw a room advertised in W10 which looked promising and I went expectantly to meet the current occupants, Tim and Len, who were about the same age as me – in their late 20s or early 30s. They were very sociable and I thought straight away that they would make good flatmates. The flat was a decent size and the rent was affordable. Tim had lived there the longest, was in charge of running the flat, and he led the questioning to assess my suitability. In telling him a bit about myself I happened to mention that I'd been to Morocco. That was the trigger; Tim's eyes lit up when he heard the magic word 'Morocco' and the room was mine. Tim made the same assumption as the driver in the Pyrenees. It's funny the way life works.

*

I'd landed, I'd got to where I wanted to be and I knew that living in North Kensington would be good – but I didn't know just how good. I celebrated my arrival by buying a Spanish feast of chorizo, olives and Manzanilla from the Portobello Road delicatessen, R. Garcia and Sons. Walking home across Ladbroke Grove and down Oxford Gardens, lined with towering, ancient trees, the sound of the Doors' great existential anthem 'Riders on the Storm' crept down the street out of someone's open window and swirled around creating a familiar, comforting backdrop. Most song lyrics are a skeleton on which to hang a tune but Jim Morrison's are much more than that, they're coded messages to be handed down the ages. If you're going to be a rock god, do it properly like Morrison did. It didn't take much to shock the Establishment at the time and Jim knew how to do it and how to grab the attention of the public which was fine by me because he had something to say.

Angela, who'd been part of the bohemian crowd I'd knocked around with in St Albans, moved in with me and stayed for a while and although we were living in a small room in a flat-share, we were in London with all the possibilities that presented. It was early summer and it felt like I was in the right place at the right time.

My feeling of being at home was enhanced when I met and started hanging out with a group of local salt-of-the-earth geezers. These were people who had been born in and lived in the area for their whole lives. It was in west London but the sense of community was how I imagined the East End to be. There was a whole load of people who were living their entire lives in North Kensington which resulted in pretty much everyone knowing everyone else. The values which guided their lives were commitment to the locality and to each other. One of them had once moved away to another part of the country but he couldn't handle it and he soon moved back.

I met them at North Kensington Squash Club of all places. I was standing at the bar chatting with Gary. We looked about the same age and he asked me when I'd been born. '1955,' I told him. He replied, 'Really so was I, what month?' 'July,' I told him. 'Me too! What day?' he responded. 'The seventh.' 'What? So was I!' said Gary. It seemed that our friendship was written in the stars.

There were six of us who hung out together as a unit and people called us the 'Six-Pack'. There was Gary (a decorator; he was into football but didn't follow a particular club), Neil and Glen (both scaffolders, both Spurs supporters), George (a taxi driver, QPR), Mick (a croupier, Chelsea), and me (Watford).

Apart from me the Six-Pack all had some sort of facial scar although I never got round to asking how they got them. We all liked a drink and we would meet in pubs and talk about football. It was an unwritten rule that whenever we met, football was just about the only topic of conversation. That suited us fine; it was exactly what we wanted. They welcomed me in and I would be invited to Gary's and fed huge roast dinners which we ate while watching the Sunday afternoon football on TV. One of our pubs was the North Pole and I won a bottle of wine there once for singing 'Green, Green Grass of Home' on the karaoke machine on a Sunday lunchtime. Most of the time I can't sing but, on that occasion I was so glad to be there, part of the group. After a few beers and with endorphins released after a Sunday morning game of squash the song came out just right and I held the tune all the way through with a smile in my voice. The crispy roast potatoes placed on the bar for customers enhanced my feeling of well-being even further.

It wasn't the first time in my life that I'd connected through football. When I was hitching in Portugal from Coimbra to the Spanish border on my 1977 trip, I got a lift from a Portuguese lorry driver who spoke no English. I only knew a few words of Portuguese but it didn't matter. When I told him that I was English his face lit up and he grinned and immediately said 'Bobby Moore'. I smiled back and gave him a thumbs up and the obvious reply, 'Eusébio.' We sat in the cab of his truck rolling through the Portuguese countryside trading the names of footballers from each other's country. His next offering was 'Bobby Charlton' to which I responded with 'José Torres'. His 'Geoff Hurst' was met with 'António Simões', and so it went. There was only going to be one winner as I have to confess that at the time my knowledge of Portuguese footballers didn't extend much beyond the national side of 1966 and the Benfica side of 1968. I ran out of Portuguese names before he ran out of English ones but by then football had worked its magic and for the rest of the journey, we sat there in a comfortable silence taking in the scenery.

Through football I also formed a bond with the locals of North Kensington. It was the summer of 1989 and football was moving back towards the centre of my universe, I was being seduced all over again. Mention a particular year to a football fan and they will immediately associate it with a football memory, maybe the FA Cup final, the greatest one-off showpiece event in the domestic game. With the league programme you can't guarantee the same climax that the FA Cup final gives you. League titles are more highly prized but they are usually won more quietly, after a long series of matches and it's not always easy to recall the game which clinched a league title. There are exceptions that spring to mind such as in May 1971 when Ray Kennedy scored the only goal of the game to clinch the championship at White Hart Lane in Arsenal's final league game of the season, five days before they beat Liverpool 2-1 in the FA Cup final. Sometimes though a club can win the title on a day when they are not even playing, like in 1972 when Brian Clough's Derby County were on holiday in Cala Millor in Majorca and learned that their nearest challengers, Leeds United and Arsenal, had failed to get the results they needed – Derby had already completed their fixtures – and that they were league champions.

1989 couldn't have been more different. Mention 1989 to a football supporter and, whatever their team, a game played on Friday, 26 May that year will probably come to mind. It was the final First Division match of the 1988/89 season and it decided the destiny of the title. It was the perfect denouement to the league season. Arsenal went into the game knowing that they needed to win by two clear goals to overtake Liverpool and lift the title. The weight of history was so heavily against the Gunners it's surprising that it didn't crush them. If Arsenal had been fully aware of the statistics which football commentators and reporters love to trot out, they probably wouldn't have bothered to turn up for the match. Arsenal hadn't won at Anfield since the 1974/75 season. Liverpool were unbeaten at home in 1989 and had won 13 of their previous 14 league games. They had won the FA Cup the previous Saturday and were reigning league champions. In the previous 25 seasons Liverpool had won the title a dozen times. Previously in the 1980s, with Everton also a force, the title had only left Merseyside once, in 1980/81 when Aston Villa won it. In the 1980s Merseyside virtually considered the Division One trophy to be its property.

Even now knowing the outcome I still get excited watching the game. When Arsenal take the lead in the 52nd minute, Alan Smith glancing in Nigel Winterburn's free kick, I think, 'Surely Arsenal don't actually go on and win the title.' I watched the game at The Pavilion in North Kensington and listened to Brian Moore deliver one of his finest commentaries. In time added on at the end of the game, he called the action, 'Arsenal come streaming forward now in surely what will be their last attack. A good ball by Dixon, finding Smith, for Thomas charging through the midfield. Thomas, it's up for grabs now! Thomas, right at the end! An unbelievable climax to the league season, well into injury time, suddenly it was Michael Thomas bursting through, the bounce fell his way, he flicks it wide of Grobbelaar and we have the most dramatic finish maybe in the history of the Football League. The top two, challenging on the night and the title possibly decided in the last minute of the whole season.'

The 2-0 win meant that Arsenal and Liverpool both finished the season with 76 points and an identical goal difference of +37. Arsenal won the championship on goals scored, with 73 to Liverpool's 65. After everything had clicked into place at the end of a 38-match season I was left with a bemused, disbelieving grin on my face, and speechless. Only football can do that to you and sometimes it's difficult to find the words to express how you're feeling. As Sir Alex Ferguson said after another dramatic finish to a game, 'Football, bloody hell.' It was an eloquent statement, the point being that the great Ferguson, normally so incisive, accurate and to the point in his post-match assessments, had been humbled and brought to his knees by the occasion. At Anfield, Arsenal staged a perfectly executed smash and grab and left Merseyside with the most valued piece of silverware in the English game.

I'd watched the pictures but the words of Brian Moore, which had expertly captured the significance and drama of the event, had been important as well.

I'd first come across Moore in 1968 when London Weekend Television launched *The Big Match*, which was screened on a Sunday afternoon and showed extended highlights of games played the previous day. It concentrated on fixtures in the London area but also showed clips of matches played in other regions. The tone was set by a bright, bouncy theme tune and a main commentator and presenter in Moore who was exuberant and more than any other commentator at the time fired my enthusiasm for football. In his early days he got so excited by football that he couldn't help going into overdrive when a goal was scored, he couldn't hold back. In later years, when he'd calmed down and become more measured, he would get embarrassed when he introduced clips of games on which he'd commentated as a young man, and with a smirk would jokingly say something like, 'I'm not sure who the commentator is in this clip.'

*

Liverpool v Arsenal was an important game for another commentator as well, Jonathan Pearce. Capital Gold Sport had launched at the start of the 1988/89 season to provide extensive and committed commercial radio coverage of London football, with Pearce as its inspiration, driving force and main commentator. With typically immaculate timing at the end of that first season Pearce found himself commentating on a game which saw a London club win the title for the first time in 18 years. I didn't know it in 1989 but I would, like others who worked with him, come to know Pearce as 'JP' and would hear many times through Capital Gold Sport headphones his commentary on the Michael Thomas goal which clinched the title for Arsenal.

Brian Moore called it the most exciting night of his television career and I left the pub after the game in a state of wonderment thinking 'somehow I have to get more involved in football'. It was only a vague yearning and I didn't know how I was going to fulfil it. I had no plan and it was Angela who, without me saying anything or telling her what I was thinking, showed me the way. She gave me a precious gift – a brilliant idea. Angela was an avid reader of the London listings magazine *Time Out* and shortly after the Liverpool v Arsenal game she noticed an ad in the 'Sportsboard' section for football reporters to work on hospital radio. Of course, she was well aware of my interest in the game and she said to me, 'You should go for that.' I couldn't think of a reason why not, so I did.

I've never sought the limelight in my life and trying to do something 'in the media' would have never occurred to me on my own. It's true that I had been on television a couple of times but on both occasions it had been without my prior knowledge. The first was in February 1969 during Watford's Division Three title-winning season. The *Match of the Day* cameras didn't get to Vicarage Road very often in the 1960s but one Saturday the weather was so bad that there were hardly any matches in England that hadn't been postponed. *Match of the Day* had to show something, so it ended up covering Watford's 5-1 win over Rotherham United. For a fleeting moment a 13-year-old was shown in the crowd in his green anorak and Watford bobble hat celebrating a home goal.

My second television appearance came some years later when Tottenham Hotspur and Manchester City drew 1-1 in the 1981 FA Cup final. Tickets for FA Cup final replays were much easier to obtain than for the original match. All I had to do was turn up at Wembley early on the Sunday after the drawn game and queue up. It was while I was waiting in line that I was caught by a television film crew and I saw myself on the news for a few seconds that evening.

Those appearances didn't lead to any offers of work and the idea of getting into football reporting would not have entered my mind if Angela hadn't suggested that I respond to the ad. Angela turned out to be the best agent I could have had and she didn't even ask for a penny.

I telephoned in response to the ad only to discover that I was too late, all the vacancies had been filled, but a seed had been sown and I began to check *Time Out* myself. Not long afterwards a similar ad appeared and this time the third-slowest person in the world excelled himself. I was on to it in a flash, the first person to respond. The main person at Charing Cross Hospital Radio was Mike Emery and he invited me to the studio the following Saturday 'to see how the programme works'.

*

I had the feeling that Mike was on my side right from the start but I still had to do enough to convince him to take me on. The first Saturday I showed up was 19 August 1989, the opening day of the 1989/90 season. I watched the show from behind the scenes and then after the final whistles had blown around the country I was invited on air for a chat with Mike, who was presenting. I didn't have to say anything particularly earth-shattering or profound but the conversation flowed and I seemed to meet expectations. It appeared that all I needed to do was talk coherently and reasonably interestingly about football, which I was capable of doing without any problem.

After we'd finished analysing the day's results I sat back and listened, entranced, on headphones as Mike interviewed Trevor Francis, then the 35-year-old manager of Queens Park Rangers. I took the interview in far more than I would have done if I had simply been listening to it on the radio, because I felt involved. The immediacy of it was electrifying. It was almost as though England's first £999,999 player, the man who headed the only goal in Nottingham Forest's 1979 European Cup final win over Malmo, was talking directly to me. I'd watched a 16-year-old Francis score for Birmingham City against Watford at St Andrew's and now I was hearing Mike ask him about his management style, which had been criticised for being overly disciplinary following Francis' decision to fine Martin Allen for missing a QPR match to attend the birth of his first child. Mike didn't mention this incident specifically, but in response to a general question about his style of management Trevor said, 'The players at QPR won't be asked to do anything I didn't have to do as a player, and if they do what I tell them everything will be all right.' That approach seemed a little simplistic to me and my involuntary response was to start softly chuckling. As he continued with the interview, Mike glared at me and waved a hand in my direction to quieten me down. Mike was quite right, I was bang out of order, and a little embarrassed I shut up immediately.

On my first day I'd broken what I came to understand is a golden rule of broadcasting – always respect your guest – but fortunately Mike didn't hold it against me. I'm sure he put my indiscretion down to inexperience and over-excitement and he let it pass without mentioning it. It was a good lesson. I quickly realised that if I was going to learn anything from coming into contact with football people I was going to have to approach them with humility. After all, how could someone who had never played at a higher level than the West Herts Sunday League Division One not be respectful of footballers who have played professionally at the highest level?

I did enough on that first day to be taken on and for Mike to tell me generously in the pub after the show that I was a 'natural'. Mike was effectively handing me a passport which would give me access to a new world.

Football had always been there but somehow it had kept me at arm's length; now was my opportunity to get closer, to touch it and to feel it, and maybe even to have a glimpse behind the veil. I'd found an opening and had darted through.

On top of that I was ready for an adventure. In the past, adventures had usually involved going abroad and travelling like in 1977. Now I was about to set out on a voyage of discovery in my homeland, and when I started out the world of football reporting was as foreign to me as years earlier the strange fairy chimneys and weird-coloured rock formations of Cappadocia in Central Anatolia in Turkey had been.

I'd had very little direct contact with footballers and I wanted to find out more about them. I'd climbed on to the Southampton team coach after watching them play Leicester City in Singapore in 1967, but apart from that I'd only collected the autographs of Watford players after home games in the early 1970s. So all I really knew about footballers was that they swore a lot and that they could just about write their names.

4

You don't know whether you can do something until you try.

I would find out on Saturday, 2 September 1989 whether I could report on a football match on the radio. The first game I covered was for Charing Cross Hospital Radio, in Division Three at Brisbane Road when Leyton Orient faced the winners in 1888/89 of the first Football League, Preston North End. It was a walk into the unknown. The instructions I was given were to concentrate on goals, sendings off and major incidents, but I didn't know what the expectations of the people running the show were and whether I would be able to meet them. It was a case of 'make it up as you go along' which I liked because it allowed me to be creative, albeit within the confines of reporting on an event. I could use my initiative; no one was forcing me in a particular direction. I was free to take decisions for myself and to begin to develop a style.

The first differences to going to a match as a spectator were that I didn't have to queue up at a turnstile or pay money to get into the ground. I had to turn up much earlier than I would have done as a paying fan, about two hours before kick-off, and so I got there ahead of the crowd. All I had to do on arrival was find the right window and collect the press pass that was waiting for me. In the ground there was a press room where I could mix with other reporters before the game. I was treated with respect by the press steward who was there to help me to do my job. He gave me a match programme and a cup of tea and told me where to find the press box.

Once in the press box I located the person I'd been told would give me some guidance, Dave Victor – great name with a persona to match – who as far as local radio coverage of the club went was Mr Leyton Orient and had been for years. Dave also worked for Charing Cross Hospital Radio but was covering the Preston game for another station. He showed me the basics like where to sit and where to connect my phone, and his friendliness, helpfulness and good humour settled me down. I thought, 'If this is the calibre of person I'm going to meet in the press box I'm in the right place.'

Once the Charing Cross Hospital Radio Sports Show started at 2pm I was on my own. Dave couldn't tell me what to say; it was up to me to set the scene, to introduce the game to the listeners and to try to stimulate a sense of anticipation. The first words I uttered were, 'Welcome to the mysterious East End of London, where we're hoping to see some of the wonders of the Orient served up in footballing form this afternoon.' Once the game kicked off it was down to me to interpret the action and to give concise, meaningful reports. It was a good outcome for Charing Cross Hospital Radio as the game ended Leyton Orient 3 (Steve Castle, John Sitton, Alan Hull) Preston North End 1 (Tony Ellis).

No one told me how I'd done and I went into a sort of suspended state as I waited to find out whether that would be my first and last game. I must have done OK because I was given a Division One game the following week and I was surprised to be told that on 9 September 1989 I would be going to a top-of-the-table clash at The Den to report on Millwall against Coventry City.

Millwall were flying at the time. In 1987/88 they had won the Division Two championship and gained promotion to the top flight of English football for the first time in their history. With a strike force of Teddy Sheringham and Tony Cascarino, and Terry Hurlock in midfield, Millwall had an amazing first season in Division One. They ended the 1988/89 season in tenth place, which was actually their lowest position all season.

Millwall made an unbeaten start in 1989/90, winning two and drawing two in their first four fixtures. Now they faced Coventry, who themselves had won three of their first four games. It was one of the games of the day. I travelled by train to The Den – Millwall's old home of the same name – to cover the game, and looking out at the bleak south London landscape of tower blocks and wasteland I couldn't help thinking how much the world needs football.

The last time I'd been to The Den had been to watch Watford lose 3-0 in the era when Millwall had legendary players such as Harry Cripps, Derek Possee and Barry Kitchener. It had been an uncomfortable experience. Away supporters are treated with hostility at any ground but at Millwall they knew how to chill the atmosphere a few degrees lower. The Den, an apposite name for the ground, had an appropriate location in Cold Blow Lane.

Now I was going to a Division One game as a reporter and I felt that the tables had been turned. There was a great mural depicting the history of Millwall painted on a wall inside the ground and as I walked past it I felt like one of the Greek soldiers inside the Trojan Horse which infiltrated the city of Troy. The match itself was hugely entertaining. Coventry City lost their goalkeeper early on and replaced him with the 5ft 7in David Speedie of all people. It ended Millwall 4 (Teddy Sheringham 2, Steve Anthrobus, Ian Dawes) Coventry 1 (David Smith) and sent the Lions to the top of Division One.

*

Not long after my visit to The Den I had my first encounter with a giant.

I'd long followed Malcolm Allison's career and considered him to be one of football's more interesting personalities. He projected a fun public image – the playboy lifestyle, the fedora, the champagne and the cigars – but on top of that he had a more serious, thoughtful side. He was multi-dimensional.

He was also unpredictable and throughout his career you never knew what he was going to do next. One constant, though, was that he never lost his love for the game. He was also a brilliant, innovative coach and he had big cojones.

Grandpa Neville had been an admirer and had made me aware of him. When Allison breezed into Maine Road in the summer of 1965, charmed into taking a coaching job there by the newly appointed Manchester City manager Joe Mercer, Manchester United were league champions. City had finished the previous season 11th in Division Two. In partnership with Mercer, Allison had the belief in his coaching methods, the ability to spot talent and powers of motivation to take on Manchester United in their own back yard in the face of the burgeoning legend of the Old Trafford club. Allison was driven by the belief that, despite the brilliance of United, there was no reason for City to live in their shadow. It was a bold ambition.

Allison combined with Mercer to give City up until then the most fruitful period in their history in terms of trophies won. They won the Division Two title by five points in 1965/66, then in their first season back in Division One they were 15th, 21 points behind champions United. The following season City won their first Division One title for 31 years, only the second in their history, finishing two points ahead of second-placed United. The success continued, with City winning the FA Cup in 1969 and both the League Cup and the European Cup Winners' Cup, the club's first European trophy, in 1970, making them the first English team to win a European and a domestic trophy in the same season.

A key part of the trophy-winning side was Tony Book, a defender whose story is one of the most extraordinary in 20th-century English football. It showed that when he was at the height of his powers Allison had a conviction that he was right when others were telling him otherwise, and also that his ability to spot a player in the unlikeliest of circumstances was unsurpassed by anyone in the game at the time.

Allison's first managerial job was at Southern League Bath City in 1963 and Book was Bath's captain. He had played in non-league football his entire career, and was not far from celebrating his 30th birthday. When Allison became Plymouth Argyle manager in 1964 he took Book with him for £1,500. In the summer of 1966 Allison persuaded a reluctant Mercer that City should part with £16,000 for Book, now 31 years old, an age at which some footballers start to think about retirement, and play him in the top flight. Book's success story mirrored City's own, as he shared the 1969 Football Writers' Association Footballer of the Year Award with Dave Mackay, and captained City throughout their triumphant years until he retired from playing in 1974 at the age of 39.

But it was the prowess of Manchester City going forward, based on the contribution of three exceptional players, which made the team so exciting to watch. Mercer signed right-winger Mike Summerbee for £35,000 in 1965 from Swindon Town and Allison gave him the licence to attack, also playing him at centre-forward. Then, just before the March 1966 transfer deadline, came Colin Bell. With Mercer prevaricating, Allison had his way and City forked out £42,000 to take him from Bury. Bell's stamina was prodigious; Allison nicknamed him 'Nijinsky' after the famous racehorse and convinced him that he could be the great player that he became. Another player Allison wanted was one whose confidence didn't need boosting – if anything, Francis Lee needed calming down. Lee arrived from Bolton Wanderers for a club record £60,000 in October 1967, scored a crucial 16 goals in 31 league appearances in his title-winning first season and for five seasons from 1969/70 was City's leading goalscorer.

In 1969, around the time of Manchester City's FA Cup final win over Leicester City, Allison had turned down a lucrative contract offer from Juventus to stay at Maine Road. For a long time Allison had wanted to be in sole charge and became increasingly frustrated as Mercer didn't keep what Allison perceived to be a promise to step aside. Their relationship crumbled and in 1972 Mercer departed to become general manager at Coventry. When Allison finally got the top job it proved too much for him; he couldn't recapture the earlier glory days and the team struggled. Although his position was not under pressure, in March 1973 Allison, feeling it was time to move on, unexpectedly resigned and accepted an offer from Ray Bloye to become manager of Crystal Palace, who were struggling in Division One.

Allison couldn't keep Palace up as they lost five of their last seven games, and the next season was no better as it ended in a second successive relegation. He couldn't get Palace promoted but his stay at Selhurst Park was illuminated by a glorious run to the FA Cup semi-final, the first time they had reached that stage of the competition, beating Leeds United, Chelsea and Sunderland – all from higher divisions – on the way. Allison's stay at Selhurst Park ended in May 1976 when he and film actress Fiona Richmond were photographed in the communal bath with the players, a stunt for which he received a Football Association disrepute charge.

There followed a couple of seasons at Galatasaray then after a spell in Memphis he rejoined the first three league clubs he had managed – Plymouth Argyle (1978/79), Manchester City (1979/80) and Crystal Palace (1980/81). Comebacks sometimes work but none of these did; he was sacked by City and his second spell at Palace only lasted for 55 days when he was fired after relegation from the top flight. He found solace in Portugal and in 1981/82 proved that he could still do it, winning the Primeira League and Cup of Portugal double with Sporting Lisbon.

Then came unspectacular spells at Middlesbrough (1982 to 1984), Willington (non-league, 1984), Kuwait (national coach, 1985/86), and back in Portugal with Vitória de Setúbal (1986 to 1988) and Farense (1988).

On 7 October 1989 our paths crossed. I hadn't been working for Charing Cross Hospital Radio for long when I was asked to take on the role usually performed by Mike Emery, and present the Sports Show from the studio. After the final whistles had blown at the matches we were covering, as usual reporters at the grounds invited players and managers to the press box to be interviewed by the presenter. We had a reporter at the Surrey Docks Stadium covering a GM Vauxhall Conference game between Fisher Athletic – who were managed by Allison – and Chorley. Malcolm's career had gone full circle and he was back in non-league football. At around 5pm I heard the producer of the show say into my headphones, 'We've got Malcolm Allison on the line.' Wow! I had a few seconds to let the information sink in and to think about what I was going to ask him. Immediately thoughts started swirling around in my head.

What came to mind was a book called *The Master Game* by Robert S. de Ropp which Malcolm called 'the most important book I've ever read'. He mentioned the book to the media after being sacked at Manchester City by Peter Swales in 1980, saying, 'The most important thing in the book to me was he said the most dangerous thing any person can have is an ego.' A reporter fell into the obvious trap and asked him, 'But aren't you famous throughout the land as having a massive ego?' Malcolm's response was spot on, 'People think so, but I couldn't be sitting here talking to you if I had a massive ego, at the moment, because I've just been sacked from my job, means that I'm incompetent at my job and er if I had an ego that would be the most destructive thing and therefore no way I could handle this situation.'

After he had been sacked, Malcolm addressed his players as a group, saying, 'I'd just like to thank you for all the hard work, and I'm sure that you'll be successful in the future, so I'd just like to say "cheerio" to you.' He then went to them individually with a message for each of them, 'See you Tom'; 'work hard'; 'look after yourself'; 'keep working'; 'don't forget what I said to you about fighting off them fucking injuries', tapping them affectionately on the back of the head, wishing them well. The players clearly meant a lot to him and he was genuinely sad that he would be leaving them and wouldn't have the opportunity to help them develop as footballers and as people. It was touching; he clearly cared.

The Master Game was a point of connection between Malcolm and myself. It was the sort of book I was reading in the late 1970s. It wasn't the type of book I thought a football manager would read, let alone describe as the most important he'd ever read; it was a book that was popular with hippies and people associated with the counterculture.

The book describes pathways to higher consciousness beyond the drug experience. It talks about the need people have to give meaning to their lives and describes several games people play to try to achieve this, and their aims, which vary – glory or victory; fame; wealth; raise family; appreciation of beauty; knowledge; salvation (religion). One of the other games has no aim while the aim of the Master Game itself is the attainment of full consciousness or real awakening.

About ten years after I'd come across the book, I found myself sitting in a studio interviewing Malcolm Allison on Charing Cross Hospital Radio.

I didn't know how I'd find Malcolm. I introduced him to the listeners by saying, 'Right now we actually have Malcolm Allison on the line, some of you might have heard of him, hello Malcolm.'

The good news was that Fisher had beaten Chorley 2-0 that day, Paul Gorman scoring both goals, and I could sense immediately that he was in a good mood. There was a buoyancy to his voice as he returned my greeting and it seemed to me that despite everything that had happened to him the zest was still there. I started by mentioning *The Master Game*, asking him whether it was still his favourite book.

'One of my favourite books, yeah,' he replied.

'Because you're a bit of a philosopher as well as a football manager, is that right?'

'I think that life's all about philosophy.'

'And you're still smiling?'

'I think the serious side of life, you deal with it, the other side of life is a happy side where you should enjoy it, and I'm fortunate enough to work at a job which I really enjoy.'

Malcolm was running mass coaching clinics at the Surrey Docks Stadium which were free to local youngsters, and he talked about this, 'I'm trying to teach them how to train, so that as they grow up, they will know how to train, for any game, whether it be tennis or hockey or football, or rugby, they will know how to train. The most important thing is flexibility and strength, if you've got flexibility and strength in any game that you're quite good at you're going to be better, and also trying to teach them concentration which is very, very important.'

I was intrigued as to how he'd overcome the language barrier when he'd coached abroad. 'I found that when I first went to Turkey, I found it very difficult in the first ten days but afterwards I didn't have any problem and from then on, I never ever used an interpreter and I found that the language barrier is not what people think it is, especially if they understand what you want and they respect you, if they respect you that's the main thing. I was very fortunate to win a championship and a cup in Portugal and I got on very, very well with the players, it's not a problem I don't think. You have to learn the language; you have to know some of the language but it's not a major problem that people think it is. I had a teacher but I found that my enthusiasm when I was coaching, I had to speak in English, I couldn't speak with the enthusiasm in Portuguese, and they soon pick up all the important words.'

I was really enjoying the exchange, which seemed to be going well, but I had a producer who rather than just let me get on with it kept barking suggested questions into my headphones while I was listening to Malcolm's replies. I ignored them as best I could but eventually, I relented and asked one of the producer's questions.

It was about nine months before the 1990 World Cup finals and England, under Bobby Robson, were on course to qualify. A question which the producer kept insisting I ask Malcolm was, 'Who is Robson's natural successor?' At the time Robson's position as England manager was not in any doubt. There was no sign of his tenure coming to an end and it was not a question which would have ever occurred to me. To try and get the producer to keep quiet, I eventually succumbed and asked Malcolm, 'Who do you see as Bobby Robson's natural successor?'

The flow of the interview was interrupted and Malcolm was momentarily taken aback. He hesitated before saying, 'When Robson finishes? Oh dear, it's a very difficult, er…' and then tailing off. It was obvious he thought it was a dumb question. I wanted to say, 'Sorry Malcolm, it's not my question,' but of course I couldn't.

With a little prompting I managed to get the dialogue back on track and he answered in general terms by saying, 'I think that the most important thing about being an England manager is being a good selector of players because you don't have much time to do actual work, training with them and I think that's the biggest mistake England ever made is not make Bob Paisley manager, because he was a good selector of players, or Brian Clough because he's proved that he's such a good motivator.'

Malcolm couldn't have mentioned a better name than Brian Clough because he was a hero at Charing Cross Hospital Radio. Before my time Clough had given a 20-minute interview and promised to take the FA Cup to the hospital if he ever won it.

Fisher Athletic wasn't quite the stature of club Malcolm had worked at for most of his career and to wrap up the interview I asked him if he wanted to get back into the big time. He gave me the answer I expected, 'I'm in the big time.' I thought, 'Of course you are,' and I said, 'I know, you're big time wherever you go.' He was quite happy for me to gently tease him, but I meant it and laughing he said, 'I love my job, I love where I work, I love making people better.' I asked him, 'And you get involved, don't you?' He answered, 'That's what life's all about, I think.'

I was not long into my life as a football reporter and I'd already made Malcolm Allison laugh.

*

The football reporting game was about to move to another level for me. The people behind the Charing Cross Hospital Radio Sports Show also ran a commercial agency, called Sportsvox. The agency covered games for regional newspapers and radio stations when the local team played away in London and they didn't send a reporter to cover the game. Sportsvox also provided coverage of all Sutton United's home, and some away, matches for County Sound Radio in Guildford, Surrey. I was assigned to cover Sutton and in return I received some of what is a precious commodity – money. It's precious because in our world the way it is, no money no life pretty much.

It would have been enough to continue reporting on matches for nothing; to get paid was something else. Having been accustomed until recently to paying to get into grounds, to receive money for watching games and saying a few words was a wonderful proposition.

Sutton United in the late 1980s were a thriving non-league club and it was a good time to be covering them. Formed in 1898 they played in junior and local leagues before progressing to the Athenian League in 1921, the Isthmian League in 1964 and then the big step to the GM Vauxhall Conference in 1986. The season before I started covering them, Sutton recorded one of the biggest FA Cup upsets of all time and they were still basking in the afterglow. Coventry City won the FA Cup in 1987. Two seasons later, in January 1989, they were drawn away to Sutton in the third round of the competition. At the time sixth in Division One, Coventry were beaten 2-1 by the non-league team in front of about 8,000 people. It was by far the greatest result in Sutton's history. The Sutton goals were scored by Tony Rains and Matt Hanlan, who were regulars in 1989/90, the season I began reporting on them.

I was more than happy watching Conference football. To someone who'd never played any higher than the second tier of the West Herts Sunday League, the level was stratospheric.

The first match I was paid to cover happened to involve Malcolm Allison's Fisher Athletic. It took place on 14 October 1989, a week after I'd spoken to Malcolm, and was played at Gander Green Lane. In a typically unconventional and imaginative move Malcolm had secured the services of a classy midfielder, Jorge Roçadas, the first Portuguese player to feature in the Conference, and an international, with whom Malcolm had worked at Vitória de Setúbal. Roçadas scored for Fisher as Sutton won 2-1. Malcolm was only in charge at Fisher for two more games, both defeats, before leaving in November for personal reasons.

Sutton had a good side and the 1989/90 season was one of their best in non-league at that time. After six wins in their final eight matches, they finished in eighth place in the Conference with 63 points.

Any reporter will tell you that the relationship with the manager at the club you are covering is crucial and I couldn't have asked for any more from Keith Blunt, who was managing Sutton at the time. One of the main pieces of information a reporter imparts before a game kicks off is the starting line-ups of the teams involved. Teams were typed out on sheets of paper by the home club and delivered to the press box. Some clubs were quicker than others at handing them out. Seeing a press officer making his way to the press box clutching a pile of freshly printed team sheets was a welcome sight and it was always a relief to be handed one. If a reporter had to use the dreaded phrase 'no confirmed team news yet' when cued to give starting line-ups on air it was because the team sheet hadn't arrived yet.

With Blunt, all that anxiety was avoided completely because he would let me know his team, starting 11 and substitutes, on a Friday morning before a Saturday game. I suppose he must have assumed that the opposition wouldn't be listening to County Sound Radio on a Friday evening.

That was typical of Sutton, a small, friendly, informal club into which it was easy to integrate. After the game both sets of players would have a drink with the supporters in the clubhouse bar. This gave the Sutton boys the opportunity to have a pop at the local radio reporter if they thought he had been out of order. Paul McKinnon had an exceptional career, mainly in non-league, but he started at Chelsea and also played for Blackburn Rovers and Malmö in Sweden. He first joined Sutton in 1977 and in no fewer than eight spells at the club he became their record goalscorer, with 279 goals in over 500 appearances. When I was watching him, he was in his early 30s and I once said on air that he was 'approaching the veteran stage'. He picked up on it and jokingly reprimanded me for my comment.

After one game between Sutton and Colchester United, I told the Colchester players that I used to watch their physiotherapist Brian Owen playing for Watford back in the late 1960s and early 1970s. They couldn't believe that Owen, then in his mid-40s, had ever been young enough to play football, and they were amazed to meet someone who had actually seen him play all those years ago.

Another Sutton player who had an outstanding career was their captain Tony Rains. While I was covering Sutton, Rains and Micky Stephens had a testimonial match against Norwich City to celebrate ten years each at the club. Both had played at Wembley in the 1981 FA Trophy final, which Sutton lost 1-0 to Bishop's Stortford to a last-minute goal, but Tony had fond memories of the day, 'The occasion was excellent, there was 20,000-odd people there, to be fortunate enough to play at Wembley, I don't think many people have experienced that, it was just a delight really to play there.' As well as scoring one of the goals which knocked Coventry out of the FA Cup, Tony played in FA Cup wins in 1987/88 over Division Three Aldershot (3-0 at home) and Division Four Peterborough United (3-1 away). That cup run was ended in the fourth round by Division Two Middlesbrough who won 1-0 in extra time at Ayresome Park after a 1-1 draw at Gander Green Lane. The win over Coventry in 1989 was the highlight of both players' careers.

As well as watching established players like McKinnon and Rains I saw a player, who went on to play league football, grow and develop over the season. In 1988/89 Efan Ekoku had scored four league goals. In 1989/90 he formed a great partnership with the experienced McKinnon and took off, using his pace and finishing ability to score 25 league goals in 39 matches, including seven in the last eight. It was obvious that Ekoku was going places, but the unknowns were when, where and for how much. The answers came when he moved to Harry Redknapp's Bournemouth for £100,000 in May 1990.

I never had a long chat with Ekoku when he was at Sutton but I did catch up with him a few years later. It was October 1994 and he'd recently moved from Norwich City to Wimbledon for £900,000. I found him thoughtful and considered. He'd just scored the only goal of the game on his home debut – against Norwich – and he was still on a high, 'I'd felt confident all week, going into that game. So, it was just a question of biding my time. I got my chance in the second half and managed to get the ball in the net.'

Biding his time was something to which Ekoku had become accustomed. He made his first league start for Sutton in February 1989 at the age of 21 and by the time of his move to Wimbledon, he was already 27 years old. 'Even at Sutton United in 1988 I always felt fairly confident that as long as I did my best I'd get there. It took a little longer than I'd hoped, but time isn't something you can control,' he said.

Being someone who moved from non-league into the Football League at a relatively late age meant that Ekoku had something in common with players like Les Ferdinand and Ian Wright, 'I've appreciated more what Ian Wright has done since I've played against him in the last couple of years or so. When you get up to the top flight you realise that it's not that easy. When someone like Ian does it year in, year out, scoring 30 goals a season, and not only that, but taking the amount of stick he gets for not doing it at a higher level, it makes you realise just how well he's done.'

When I'd watched Efan play for Sutton with other reporters, and it had become obvious that he would play at a higher level, there was inevitably speculation as to which league club he would choose. There was general surprise that his first move had been to Bournemouth, but he said, 'I would have liked to have stayed at Sutton for one more year, but the lure of playing in the Football League is often too much for any part-time player. You want to play full-time, because training every day can only improve you. I had the opportunity to join Sheffield United and one or two other clubs in the First Division as well. Possibly with hindsight I should have joined one of them, but it doesn't really matter now. At the time I thought I'd made the right decision and I still think so. Injuries restricted me to only 75 games in almost three seasons. If I'd been able to stay fit and the team had done well in the first year or so I was there, then maybe I'd have left a lot sooner. But each time I came back from injury I felt I was coming back a stronger player for watching so many games, and not really staying away from football. A lot of players when they get injured, especially when they're younger, don't want to watch football because it's almost painful, but I think the more you watch the more you learn.'

In his final days at Bournemouth Ekoku scored 11 goals in 18 games and in March 1993 he moved for £500,000 from Bournemouth to Norwich. What a time to arrive at Carrow Road! In the Premier League's inaugural season Norwich, with Mike Walker in charge, had topped the table going into 1993. Ekoku's first game, for which he was on the bench, was at home to Manchester United, who went on to win their first league title for 26 years. 'Losing to Manchester United in the first game I was there took the title away from us. I think if we'd beaten United that night we might have won the league. I could have been part of a championship winning team within weeks of joining. But finishing third was a great achievement considering the size of the club,' Ekoku said.

Due to his late-season arrival at Carrow Road, Ekoku might not have had time to make a huge contribution but he still managed three league goals from one start and three substitute appearances.

Third was Norwich's highest ever finish in the league and meant a place in the 1993/94 UEFA Cup. 'The following year things went really well, at least in the beginning. Norwich were in Europe for the first time and I scored some good goals as well,' he admitted. On 15 September 1993 Efan scored Norwich's first goal in European competition, against Vitesse Arnhem in the UEFA Cup, and ten days later he became the first player to score four goals in a Premier League match, in Norwich's 5-1 win at Everton.

But events beyond the control of a player can change circumstances quickly in football. In December 1993 Howard Kendall resigned as Everton manager. The following month Walker resigned from Norwich and was appointed at Goodison amid accusations by Norwich chairman Robert Chase of poaching. Ekoku said, 'It was a shame when the manager had to leave at the time he did. These things happen in football and you've just got to get on with it. Him leaving upset a few things, and one or two key players left, or it was almost inevitable that they were going to leave within a few months, or at the latest by the start of the next season. Stability was never achieved again and things just petered out.'

John Deehan took over from Walker and Ekoku became a disaffected footballer, 'Sometimes managers have to show a bit more confidence in their players and that was the case at Norwich. You can't be too fickle about choosing your team and changing it every other week. You've got to give players the time to establish themselves amongst each other, especially strikers because they live on confidence. It's not good long term to chop and change. You score one goal and win one game and you're everybody's hero again. You obviously want the crowd to like you, but the main thing is that you like yourself, and the manager likes you as a player. If the manager can't make his mind up, whether you're good, great, superb or awful then you've got problems.'

Efan got his move to Wimbledon in October 1994 and went on to score nine Premier League goals for his new club that season, outscoring every Norwich player. Wimbledon finished the season in ninth place while Norwich ended 20th and were relegated.

5

From watching him on television I knew Terry Cooper as a player who was converted from a winger into a marauding full-back, and who was the first-choice left-back in Don Revie's highly successful Leeds United side in the late 1960s and early 1970s. Cooper never lost his attacking instincts and many a time he would overlap Eddie Gray, himself an outstanding winger, and send in a telling cross. Leeds won trophies but they didn't win over the general footballing public, me included, because they were perceived as having a cynical edge to their play. It didn't appear enough for them to beat opponents; sometimes they had to humiliate them as well.

After covering a game at Luton Town once I walked past John Moore, at the time first team coach at Kenilworth Road, who was leaning against a wall reflecting on Revie's Leeds with a group of reporters. Moore had played for Luton at the time when Leeds were a major force. As I walked past I caught Moore telling his audience, 'They didn't have to be like that,' which summed Leeds up for me in one short sentence – their players had been so good and so talented that they could have relied on their ability to win games, without resorting to the underhand stuff.

In May 1988 Cooper became manager of Exeter City. The first major trophy in Exeter's history was the Division Four championship which they won under Cooper in 1989/90. In that season, City won 20 out of 23 league games at St James Park.

Exeter made a good start to the 1990/91 season. They won four of their first six matches and at one point were sixth in the table. Going into the game at Fulham on 27 October 1990, which I was sent by Sportsvox to cover, they were on a run of six without a win. That was to extend to seven.

I liked going to Craven Cottage, overlooking the Thames, and I enjoyed Fulham v Exeter. The ground did not have impressive modernity but it was quaint and historic. The walk through Bishop's Park from Putney Bridge tube station meant arriving at the ground in a buoyant mood, although during the time that I worked for Sportsvox there was no guarantee that the quality of the game would live up to the expectation. In my first season as a reporter I covered a joyless 0-0 draw between Fulham and Blackpool, played on 21 April 1990. It was near the end of the season and both sides were battling against relegation. The match was choked by fear, the great inhibitor, and was a reminder that to be a winner you have first to overcome the fear of losing. At the time some prisoners were staging a rooftop protest at Strangeways prison in Manchester, and I suggested in one of my full-time reports that 'if the authorities want to get the prisoners down from the roof top at Strangeways they should show them the full unedited version of this match'. An advertisement behind one of the goals at the Putney End of Craven Cottage seemed apt. It read, 'Lonely, suicidal, depressed? Phone the Samaritans.'

In comparison Fulham v Exeter, which I was covering for a West Country radio station, was free-flowing and entertaining with plenty of goals. Fulham won 3-2 and the brilliant Gordon Davies, their record scorer with 178 goals in 450 appearances, played excellently, scoring two goals. For one of them Davies received the ball in the Exeter half, yards clear of their defence which was trying to play him offside. From my position in the press box I couldn't tell whether Davies had been offside when the ball had been played, or whether he had just beaten the Exeter offside trap. Exeter were furious that the goal was allowed to stand and one of their substitutes who was still on the bench, Ben Rowe, was sent off for his protests.

Press conferences at Fulham were informal gatherings of journalists outside the Cottage. At the start of press conferences there was often an awkward silence when reporters looked at each other waiting for someone to break the ice by asking the first question. I always thought that this was crazy – we've got the manager here and have the opportunity to ask him questions about the game, let's get it on. I had no problem asking the opening question to get things going, so I asked Cooper whether he thought the match would have been enjoyable from a neutral's point of view. He responded in his archetypal Yorkshire accent, 'It wasn't enjoyable for me,' and got straight to the point of his dissatisfaction, 'not with a linesman like that on that side. He weren't one yard he was ten yards offside, twice in the second half, he never give either.'

There was a long pause as it sunk in how wronged Cooper was feeling. It eventually dawned on me that because I'd asked the opening question everyone was waiting for me to ask the next one. I was struggling to think of a question. The game had ended, it was all water under the bridge and nothing could be done to change what had happened. We were all, including Cooper, stuck with it and we hadn't been able to see a television replay of the contentious incident to get a definitive view on whether or not Davies had been offside when the ball was played. Eventually I said, 'Are you going to make any complaint about it?' Cooper answered, 'You can't win, if I make a complaint the FA will fine me. It would be nice if Fulham have videoed it just to send it to the FA, not for the FA but just for the linesman.' Then he delivered a cutting comment, 'He'll be off out with his wife tonight and have a bottle of wine, he's spoiled our weekend.'

Another pause before Cooper turned the tables by asking me, 'Did you have a good view of it?' I bottled it; instead of answering honestly and simply saying 'no' I felt that Cooper was looking for sympathy and I replied somewhat lamely, 'Yeah, it did look offside.' This only encouraged Cooper who came back with, 'Oh steady, be careful, "it did look"; be careful, it weren't one yard it was ten yards offside, Gordon Davies even stopped and had a look, he couldn't believe it.'

For the first time since the exchange began another journalist spoke up but I'm not sure his contribution was too helpful, 'He took it well though.' Cooper's response was, 'Oh great, I wish I could get one against one on the keeper, I'm 46 I could stick it in as well. Anyone like Gordon Davies, what's that 300 goals he's got?'

A few more questions were asked which Cooper answered dismissively before he got back to the bone of contention, Fulham's second goal. He seemed ready to discuss it individually with each journalist present. 'I've got nowt against the referee, it was the linesman. Did you see Fulham's second goal?' he asked another press man who answered, 'Fulham's second goal? Yeah.' 'Well how far was he offside?' The journalist gave an answer similar to mine, 'He certainly looked offside.' Of course that wasn't good enough for Cooper, 'No, he didn't look, how far was he offside? He was ten yards.' The journalist responded, 'Well I wasn't watching the player when the ball was passed,' to which Cooper just said, 'Eh, eh, he was ten yards.'

Cooper then turned to another reporter who claimed that Davies had been level with the last player when the ball had been played. 'I tell you what, I'll send you the video as well. Just send me the price of a pint back. Fulham's second goal turned it upside down. I thought they'd gone at the time. We were containing them, they're obviously not playing with much confidence at the minute and we were containing them but it's turned the game upside down.'

The press conference descended into farce when someone asked, 'Overall apart from the decision were you pleased with the performance?' Cooper's response blackened the mood even further, 'No I'm never pleased, we expect a battle, we expect when we come away that the referee will lean towards the home side, I admit because we get that at home, we get that, but not as blatant as that and to get a bloke from the press saying he was level I mean that just sums the game up. What chance have you got? He's not an FA councillor, is he? He's old enough to be one.'

An aircraft flew low over the Cottage and the press conference disintegrated. The incident reminded me how completely different to mine a manager's view of a game could be. To me watching and reporting on matches was fun, the result didn't really matter. As long as I did my job I would be all right, but a manager had a different, sometimes terrifying perspective. I imagined a doom-laden Terry Cooper that evening sitting on a coach back to Devon, staring out at a darkening sky and ruminating about how unjust the day had been for him and his team.

*

Not long after witnessing the Terry Cooper Show at Craven Cottage I covered my first game involving Watford. It was played at Vicarage Road on 8 December 1990, against Plymouth Argyle and I was working for Plymouth Sound radio station so I had to come at it from the away team's angle.

It was a few years after the end of the incredibly successful Elton John/ Graham Taylor era which had lasted for ten years. Unsurprisingly none of Taylor's successors had managed to hold the job down for long – Dave Bassett, the first to try, was sacked after nine months in January 1988 with Watford bottom of Division One; Steve Harrison oversaw relegation that season and a failed attempt to come straight back up in 1988/89 via the play-offs before acknowledging that he wasn't cut out to be a manager and he left after just over two years; Colin Lee signed players in the summer of 1990 then when Watford lost the first seven home games in 1990/91 he went in November 1990. When I covered the Plymouth game Steve Perryman, having been in charge for two games, was looking for his first win as Watford manager and the club's first home win of the season. They got it. One shining light in the post-Taylor years was Paul Wilkinson, leading scorer in three successive seasons, and he got both goals in a 2-0 victory. Despite that Watford remained bottom of the table.

The press box was a long enclosed section at the back of the main stand. When Watford moved to Vicarage Road in 1922, two years after joining the Football League, the main stand was a state-of-the-art structure. Sixty-eight years later it had hardly changed and could only be described as 'dilapidated'. No matter, for me climbing the big wooden steps to reach the press box from the press room underneath the stand was a surreal and exhilarating experience. To be sitting in the press box at my club to report on a game was an enormous privilege.

I covered more games at Watford that season, all for the away team's radio station. One, in midweek on 19 March 1991, was for a Lancashire station. Watford lost 3-0 at home to Blackburn Rovers to extend their winless run to 12 league games. After the game Dave Victor, who'd also covered the game, said to me, 'It'll be a shame to see them in Division Three next season.' I didn't really feel I could make a convincing case to oppose his view. One of the eternal fascinations of football is that it so often throws up the unexpected. The following Saturday Watford went to Middlesbrough, who were in fourth place going into the game, and won 2-1. That was the beginning of a run to the end of the season which saw Watford win seven, draw two and lose two and finish safely in 20th place.

One of the games in that run, on 23 April 1991, provided me with a moment of truth.

A day or so before the game I received a phone call from Mike Emery at Sportsvox, asking, 'You've done commentaries before haven't you?' It was an interesting and at the same time perplexing question because I'd never commentated on a game and surely Mike must have known that. Maybe he did. People don't always say what they mean, they have roundabout ways of saying things and this might have been Mike's way of saying, 'I know you've never done a commentary before but that doesn't matter, I need someone to do one now and I think you can do it.' It was a big moment, one I'd been waiting for ever since I'd started reporting on games. When I began as a football reporter my ambition was to go all the way to the top. I remember getting drunk once and telling someone that I wanted to become the greatest commentator ever.

When I was a kid I'd commentated on Subbuteo matches played between my mates. We would record our commentaries and play them back and laugh at the way we got excited. Until then that was my only experience of football commentary.

Mike wanted me to commentate for Clubcall on a game between Watford and West Bromwich Albion. There was no way I was going to turn it down; apart from anything else I never once rejected an offer of work in my time as a football reporter, however short the notice, whatever the game, wherever and whenever it was going to be played. If I'd been asked to cover a Simod Cup tie between Rochdale and Bury to be played on the Moon I would have taken it and found a way of getting there.

I'd already proved that I could report on games, now I would find out whether I could commentate on them as well. It helped that the match was at Watford, where I felt at home, and that I'd already reported from the Vicarage Road press box.

It was an important game for both clubs. Despite having only lost once in their previous seven outings Watford were still 23rd in Division Two, while West Brom were one position higher in the table.

I found out that there is a world of difference between reporting on a game and commentating. Generally speaking a reporter informs the listener of events after they have already happened, maybe only just after, but crucially there is a delay which is long enough to allow the reporter to take in the events, make sense of them and then recount them. A commentator talks about the game as it is happening, a much more complex and difficult skill. The match is perceived via the senses and immediately explained to the listener by the commentator as it happens; there is little or no time for reflection.

I got through Watford v West Brom OK but I didn't feel that I'd set the world of football commentary alight. My approach was not quite right. The best commentators are bursting with words and they can't get them out fast enough. To keep pace with the game they speak quickly. Ninety minutes is a long time to talk with only a 15 minute break at half-time and at the back of my mind I kept thinking that I might run out of words. After all I am unofficially the third slowest person in the world and I spun out my words by speaking s l o w l y, in a slightly drawn-out fashion. The substance of what I said was all right, factually I was accurate, but my presentation probably wouldn't have thrilled anyone. I was glad that I'd had the opportunity to give it a try it but I realised that I probably wasn't going to make it as a commentator.

The game was interesting because the most influential player for each team was a centre-back, Glenn Roeder for Watford and Graham Roberts for West Brom. Roeder actually scored Watford's goal, with Don Goodman netting for the Baggies in a 1-1 draw. It showed that if you're a good enough player you can dominate a game no matter what position you play.

After the match I got my first taste of Glenn's dry sense of humour. It was about the time when Paul Gascoigne was being transferred from Tottenham Hotspur to Lazio and there had been a suggestion that Glenn would be part of the arrangement and go to Italy as Gazza's 'minder'. It was the sort of story the press, particularly the tabloids, jump on and after the game a reporter asked Glenn if it was going to happen. He replied, 'After the way I played tonight I might be going to Lazio with Gazza as my minder.'

*

There are occasions when a reporter does get to describe the action exactly as it happens and later the same season I experienced one of those golden moments. On a warm evening in west London on 10 April 1991 I was covering a Division

One game between two good teams, Queens Park Rangers and Graham Taylor's Aston Villa, for the Birmingham radio station BRMB. The previous season Villa had finished second to Liverpool in Division One and David Platt had been voted PFA Players' Player of the Year having scored 21 goals from midfield. At that time Rangers were consistently finishing in mid-table or better in the top flight. I looked up from my notebook just as I was finishing a report during the game, and as I lifted my eyes and finished the last sentence of the update, Platt gloriously volleyed in a goal from just outside the penalty area to put Villa ahead in the 33rd minute. With the away fans going mad in the background the listeners could instantly hear that Villa had scored and as I described the goal, finishing with 'and that's why David Platt is an England international', I felt like a surfer who'd caught a huge wave and ridden it all the way to the end.

QPR turned the game round in the second half to win 2-1 through goals from Bradley Allen and Andy Tilson.

*

After I'd started watching Watford in 1968 occasionally me and my mates would venture up to London to take in a match at one of the capital's great football cathedrals. We saw the supremely well-drilled Arsenal side of McLintock, Armstrong, Radford and Kennedy in the 1970/71 season when they won the double. Cooke, Osgood and Hudson dazzled us in the blue of Chelsea, and at White Hart Lane one midweek evening in 1973 I was in a crowd of 52,000 which watched Brian Clough's Derby County win an incredible FA Cup tie. It was a fourth round replay which was 0-0 at half-time and with just over ten minutes to go Spurs were 3-1 up. Then Roger Davies scored twice to send the game into extra time during which Davies completed his hat-trick, Derby ending up 5-3 winners.

The London venue I enjoyed visiting most though was Upton Park. The East End was more real and there was such a close connection between the supporters and the players. The appreciation of good football seemed to be keener at West Ham. The players repaid the supporters by being loyal to them. Someone as extraordinarily talented as Trevor Brooking, with his midfield poise and finesse, chose to spend his whole career with the Hammers. Bobby Moore had his ups and downs at West Ham but he wouldn't have spent nearly 16 years at the club if it didn't have something about it.

Billy Bonds didn't spend his whole career there but he was still 27 years with West Ham as a player and a manager, playing a club-record 799 first-team games over a period of 21 seasons between 1967 and 1988. A £47,500 Ron Greenwood signing from Charlton Athletic, for whom he made his league debut at the age of 18, Bonds played for West Ham at right-back, in midfield and at centre-back. In 1973/74 he was West Ham's leading scorer with 13 goals. After Moore left in March 1974 Bonds was made captain, a position he held for ten years. Bonds led the club to an FA Cup final victory over Fulham in 1975, and to the final of the 1976 European Cup Winners' Cup. There's something in the DNA of West Ham which makes them unpredictable though and in 1977/78 there was a relegation. Just as perversely they won the FA Cup as a Division Two club in 1980, beating Division One Arsenal 1-0 through a Brooking header. Bonds again captained the side, making him the only West Ham skipper to lift the FA Cup on two occasions. He played his last game for the Hammers at Southampton in April 1988 at the age of 41 years and 255 days.

When Lou Macari resigned as West Ham manager in February 1990, Bonds was appointed as his successor.

After I'd finished covering Sutton United my next regular gig for Sportsvox was to report on West Ham home games for BBC Essex. It was a doddle; all that was required of me was one two-minute piece at five o'clock. Mike Emery would make my week by phoning a few days before the game and asking, 'Two minutes at five o'clock?' I'd say, 'Yes please, Mike,' and would put the phone down on a high at the prospect of another trip to Upton Park.

Doing just one long report after the final whistle meant that I could sit back and take in the game. There was no pressure because I had a long time to write my report after the match had finished. My assignment coincided with Bonds' first full season in charge, in 1990/91 when they won promotion, finishing second in Division Two to Oldham Athletic. On the way West Ham beat Leicester City 1-0 at home, on 19 January 1991. George Parris scored the goal but Ian Bishop caught the eye with a virtuoso passing display.

As usual I went to the post-match press conference. It wasn't long before someone mentioned Bishop which inspired me to chip in and ask Billy what I considered to be a sensible question, 'Does he remind you of Glenn Hoddle at all?' My thinking was that Hoddle had been the best passer of a ball of his generation and I wondered if Billy thought Bishop was anywhere near his class. Billy decided to have some fun at my expense and he replied with a smile, 'No, he reminds me of Ian Bishop.' Everyone thought it was hilarious, which I can understand, and they fell about laughing. One reporter, rather than leaving it and moving on, decided to prolong the moment. With a big smirk he said of Bishop, 'Well, he has got long hair.'

I had the pleasure of working with Billy on several games, including in the press box at Wembley on the glorious occasion of Watford's 1999 Division One play-off final win over Bolton Wanderers. At Watford we would park at the bottom of a hill and walk up past the allotments to the ground. Billy's stride was such that going up the hill I would virtually have to run to keep up with him – he was so fit and strong even in his 50s. He once told me that he regretted packing up playing as early as he did, at the age of 41. With his suntan, his hair still over the collar of his shirt and his relaxed, amiable manner with a pair of shades on he could easily have passed for a chilled-out surfer dude.

*

A report I did on a Watford v West Ham game in January 1991 was instrumental in my moving to a different sphere of operation. The week before the Hammers' home win over Leicester, they had won 1-0 (Trevor Morley) at Vicarage Road and I'd been there reporting for BBC Essex.

After the 1990/91 season ended I began to have doubts that Sportsvox would continue as an entity. It wasn't making any money. In the previous close-season a meeting had been held to discuss plans for the forthcoming campaign. As 1991/92 approached no similar meeting had been called. No one had said anything and the silence was disconcerting. I had to act, I had to somehow make sure that I continued to report on football matches. The activity thrilled me and I was hooked. I needed the excitement and the buzz it gave me.

After starting as a reporter I looked around at the radio coverage of football that was on offer in London. It wasn't long before I discovered the newly formed Capital Gold Sport and started to tune in regularly.

I had first reported on an Arsenal game in September 1989, a 2-0 League Cup win over Plymouth Argyle, just before my first visit to Sutton United. The contrast between Highbury and Gander Green Lane was extreme. At Highbury a uniformed commissionaire handed reporters their matchday programme and in the press room we drank tea from bone china cups. I don't remember much about the Plymouth game, and the air of formality was a little stifling. It was in the concourse of the ground at that match that I recall seeing Capital Gold Sport reporters for the first time. They were carrying huge sky blue bags containing expensive-looking broadcasting equipment. They were in a hurry, like they were on some kind of important mission. When I saw them my immediate thought was, 'I'd love to be part of your world.'

Capital Gold Sport was just what London football needed, and exactly what I needed. It was fresh and new and was ready to blow away the cobwebs of the old order. In some ways it was to football reporting what punk had been to music in the previous decade. The coverage had energy although at the same time it was respectful. It was different to any radio coverage of football I had previously heard. It was edgy, alive and enthusiastic. Jonathan Pearce reminded me of the young Brian Moore in the 1960s, when Brian had been at his most uninhibited in the early days of *The Big Match*.

The Capital Gold Sport approach to football was similarly unrestrained, free flowing and raw. It didn't hold back and went straight for the target, which was the heart, mind and soul of the football fan on the terrace. It was the sort of noise you might expect to hear in a favela in Rio de Janeiro if you tuned in a transistor radio to listen to coverage of a game between Santos and Fluminense at the Maracanã. It was passionate, as loud and proud as the sovereign ring on a market trader's finger. Hearing it woke me up and started me dreaming at the same time.

About a week before the start of the 1991/92 season I sent a tape of my full-time report for BBC Essex on Watford v West Ham, which a friend had recorded, to Capital Gold Sport. I soon got a call from Jonathan Pearce, telling me, 'You can come and work for us but you'll have to speed up your delivery. Come to the studio this Saturday and we'll show you how the programme works.' At first, I was surprised by how quickly JP had called me but later I discovered that he doesn't hang around and he acts decisively. On the other hand as I'm the third-slowest person in the world it wasn't a surprise that he told me I needed to speed up my delivery. With typical astuteness and acumen, he'd immediately identified a weakness, which I already knew about. I assured him that I would work on it and I gleefully accepted the invitation without hesitation.

Arriving at Capital Gold Sport's Warren Street studio at about midday on Saturday, 17 August 1991 reminded of my first day at Charing Cross Hospital Radio a couple of years previously, only this time, it seemed, it was for real. Charing Cross Hospital Radio and Sportsvox had been something of a rehearsal and a learning curve; now my apprenticeship was over and I was entering the world of actual money making commercial radio. This was showbiz and listening figures counted. Everyone was friendly and welcoming but I could tell straight away that they were professional and were there to get the job done.

It was always frenetic in the Capital Gold Sport studio on a matchday; this particular day being the opening day of the season it was especially so. At the request of Pete Simmons, the show's producer, I did a voice test by scripting and reading a preview to one of the games to be played that day. After I'd passed the test Pete told me that the reporter who was due to cover Brentford v Leyton Orient hadn't turned up. He said, 'If he's not here by one 30 we'll send you to Griffin Park.' I thought that he was joking and laughed; at a quarter to two I found myself on my way to west London for a three o'clock kick off carrying one of the big sky blue bags I'd seen at Highbury, full of unfamiliar, sophisticated radio equipment. I didn't get to the Griffin Park press box until about 2.30pm, half an hour after the show had started. I managed to work out how to plug in the equipment and got a line to the studio about 15 minutes before the match kicked off.

For my first game, a nice, quiet uneventful occasion, ideally a 0-0 draw, would have been welcome. Instead I got a frantic London derby which Brentford won 4-3. Dean Holdsworth scored a hat-trick, Terry Evans got the other Brentford goal and for Leyton Orient Kevin Nugent scored twice and Andy Sayer once. I worked out what was going on in the show as it went along, just about keeping my head above water as I adjusted to a much faster pace than I'd been used to on other radio stations. There'd been no time for anyone to explain how many reports I would be doing and when and I came a bit unstuck after the game had ended. The Capital Gold Sport format was to do a full-time report on the final whistle which relayed the facts of what had happened and then about half an hour later to give a 'considered' piece which was more reflective and put the game into context. I didn't know this and my considered piece was more or less a rehash of the report I'd given at full-time. It was great to be part of the show I'd listened to so often, and to be swept along by the tide, but as with the first time I'd worked for Charing Cross Hospital Radio I didn't know whether it would be a one-off or whether I'd done enough to be taken on.

Having had a taste of it and enjoyed it immensely I desperately wanted more, and I was in limbo until Pete Simmons told me after the dust had settled, 'We'll have to work on your considered report, but you did all right.'

I was in. I'd got the move I craved – I was working for Capital Gold Sport, London's legendary soccer station.

6

Capital Gold Sport suited me absolutely down to the ground and for the second time in my life I was part of a team. The first time had been when I'd played for Longdean Invaders Reserves in the West Herts Sunday League in the 1970s. I'd started going to training with Longdean on a Wednesday evening at a time when there was only one team. Then one evening the first team captain Howard announced that there would be a meeting after training without telling us what the meeting would be about. After we'd showered and got dressed we went into another room and waited for Howard to enlighten us and dispel the mystery. Howard told us that a decision had been taken to start a reserve team – and he invited me to be captain. I felt incredibly honoured because I was being asked by someone who knew me to take on a position that came with great responsibility. Howard knew exactly what I would give to the role if I agreed to take it on. I knew that the way I performed would have a big influence on how successful Longdean Invaders Reserves would be. I accepted the invitation gladly and immediately.

The Capital Gold Sport team was similar to Longdean Invaders Reserves in several ways. There was a shared goal, although instead of having fun trying to win matches at Capital we were having fun striving to give the best possible coverage of matches involving clubs in the London area. As at Longdean Invaders Reserves there was competition; this time people were competing with each other to be given the best game to cover instead of a place in the starting XI.

There was a hierarchy at Capital Gold Sport, with JP at the top, always commentating on the game of the day. From there the match you were allocated was to an extent determined by how good you were perceived to be, although certain reporters were assigned to cover particular clubs. There was a lot at stake in that big careers were being forged. For many people at the station what they were doing was a stepping stone on the way up in their profession.

As captain of Longdean Invaders Reserves I was part of a three-man committee which comprised Howard, Bert – who was club chairman and the father of one of the players – and myself. Bert was also our number one and often only supporter who stood out in all weathers watching us play on a Sunday morning. The committee sat down after training and picked two teams, a first team and the reserves, for the following Sunday. I felt the sense of power and responsibility acutely. The reserves had a decent team and players wanted to play. We entered the West Herts Sunday League in Division Three and in our first two seasons we were promoted twice before we found our level in Division One, a level below the top. There was competition for places to play for the reserves. Players would go to the pub after training and wait for the committee members to walk in and announce the teams. Handwritten pieces of paper with the teams on them were passed round from person to person. I once received a phone call at home from a disgruntled full-back who was furious that he had been left out of the reserve team starting line-up, which I thought was great because it showed how much he cared and wanted to play.

The difference for me between Longdean Invaders Reserves and Capital Gold Sport was that instead of being involved in deciding who would represent us, my fate was now in the hands of someone else.

*

In the early 1990s, when I joined, Capital Gold Sport was strong as a collective. We all went off and did our thing on a matchday but in the early days we always made the effort to meet up for a beer after the show had finished, the Prince of Wales Feathers in Warren Street being our favoured meeting place, which was fine with me because it was a down-to-earth boozer and it served a good pint of Fuller's London Pride.

One evening in particular, not long after I'd started, stands out when we bonded like I'd never seen a group bond before, during a riotous and glorious drinking session at the Feathers. It was our Christmas gathering, on an evening when no matches were being played so everyone could be there and chill. As the evening gained momentum it turned into a spontaneous and heartfelt display of everyone's commitment to, appreciation of, and respect for one other. Admittedly it was alcohol-fuelled but the sentiments expressed were genuine. We started off just chatting but I suppose that, as we were all football fans getting drunk, it wasn't surprising that we eventually started to sing. The same song was sung in turn about everyone in the group, at the same volume and with the same gusto:

'We've got Tony Incenzo in our team,

We've got Tony Incenzo in our team,

We've got Tony Incenzo in our team,

We've got the best team in the world.'

Tony was the Queens Park Rangers reporter. He'd been with Capital Gold Sport since the start and knew his job inside out. He was professional, precise and concise and he could be clever, original and amusing. On one occasion after a 0-0 draw at Loftus Road, which had been uninspiring, his considered report was, 'Gavin Peacock has just run the length of the pitch playing one-twos with his son who finished with a low shot into an empty net. It was more entertaining than anything we saw in the game.' After another match, which Rangers won 1-0 through a Kevin Gallen goal, he said, 'One Gallen equals three points for Queens Park Rangers.'

'We've got Ian Crocker in our team,

We've got Ian Crocker in our team,

We've got Ian Crocker in our team,

We've got the best team in the world.'

Crock knew where he wanted to go and he got there. He believed he was good enough to be a commentator and eventually he became one. At first he used to be stuck in the studio on a matchday, rounding up the scores from matches being played every 15 minutes or so. He was good at what he did but he really wanted to get out there and be at games. He asserted himself tactfully without upsetting anyone. JP recognised his talent and when he got the opportunity to commentate, Crock became a major asset to the station. When he left he became one of many who made the journey from Capital Gold Sport to Sky Sports.

'We've got Julian Waters in our team,

We've got Julian Waters in our team,

We've got Julian Waters in our team,

We've got the best team in the world.'

Julian was an accomplished commentator who once held the number two spot behind JP. He was amiable and easy-going and he went with the flow. He was never allowed to forget that he once made a schoolboy error and got off the train at Grimsby instead of Cleethorpes when on his way to cover a Grimsby Town game at Blundell Park. He eventually found a long-term home at Sky Sports News.

'We've got Deano Standing in our team,

We've got Deano Standing in our team,

We've got Deano Standing in our team,

We've got the best team in the world.'

Deano was Capital Gold Sport's Millwall reporter and was well-placed to do the job because he worked as the club's press officer. Deano was articulate but his rough-and-ready south London accent made him an ideal voice of The Den. Deano ran a great press room at the new Den, which opened in 1993. It had everything you needed – a warm welcome, a match programme, printed team sheets in good time, tea before the game, soup at half-time and beer at the end, a TV with Sky Sports News so you could get the scores in the other matches being played that day and because it was a new stadium it was spacious and comfortable.

'We've got Mick Conway in our team,

We've got Mick Conway in our team,

We've got Mick Conway in our team,

We've got the best team in the world.'

Every group has an entertainer who keeps the others amused and we had Mick. For a start there was the 'Whelan Test' which was novel, reflected Mick's passion for the game and endeared him to us. When Mick met anyone for the first time he had a way of assessing whether or not they were worth talking to about football. He gave them a unique test which he'd invented. Out of the blue he would come and stand about six inches away from you and jab you in the chest, while in his Irish accent hollering, 'Whaddya tink of Ronnie Whelan, whaddya tink of Ronnie Whelan?' When Mick gave me the 'Whelan Test' I was, like most people, a little taken aback. Not having a clue what was going on, I replied, 'Ronnie Whelan was a very good player, Mick.' Wrong answer. To pass the test you had to move closer to Mick, jab him in the chest and yell, 'Ronnie Whelan was absolutely by far and away the best midfield player on the planet in the 1980s bar no one at all!' Although I failed the test, Mick decided that I was worth talking to about football anyway and I was glad that he did. Mick was great company and we spent many hours together after games in the Feathers.

I used to prick up my ears when Mick was on air, I enjoyed listening to his reports, they were interesting and were delivered punchily in exactly the style Capital Gold Sport liked.

Mick was passionate in his opinions, which were usually extreme: a player was either the best thing since sliced bread or completely hopeless. When he liked a player he let everyone know and generally he was a good judge. In July 1996 Leeds paid £2.8m for Lee Bowyer to make him the most expensive teenager in British football history. Mick had been the first at Capital Gold Sport to rave about Bowyer when he broke into the Charlton Athletic side as a teenager.

Like me, Mick was knocked out by the whole Capital Gold Sport experience. We couldn't believe how fortunate we were to be working for the station. There was some friendly rivalry between us because we started working for Capital at the same time and we were vying for the best games but that didn't stop us being mates, even though he went ahead of me in the pecking order.

'We've got Rob Wotton in our team,

We've got Rob Wotton in our team,

We've got Rob Wotton in our team,

We've got the best team in the world.'

Rob was another who moved from Capital to Sky Sports. As well as being a very able broadcaster, Rob was a gentleman, a superb facilitator and a diplomat, who through his humour, empathy and understanding had a way of diffusing tension, easing friction and dealing with tricky issues.

'We've got Dave Clark in our team,

We've got Dave Clark in our team,

We've got Dave Clark in our team,

We've got the best team in the world.'

Clarkie had the loudest laugh of anyone at the station and he was always laughing. He was a big bear of a man with a twinkle in his eye who trod the same path as others from Capital Gold Sport to Sky Sports.

'We've got Steve Wilson in our team,

We've got Steve Wilson in our team,

We've got Steve Wilson in our team,

We've got the best team in the world.'

I first met Steve at Griffin Park in March 1991, at a game between Brentford and Bradford City, during my second season with Sportsvox. Steve was doing what I would go on to do many times for Capital, covering a home match involving Brentford. He was serious about his work and he had class and refinement. He was nurtured by JP and he eventually hit the jackpot and went on to work for *Match of the Day*.

Steve handled every challenge calmly and coolly. One evening in the Feathers he told Mick and I the story of his first commentary for Capital Gold Sport. It had been a midweek game at Leyton Orient. His pundit had been to a lunch earlier in the day where he'd met a lady. In his inebriated state and being a complete romantic the pundit invited the lucky lady to accompany him to Brisbane Road, and they sat next to each other in the press box. At one point during the match Steve cued the pundit for his views on a particular incident. When there was no immediate response Steve glanced sideways and saw that the guy was in the middle of a passionate clinch with his lady friend. It all happened in a split second and Steve just continued with his commentary unperturbed.

'We've got Pete Simmons in our team,

We've got Pete Simmons in our team,

We've got Pete Simmons in our team,

We've got the best team in the world.'

Pete was a senior producer who, with the help of a team of assistants, coordinated everything from the studio. During the week they had to make sure that the right person would be at the right ground at the right time the following Saturday. When they were there, Pete had to press the right buttons and pull the right levers to ensure that the right person was on air at the right time. As games were being played snippets of commentary had to be prepared ready to be used just before we went off air at the end of the show.

Pete ensured that the overall tone and sound of the broadcast were of a high quality. Capital Gold Sport's aim was to remove the separation between reporter and supporter. The broadcasting equipment we used helped us to achieve this.

As well as wearing a headset which comprised headphones and a hands-free microphone, we also had an effects mic which we positioned strategically to pick up the roar of the crowd which is an intrinsic part of the theatre of football and combined with our words completed the overall colourful picture. Pete did his job brilliantly and when appropriate he enjoyed yelling at commentators and reporters which helped to relieve the stress.

'We've got Simon Michaelson in our team,

We've got Simon Michaelson in our team,

We've got Simon Michaelson in our team,

We've got the best team in the world.'

I felt honoured and privileged to be part of it.

I was born in London and have always had a strong affinity with the city, the London of 'Waterloo Sunset' and 'Maybe It's Because I'm a Londoner'. To be working for Capital Gold Sport, a radio station whose raison d'être was to cover London football in a way that was as bouncy as a football itself, was mindblowing.

When I started in 1991 there were 14 Football League clubs in the London area for Capital to cover, each with its own unique story. The clubs were as diverse as the city itself, from the north London giants Arsenal and Spurs to the Football League's newest club Barnet.

Arsenal were a model of well-run consistency with an unbroken run in the top flight which stretched back to 1919, the longest of any club in the country. Under George Graham they were enjoying a very successful period and they had followed up their dramatic triumph in 1988/89 with another title win in 1990/91 when they lost only one league match all season.

Spurs had won the double in 1960/61 but their thirst for glory had mainly been quenched through triumphs in cup competitions. In 1901, while members of the Southern League, they had become the first (and so far only) non-league club to win the FA Cup and in 1963 they became the first British team to win a European trophy when they beat Atlético Madrid 5-1 in the final of the European Cup Winners' Cup.

Chelsea, the Kings Road playboys whose triumphs before 1991 had been sporadic but spectacular, had a history of highly talented flair players like Peter Osgood, Charlie Cooke and Alan Hudson who were more suited to winning cup competitions than triumphing in arduous league campaigns.

Crystal Palace had ended the 1990/91 season third in Division One, their best ever finish, with a side that included Nigel Martyn in goal and the telepathic Ian Wright/Mark Bright partnership up front.

Queens Park Rangers were enjoying a golden spell in their history and between 1983/84 and 1992/93 they finished the season as London's top side on three occasions and had reached the FA Cup final in 1982.

West Ham were a wonderful mystery of a club that I couldn't fathom. Their supporters maintained that they had won the World Cup for England in 1966.

Wimbledon were one of the most remarkable stories in 20th-century English football. They won the FA Amateur Cup in 1963 and 25 years later they won the real thing. They were elected to Division Four in 1977 and by 1986 had incredibly worked their way up to Division One.

In Division Two were Charlton Athletic, whose supporters did an amazing job to get the club back to their spiritual home at The Valley after they'd been forced to vacate it in 1985 due to financial problems. They formed The Valley Party and took on Greenwich Council which opposed the renovation of the stadium. This led to a joyous homecoming to The Valley in 1992.

Millwall had fallen from the top division in 1989/90 but still had the great Teddy Sheringham, in 1990/91 the leading scorer in the Football League.

Although they weren't actually located in London, to my delight Capital Gold Sport also covered my club Watford.

In Division Three we had Brentford where I'd had my first experience of working for Capital Gold Sport in August 1991. They went on to finish the 1991/92 season as champions, Dean Holdsworth netting 24 league goals, which led to a return to the second tier for the first time since 1953/54.

Fulham, founded in 1879, were London's oldest club and had been at Craven Cottage since 1896. They were going through a fallow spell but their supporters were just glad that they were still in existence in their own right after a failed plan in 1987 to sell off the Cottage for housing and merge the club with Queens Park Rangers, a plan aborted by action taken by Jimmy Hill.

Leyton Orient had had been promoted from Division Four in 1988/89 under Frank Clark and followed this up with solid finishes in the higher division over the next five seasons.

London's only representatives in Division Four in 1991/92 provided a riotous and colourful story. Barnet were founded in 1888 and became a prominent non-league club. They reached the third round of the FA Cup in 1965 and in the 1970s players like Jimmy Greaves, Bob McNab and Marvin Hinton played for them. In 1986 Barry Fry became their manager for the second time and in 1990/91, after they'd finished runners-up three times, he guided them to the GM Vauxhall Conference title to finally take them into the Football League. Barnet scored 103 goals and averaged crowds of 2,918 at Underhill in that championship-winning season. Their final game in the Conference was a 4-2 win at Fisher Athletic and their opening fixture in the Football League a 7-4 home defeat to Crewe Alexandra in front of 5,090 people, which set the tone for the season and said much for how Fry got his team playing and how the public responded.

I was part of a strong team at Capital Gold Sport and although I was only a small cog in a big wheel I was part of what made the wheel go round. Before working for Capital I was often the main reporter for whichever station I was working, so if I was at Leyton Orient v Plymouth Argyle for Plymouth Sound I would be covering the main game for their sports show and would have given three reports in both halves each lasting about two minutes. In a match in which there might not be a shot on target until say the tenth minute you had to be creative to give reports of that length and frequency. Working for Capital demanded creativity of a different type. There were more games being covered and my half-time and full-time reports had to be no longer than 30 seconds, goal flashes during the game even shorter. My approach was not to think, 'Thirty seconds, what can you possibly say in 30 seconds?' Instead it was, 'Let's see how much I can pack into 30 seconds.'

But there was no doubt about who the focal point was, the driving force.

'We've got Jonathan Pearce in our team,

We've got Jonathan Pearce in our team,

We've got Jonathan Pearce in our team,

We've got the best team in the world.'

And then there was JP.

7

Jonathan Pearce was born in the West Country in 1959. He told us many times that he was robbed of a career in professional football when, while with Bristol City, he broke a leg in two places as a teenager in 1974. The local radio station needed someone to cover City and a career in broadcasting began. JP moved to London in 1987 and helped to launch Capital Gold Sport in 1988.

JP held it all together; he opened the show, cued reporters at the other grounds, commentated on the main game, kept track of the other matches being played that day and put the results into context, and he hosted a phone-in before closing the show four and a half hours after it had started. Sometimes he would commentate on four matches in a week. I worked with him once when, as a stunt, he commentated on a morning kick-off at Vicarage Road and then went by motorbike to Stamford Bridge where he commentated on a Chelsea game that started at 3pm.

He lived it, relishing every second. He loved watching football matches and commentating on them and he did it better than anyone else around at the time, more fluently, more cogently, more passionately, more excitedly and in a way that was more relevant to the contemporary football supporter.

Watching JP work at close quarters, I was amazed at the way he would stay on top of the game. He didn't miss a beat and he always described the action in real time, as it happened without any delay. If he said that Gavin Peacock had the ball he would actually have it at the time and he was accurate and concise with the detail as he described the game. It was almost as though he was controlling the players who responded to whatever he said, it was a wonderful illusion to watch.

Top sports broadcasters have an ability to assimilate and contextualise huge amounts of information instantly and JP was up there with the best. I'm convinced that he has more than one brain.

After the games had finished on a Saturday and all the final scores were in, four of us would quickly work out how the results had altered the English league tables and would read out the updated positions and points of teams in each of the four divisions. I would regularly be given one of the lower-division tables to do. When I went to the studio to collect my broadcasting equipment on the way to the game, Pete Simmons would say to me, 'Can you do the Division Three table today?' I would take with me two specially prepared, neatly typed pieces of paper. One would list that afternoon's Division Three fixtures and the other would show the table at the start of play in an appropriately abridged format – team name, number of games played, number of points and goal difference.

When the final whistles had blown Pete would quickly yell the results down the line to me – 'Brentford 1-0, Cambridge 0-0, Cardiff 1-3, Darlington 1-1, Exeter 4-0, Hull 3-3, Mansfield 0-0, Plymouth 2-1, Rochdale 3-0, Southend 0-1, Swansea 2-1, Torquay 2-2.' As he did so I would write the scores down and would then have what seemed like about two seconds to work out how the top and bottom of the new table looked taking into account that afternoon's results. When cued I would read out the top six and bottom six clubs, their position, points total and if necessary, goal difference. I enjoyed the challenge but it wasn't my favourite part of the afternoon. While I was working out the new table I would feel like a man being chased down a dark alley by a psychopath wielding a machete, although as the tables were gone through in order I actually had longer to work out my table than those doing the Premier League or Division One and Division Two tables. JP would do the Premier League and read out the whole table, not just the top six and bottom six. I was always relieved when I'd finished and could get on with writing my considered piece on the game I was covering.

As well as working as a reporter, I used to act as what was known as 'third man' at some games. This involved playing a supporting role to the commentator and pundit. On one occasion I was with JP at Vicarage Road for a midweek Division One match between Watford and Crystal Palace. There were a lot of games being played in Division One that evening. Just before kick-off JP turned to me and unexpectedly asked if I would, after the games had all finished and the results were known, work out an updated Division One table.

The difference this time was that because it was a last-minute request I wasn't prepared and I didn't have the usual typed-out pieces of paper listing fixtures and showing the Division One table before kick-off. All I had was the table in the matchday programme which was not in a format which would easily allow the task to be performed. I agonised during the game about how I was going to work out the new table. I was half hoping that JP might forget that he'd asked me to do it. No chance. After the game had finished, during an ad break, just as he was about to do a live interview with someone who was on a phone somewhere, JP turned to me and said, 'Have you got that table ready?' I'd sort of managed to part work it out but what I'd done wasn't complete and couldn't be used as it was. I said, 'I've done some of it,' and feeling like a naughty schoolboy who hadn't finished his homework I showed him the page in the programme on which I'd made annotations. JP rolled his eyes, took the programme from me and started his interview. While the guy he was interviewing was answering his questions JP set about the job of working out the new table. By the time the interview was over he had finished, and he read the new table out on air before wrapping up the show with his usual panache.

JP could be wickedly funny as well. On one occasion he came out with a joke which only those in the know would have got. A reporter had been into hospital for shall we say a delicate operation. For his first game back, when he was able to sit down again without discomfort, he was sent to White Hart Lane. JP's cue to him for his preview was, 'Spurs have been doing well recently, but they're perhaps lacking a defensive midfield player. Maybe they would benefit from bringing someone in to play in that position, possibly a player a bit like Nobby STILES?' Ouch. I winced when I heard that.

Working with JP as third man allowed him to assess my potential first-hand. At a Wimbledon match early on I said on air something like, 'It's worth making the point that Dean Holdsworth hasn't scored in his last six games.' I thought it was a sound Motty-type stat worth relaying to the listeners but as he continued commentating JP wrote a note which he passed to me, which read, 'Observations not points.'

After the game JP said to me, 'You've got to want the microphone.' It was the broadcasting equivalent of a coach saying to a footballer, 'You've got to want the ball.' I didn't want to admit that I wasn't particularly ambitious so I nodded sagely in agreement and didn't say anything but I was thinking, 'JP, football reporting to me is a bit like when I played football for Longdean Invaders Reserves. I was never a star player. I would sometimes play an incisive, defence-splitting through ball and I used to chip in with about three goals a season but usually when I received the ball in the penalty box the prospect of scoring a goal was too much and I would get over-excited, lose composure and fluff the chance. I played in midfield but I never really demanded the ball and I didn't run the game. I would take up a position where I could receive it and if a team-mate passed to me, great, I would do my best with it but I didn't have any special ability and I would usually fairly quickly play a safe pass so that we kept possession. I was more of a continuity player, my role was to give the ball to someone else and let them create some magic. I'm the same as that as a football reporter. I've accepted that I'm not going to be a big, famous, star commentator like you, but like you I love football and for me just to be involved in all this, to play a part and to make a constructive contribution is enough.'

JP wanted the microphone so much that I reckon if he could have done he would have covered every game himself. He would have been at the main match, which he always was anyway, and he would have been at all of the others as well. He would have said in his commentary, 'With 14 minutes played on Capital Gold Sport it's Chelsea 0 Manchester United 0, the last we heard it was goalless at Highbury, what's been happening there Jonathan Pearce?' 'Jonathan, it's still goalless here, the closest we've come to a breakthrough was on 12 minutes when Ian Wright brilliantly dribbled through the Newcastle defence and shot narrowly wide, any goals at Goodison Park where Spurs are the visitors, Jonathan Pearce?'

But Capital Gold Sport employed other people and JP had to make sure that they were the right ones. The tape I'd sent to him was one of many he received as the hirer and firer of reporters. JP once told us about a tape that had been sent to him by a Millwall supporter. It contained a clip of commentary which had started promisingly, 'Alex Rae has the ball on the left, Rae's gone past his man, that's a great cross to the far post for Tony Cascarino … Cascarino with a downward header past the keeper … GET IN THERE YOU FUCKING BEAUTY!'

People play fantasy football but to me football itself is a fantasy in the way it delights and transports me to other realms, never more so than when a goal is scored. I never tire of football and I never tire of seeing goals being scored. When I watch a goal going in it's like it's the first time I've ever seen it happen. Somehow, no matter how many of them I see, goals retain their freshness and capacity to amaze. Football in general and goals in particular create a never-ending source of wonderment.

Goals scored by their team send supporters into raptures and give them fleeting moments of ecstasy. Goals were the lifeblood of matches covered on Capital Gold Sport and they demanded an emotional response. The show was never more alive than when an important goal was scored in one of the games we were covering. Goals were celebrated joyfully in an unrestrained fashion. No one did it more theatrically, entertainingly and flamboyantly than JP with his long, drawn-out Brazilianesque goal celebrations which became his trademark, each one a unique rubber stamp. JP's voice was explosive and when a goal was scored he erupted like a volcano. Through his words and tone of voice JP conveyed the significance and uniqueness of the goals he commentated on and the better and more relaxed he got the more he opened up and let go. His commentary would build and reach a crescendo when a goal was scored and his routine could be pure pizzazz.

After Lee Chapman had scored for West Ham away to Blackburn Rovers on 18 September 1993, 'Marsh stabs it forward, it's all a bit tight in there, Gordon plants his header back into the box, Chapman! Lee Chapman on his debut, West Ham are ahead, oh it's luverlee!'

Arsenal won the FA Cup in 1992/93, beating Sheffield Wednesday in the final after a replay. In the semi-final Arsenal beat Spurs at Wembley through a 79th-minute Tony Adams goal. When the goal went in JP cleverly used in his commentary the donkey taunts which opposition fans often directed at Adams, 'It's a free kick now, Merson chips it over the wall – the header down, Tony Adaaaaams, Captain Marvel, ee-ore, ee-ore, he always does it for Arsenal!'

At Watford they particularly liked 'On the night of the full moon it's a howling, prowling, roaring, scoring David Holdsworth' when the centre-back scored a goal which helped to knock Leeds United out of the League Cup at Vicarage Road in a 2-1 win in 1992.

The pinnacle for JP was commentating on England and 'Lineker scores!' took on an extra dimension when it was for England rather than Spurs. Perhaps JP's finest moment behind a Capital Gold Sport microphone came as a wave of euphoria swept over the country and England made it to the semi-final of Euro 96. In a group match England demolished the Netherlands 4-1 with a breathtaking display of intricate, attacking football. England's second goal put daylight between them and their opponents, 'Gazza – Sheringham heads it on, it's a second goaaaaaal, it's double Dutch delight, Gazza went to take the corner and the Dutch weren't ready, the defence wasn't steady and there was good old Teddy and toast tonight with a glass of Sheriiiii, England 2 Holland 0!'

JP was gutted when Capital Gold Sport lost the rights to cover England internationals. A story circulated that during Euro 96 his commentaries on England goals were played to the players on the team coach to inspire them. I never found out if it was true but I wouldn't be surprised if it was.

For me Brian Moore was *the* football commentator of the 1960s, 1970s and 1980s. He became calmer in later years but he never lost his passion for the game. He seemed to get just how much football means to players and supporters. There have been many excellent, even brilliant, commentators over the years to whom I can happily listen, who more than adequately describe the action, but Moore had something extra that set him apart and so did JP. Both of them excited and enthused me and stimulated my interest in football in a way that no other commentator did. At some point Moore handed the baton to JP. I don't know when it happened, but I like to think that it might have been during that climactic night in 1989 at Anfield when Arsenal won the title.

At Capital Gold Sport JP encouraged us to think big, beyond the confines of local radio. We broadcast in London and the south-east but he saw our main competitors as BBC Radio 5 Live, a national station, and his main rival as Alan Green. I never took a particularly close interest in listening figures myself but I did hear people talk about audiences of more than two million and I know that JP and Capital Gold Sport won quite a few Sony Radio Awards, which apparently are very prestigious.

As much as anything, JP characterised us as fans with microphones, and our responsibility was to reflect and embody the passion felt for the game by the supporter on the terraces.

8

Nobody likes a postponement and as a football reporter they were particularly unwelcome, especially when they were unexpected and at short notice. I would spend all week looking forward to the match, build myself up, do my preparation, make my way to the ground, and then it would all get taken away. One day, though, early in my time at Capital Gold Sport, a postponement worked beautifully in my favour and led to a meeting with for me the English game's ultimate 20th century icon.

The first FA Cup final I can remember is the one played in 1964, when West Ham United beat Preston North End 3-2, in which Preston's Howard Kendall became the youngest player to play in a Wembley final in the competition, aged 17 years and 345 days. Bobby Moore, born in Barking on 12 April 1941, was West Ham's captain that day. Moore joined the Hammers in 1956 and made his debut two years later. He made his England debut in 1962 and became the regular captain of his country in the summer of 1964. The FA Cup win was the first of three successful Wembley finals in as many years for Moore. In 1965 he lifted the European Cup Winners' Cup after West Ham defeated 1860 Munich 2-0 in the final, then on 30 July 1966 he wiped his hands clean before accepting the Jules Rimet Trophy from The Queen. He played his last game for West Ham in 1974 and moved to Second Division Fulham for £25,000. During his first full season at the Cottage Fulham reached the FA Cup final, losing 2-0 to West Ham.

Moore retired from playing professionally in 1978 and eventually joined Capital Gold Sport in 1990 to work alongside JP. Harry Redknapp told an anecdote about how, when he was managing West Ham, he took the Hammers to Grimsby for a midweek fixture. Before the game Redknapp looked up at the press box, saw Bobby and thought what a waste it was for someone of his stature to be working as a radio pundit when he should have been in a job where he could have made a much more significant and meaningful contribution to English football. I wouldn't deny that Harry had a point, but I couldn't help but contrast the story to my own situation and to find it amusing and ironic. Booby had reached the pinnacle of the game as a player and the perception was that for him to be working as a radio pundit at a midweek match between Grimsby and West Ham was somewhat demeaning, whereas for me to be reporting on a game at Blundell Park between Grimsby and a London club meant that I had made it and had fulfilled a dream.

In my first season at Capital, I was given Leyton Orient v Bury to cover, which was to be played on 14 December 1991. The weather was bad that day and as I drove to the ground I heard on the radio that games were being called off right, left and centre. As I approached the ground at just before 1.30pm it was the only fixture in London which had not been postponed. My preparation for the game had been on the basis that I would be doing the usual number of short reports. I didn't know what would happen if my match was the only one left on and I started wondering if I might be asked to present the whole show live on my own and do a 90-minute commentary as well. As it turned out the game was postponed just as I arrived at the ground so I was off the hook. I drove back to the studio at Warren Street to drop off my kit and walked in to the office, where I saw Bobby Moore.

When England won the World Cup in 1966 to become world champions for the first time I couldn't have been much further away from the action. I listened to commentary on England v West Germany on the BBC World Service in the middle of the night in Singapore. Now I was in the same room as the man who had captained England to victory.

JP and Bobby were the only two people there; everyone else had gone home as all the postponements meant that there would be no programme. The office was silent as I walked in and clocked him. I didn't have to answer the question, 'How do you start a conversation with Bobby Moore?' because on seeing me Bobby immediately sparked one up with me. Just small talk about why my game had been postponed and what I would be doing with a free afternoon, but he was genuinely interested. I asked him a bit about his career and he told me that he'd been lucky with injuries.

Blond hair, blue eyes, there was an air of calm authority about him. Sometimes in this country we get things just right and we did when it was decided that there would be a statue of Bobby outside the rebuilt Wembley stadium. If there was going to be a statue of anyone there it had to be him.

They say that you should never meet your heroes but Bobby Moore was all I could have wished him to be that day.

*

When I started working at Capital Gold Sport they had someone who reported on Watford matches, a guy called Jon Desborough, and he was good. When I found out that the station had a dedicated Watford reporter, even though I was happily reporting on any game I was given, I wanted his job. Some people are never satisfied. There was no way I was going to get it, or would have expected it, while Jon was still around. However, once Capital knew that Watford were my team, when Jon wasn't available I was given their matches to cover. Eventually, as luck would have it, Jon left to go elsewhere and I started covering Watford. I couldn't have asked for any more.

It was in Steve Perryman's first full season as Watford manager, 1991/92, that I covered my first Hornets game for Capital Gold Sport. In comparison to the heady triumphs of Graham Taylor's first spell it was a very low-key affair – a Zenith Data Systems Cup first round tie at Vicarage Road against Southend United, played on 2 October 1991 in front of a crowd of 1,700. David James played in goal for Watford and Andy Sussex scored the only goal of the game for Southend. But it didn't matter to me. I felt like Charlie George must have done when he climbed off the Highbury terraces to pull on an Arsenal shirt.

I was at Vicarage Road on 22 February 1992 for a 0-0 draw with Port Vale. It was a dull game but from a long post-match conversation with Steve Perryman I gained an insight into what it was like to manage the club at the time. The result left Watford 18th in Division Two. After the game I waited until all the other reporters had finished talking to Steve and had gone. There was just Steve and me left in the press room.

When Steve became manager in November 1990 Watford were bottom of Division Two, and I started by asking him what sort of progress he thought had been made since he'd arrived at the club. His response went into depth, 'Well not enough progress as I would like, put it that way. We managed to scrape out of the relegation issue last year by the skin of our teeth, which bearing in mind the position I took over was a phenomenal sort of exercise to actually achieve that. During the close-season we then lost three of the 11 players, it's more than 11 but I knew what my best 11 were, Wilkinson, the 20-goal-a-year man, Falconer, 6ft, left-footed midfielder, and Glenn Roeder who's out with an injury and at one stage decided to leave us to join Gazza in Italy. So bearing in mind there must have been reasons why we were bottom of the table all year to eventually scrape out and then to lose three of the more positive players in the team was quite something to overcome.

'I always knew this season was going to be difficult. It's certainly proving that way. We haven't had the deep traumas of last year in terms of our position and points adrift of everyone else and yet I don't think it's as good a league either. I think there's more poor teams in the Second Division this year than there were last for instance. So, it's very difficult in the sort of recession times that we're in being able to replace a bulk of players, I suppose if you look at Aston Villa they're a club that have done it, they've took in a hell of a lot of money for one player, to Italy, and then spent most of it by getting in lots of different players and shifting players around and moving them on, but it's very unusual in this day and age. So we have to make the best of what we've got.

'I'm pleased with quite a lot of it, I think the spirit of the side is much better this year than it was last year, but bearing in mind I took over at a time where if you're bottom of the table there are lots of different people that can separate you in terms of supporters and press and whose fault is it that you're bottom of the league. So the spirit's much better, I would like us to be a better football side than we are, I think that we lack a bit of cohesion, we certainly don't produce enough thrills and goalmouth excitement that you're entitled to get at home and yet away from home our form has been good, our results have been good, we've played some particularly good games away and got decent results. To go and beat Cambridge is no mean feat, to win 4-0 at Millwall, although Millwall are struggling at home themselves, but there are signs that we're getting it together.

'I think it would have been too much to expect for us to just miss falling over the edge of the cliff last year to then get up from that situation and go and climb a mountain, i.e. promotion. But having said that, that's not taking an easy way out. I would have expected us to be better-placed than we are at the moment, certainly a better football side, and I certainly expect to see signs of improvement particularly football wise and points wise between now and the end of the season. A lot of that depends upon luck with injuries and whatever, that's certainly not been the case that we've got anything to moan about in that department, we've been very lucky in that area. But I think the understanding is coming, it's just a shame that we do lack that confidence at home, the supporters lack confidence in the team, they don't see any big name coming here for a million pounds or half a million pounds as a new striker or whatever, so they have not been really fired up.

'The one that has given a bit of fresh air to it is Hessenthaler, a £65,000 player from the non-league who's shown that his urgency of legs and desire are something to cling hold of and improve upon. So in certain ways there's been improvement, in other ways I've been disappointed, obviously.'

Andy Hessenthaler was a phenomenon. He didn't play as a full-time professional until the age of 26. Before that he worked as a builder and played as a part-time semi-professional for Dartford, Corinthian and Redbridge Forest. It was on the recommendation of Peter Taylor, Perryman's assistant, that Watford signed Hessenthaler from Redbridge in September 1991. He had impressed everyone at Watford and probably because of his late arrival in league football there was a hunger and appetite about him. Tongue in cheek, I asked Steve what he thought of the idea of building a team of players all plucked from non-league football. He laughed and said, 'The accountant would be quite happy with that and the bank manager I'm sure. There are players in the non-league for sure and we're actively scouting those regions as everyone else is. You do get that hunger in the players outside the league, they do realise what a joy it is to be a professional footballer and go to work every day earning their living at something they wish to do. But you still have quality in the professional ranks as well so it's just a mixture of all those things. We've got to be available to buy the chance buy as Tranmere bought [John] Aldridge who's scored so many goals for them this year. You have to be available to accept players from our own youth ranks. When you consider David James is going to go for a million-plus that tells you something about the development here at Watford and a number of good players in the league now that have been taught their football here.

'We have to go and look for experienced players like Luther Blissett and [Peter] Nicholas who have been for whatever reason let go by their own clubs and we've decided to bring here to up our level of experience. And certainly non-league's another area where we have to scout and trawl if you like and make sure that we are there fighting with other clubs when a good player becomes available. Andy Townsend at Chelsea from the non-league, terrific player, it's not to say that because you're a non-league player you lack quality, there are qualities down there and when you surround them by other professional players with full time training they can actually improve a hell of a lot.'

I wondered whether Steve had set any targets in terms of how long it would take to build a winning side at Watford. Did he think that it would take, say, three years to turn the club round from being a bottom club to one challenging for the Second Division? 'Yes, within all the traumas of relegation, from the first day I took over, you look at the contract situation because of freedom of contract being as it is. Wilkinson, [Willie] Falconer, [Jason] Drysdale, [Gary] Porter all contracts up. Four players who again were four of the 11, what I would consider the first 11 if I had to put my name on that 11, not always possible because you get injuries and whatever. So we had the normal wrangles, no one was going to sign before the end of the season because they didn't want to sign for a Third Division club, probably rightly so with all their ability. So we had all these wrangles, and eventually Falconer and Wilkinson left us very, very late, made it hard to sign replacements before they actually left.

'I haven't got that this year, I've got two younger players, two good players who I hopefully will sign before the deadline time, so that we can have a fresh summer looking for new talent, looking to top up on what we've got, maybe looking to do deals with players that I'm not so sure about or keen about, hopefully the recession days fade into the past and clubs look as though they're going to spend a bit more money to get a surge going for the possible super Premier League or whatever it is, so yeah as I say I spent too long in the summer haggling over contracts and you've only got so much time, there's only so many hours in the day and only so much money available, until your player actually leaves you, then you don't know what money you've got. So I would like to think that because of the lack of problems we have between now and the end of the season with contracts that I can concentrate on getting us a side during next season that is pushing for the First Division.'

The amount of money available to a manager is a crucial factor and I asked Steve whether the sort of funds that he would have liked to have been able to spend were available to him at Watford. 'My brief from the chairman is that I have to balance the books in terms of the transfers in and out. When you consider that we have David James who is probably going to leave us at the end of the year, we're going to get decent money in for him, so there is money available obviously but it's also directed by the fact that our last couple of gates have been 6,000, upper 6,000s and 7,000s, which is not good enough, we need 10,000 to break even here, so you know that will be a drain on resources as well, because there's money walking out of the gate every week or every fortnight when we play at home. So it's up to me to try and produce a side that people want to come and watch, but I still say that the first priority is to have a season of stability if you like for a chance for my ideas to filter through.

'I remember John Lyall going to Ipswich and there being, in your words, lack of patience and people calling for his head. John Lyall is an exceptional coach and a very good man at putting a team together and you can see now by their position in the Second Division that that patience has been rewarded if you like. So it does take time, you can't just change things from one day to the next, it can't be done unfortunately, supporters would like it but it can't happen so unfortunately you have to go through a bit of, er, you know just avoiding relegation was not the end of the issue. There is more to it than that and so there are going to be a few frustrating Saturdays and midweeks, hopefully there's going to be some good ones along the line as well and hopefully we're going to whet the appetites of the supporters that we have left to encourage them to buy season tickets and support us next year when I would suggest from my knowledge of the game that we'll be pushing.'

Like Dave Bassett, Steve Harrison and Colin Lee before him, Steve was walking in the shadow of Graham Taylor and I asked him how conscious he was that Watford had enjoyed tremendous success in the Taylor era under the guidance of an exceptional manager. 'Well it's something to be pleased about because it meant that when I took over a club however perilous the position it was a Second Division club and Graham Taylor had been responsible for getting them not to the Second Division but to the First and for whatever reason they'd come down to the Second. So there was a lot of quality at this club, I'm not talking necessarily of the professional staff but qualities of commercialism, of the way people looked upon the club, the way that the backroom people acted, physio, kit man, my secretary who was Graham Taylor's secretary. So there was a lot of good things left from that era and therefore to a certain degree although it was as I said a perilous position there was also a good feeling about the club as well when I came here in terms of you know assets to use so I'm not really worried, I had to be a player at Tottenham for many years with the shadow of the 50/51, 60/61 side and whatever we did we were never going to be as good as those albeit you know we had a special team in the eighties and won some decent trophies but it's something that people always look back with fond memories and they deserve to look back with fond memories on the Taylor era at Watford because he did so many good things. But I have to see the positive side of that rather than the negative.'

At the age of 40 Steve was still a relatively young manager. I always wonder to what extent players, when they become managers, are influenced by the managers they played under, and to what extent they are able to develop their own style. Steve had played under successful managers at Spurs including the great Bill Nicholson and I asked him about who had influenced him. 'I think you pick up from anyone you work with, for good and for bad. Bill Nicholson for instance as a 17-year-old coming into the first team there, Bill Nicholson I don't think ever fined a player for being late, if you were late one look from his granite type features were enough to say to you "I'd better not do that again" because he's going to, not only is he going to look at me he's actually going to say something next time. So there was this aura of discipline that he carried around him, rightly so because he was a very great manager who did some fantastic things. Very organised the way that he approached it, with the training ground at Cheshunt and travelling etc., very, very organised.

'I had Terry Neill when I was there, I had Keith Burkinshaw, I had Peter Shreeves, all good things in their own ways. Peter Shreeves tactically I felt was very, very good. Keith Burkinshaw for his honesty, fine, Terry Neill came and we were in a bit of a relegation issue at the time and he managed to save us from that albeit in the last game, he brought a freshness to my game that I felt had been overpowered a bit by the real strong influence of a disciplinarian like Bill Nicholson. He sort of opened the doors to me to a bit of freedom and so I have to thank him for that, but you learn from all of them but eventually you have to become your own type of manager and you know we'd all like to copy [Brian] Clough and his success but we can't all carry it off in the way that he does it, so you have to do it your own way and hope that's good enough.'

I would have been happy to carry on the conversation long into the night but I didn't want to overdo it. I wound up by thanking Steve and wishing him good luck for the rest of the season. He responded by saying, 'I enjoyed doing that.'

Watford had another great end-of-season run, winning eight, drawing three and losing one of their last 12 matches to finish 1991/92 in a comfortable tenth place. Steve had said in our discussion that David James would probably leave Vicarage Road at the end of the season and that was exactly what happened. James, who had helped Watford to win the FA Youth Cup in 1989, moved to Liverpool for £1.25m in June 1992.

Watford finished the 1992/93 season, which turned out to be Steve's last as manager, in 16th position in Division One. Steve had been Spurs' longest-serving player and his heart was in the north London club. The lure of White Hart Lane proved too much and at the end of 1992/93 he resigned as Watford manager and rejoined Spurs, becoming assistant to his former team-mate Ossie Ardiles.

9

As Mick Conway was ahead of me in the pecking order, I had to wait until he was unavailable to cover my first topflight game for Capital Gold Sport. It was in Division One, between Southampton and Crystal Palace at The Dell on Wednesday, 11 March 1992. I was there to focus on Crystal Palace as the London team but I ended up being dazzled by the sublime skills of Matt Le Tissier. His weight of pass and vision were unreal. If a Southampton player made a run Le Tissier would pick him out. He stood out even in the company of Alan Shearer and it was Le Tissier who scored the only goal of the game from a Shearer pass.

A few years later, in the summer of 1995, I was sent by Capital to interview Le Tissier who was in London to promote a video compilation of his greatest goals, aptly entitled *Unbelievable*. A room had been set aside for the interviews at HMV on Oxford Street and he was there with a small entourage. When I was introduced to him, I felt like I was being ushered into the Court of King Matt.

What a gift to be able to play football like Matt Le Tissier. What a gift for the Southampton supporters that he spent his whole career at the south coast club. I wondered what it was like to be able to play football with the ability he had, and when we sat down to talk I suggested to him that it must be an amazing experience and give him a lot of pleasure and satisfaction. 'Yeah, it gives me a great deal of pleasure. The main thing I enjoy about football is sticking the ball in the back of the net like anybody but it is nice to see the pleasure on the faces of the people in the crowd when that happens.'

Le Tissier was treated like a god at Southampton and the rapport he developed with the club's supporters had to be a big reason he'd stayed there for so long. 'Yeah, they've been great to me ever since I made my debut as a 17-year-old, they've been fantastic, never erred in their support of me and it's been wonderful down there.'

I was keen to learn about Le Tissier's mental approach to the game. He was sometimes criticised for being 'laid-back' but to me that was an asset rather than a handicap. Le Tissier appeared to me to be relaxed on the pitch, to be able to play without any tension, and to be in control of what he was doing. I told him this and asked him how he felt when he was out there. 'Yeah it is, it's a totally relaxed state of mind that I play in because I believe that's the way to get the best out of yourself. I see some people and they hype themselves up and they're a bag of nerves before a game but I don't think that's the best way to get the best out of me. It may work for them but from a personal point of view if I'm relaxed in my mind then I know I can play to the best of my ability.'

At Southampton, Le Tissier was a massive fish in a relatively small pool. As such he would be in a good position to call the shots. He had his own ideas about how he wanted to play the game. I asked him whether he would say that he was a person who liked to play to his own rules, and if so whether that brought him into conflict with coaches and people who maybe tried to make him play in a certain way. 'Probably to a certain extent, yeah, if the manager asks me to do something I won't totally ignore what he says, I'll try and do the best for the team, but there are occasions where if I think that something else is on, the manager has to have the belief in me that I know what I'm doing when I'm out on the pitch and he's got to have confidence in that ability.'

One of Le Tissier's great strengths was his ability to improvise and I asked him if he thought football should be played 'off the cuff' and not to a rigid system. He gave me an interesting and thoughtful answer which made sense. 'In certain areas of the pitch, obviously when you're in the defensive third which doesn't happen very often to me, but I like to think in the last third of the field it is very much off the cuff and I think that's the way to unlock defences because you can be very predictable sometimes in the way that we play the game and I think the only way to unlock good defences is to be a bit unpredictable.'

THE MAN WHO SHOUTS

Matt enjoyed scoring goals the most but like Stanley Matthews there was an element of selflessness to his play. 'Scoring goals gives me the greatest pleasure, putting the ball on a plate for somebody else to score isn't that far behind, it's very close but there's no better feeling than sticking the ball in the back of the net.'

Matt's career ran counter to the popular perception that footballers are in the game to make money and win trophies and I asked what motivated him. 'I think everybody would laugh if I said I was in it to win trophies and earn money because I've stayed at Southampton so long. I do it because I enjoy doing it and I enjoy it because I know the way I play gives people entertainment and value for money when they pay a lot of money to come and watch the games.'

Le Tissier did more than anyone else to keep Southampton in the top flight throughout his career. He was adored by Saints supporters but the same cannot be said of England managers; he played eight times for England between 1994 and 1998.

9 March 1994: England 1 Denmark 0, as a substitute for Paul Gascoigne in the 66th minute

17 May 1994: England 5 Greece 0, as a substitute for Darren Anderton in the 62nd minute

22 May 1994: England 0 Norway 0, as a substitute for Darren Anderton in the 76th minute

12 October 1994: England 1 Romania 1, playing the full 90 minutes

16 November 1994: England 1 Nigeria 0, as a substitute for Peter Beardsley in the 79th minute

15 February 1995: Republic of Ireland 1 England 0 as a starter (match abandoned after 23 minutes)

1 September 1996: Moldova 0 England 3, as a substitute for Nicky Barmby in the 80th minute

12 February 1997: England 0 Italy 1 as a starter and was replaced by Les Ferdinand in the 61st minute

Despite his ability and his achievements for Southampton, Le Tissier simply wasn't given the chance by England to prove himself at international level. His first three appearances were all as a substitute and he played the full 90 minutes only once. In his two other starts, one match was abandoned after 23 minutes and in the other he was substituted after about an hour. Le Tissier played a total of 229 minutes for England, the equivalent of about two and a half games.

I asked Matt whether the England manager at the time, Terry Venables, had told him where he fitted into his plans. 'No not at the moment, he's not said anything to me for a long time now and I don't suppose he has to, if he doesn't want me in his squad that's up to him.'

Venables was succeeded as England manager by Glenn Hoddle in 1996 and you would have thought that if anyone would have appreciated the talents of Le Tissier it would have been Hoddle, himself one of the most gifted players of his generation. But Le Tissier won only two caps under Hoddle and he was omitted from the England squad for the 1998 World Cup in France. It had seemed highly likely to many people including Le Tissier that he would go to France when in April 1998 he scored a hat-trick for England B against Russia at Loftus Road, as well as hitting the woodwork twice and finishing the game with the captain's armband. But that wasn't enough to convince Hoddle who acknowledged that Le Tissier was abundantly talented but felt that he didn't have enough mentally or physically to reach 'the top', and that he needed to contribute more over 90 minutes. Choosing to play for Southampton for his whole career did not help Le Tissier's England chances under Hoddle, who would have liked to have seen him play for one of the big clubs where the crowds were more demanding than at The Dell.

I watched England play Argentina in the second round of the 1998 World Cup finals on TV at the Aldgate Exchange in east London on 30 June 1998. It was an enthralling, ultimately frustrating spectacle with an excruciating conclusion. With the score 2-2 after extra time the game went to a penalty shoot-out in which Argentina took a 4-3 lead. In 540 career appearances for Southampton Le Tissier scored 209 goals, of which 48 were penalties. He missed once from the spot, when his kick was saved by Nottingham Forest's Mark Crossley. I would have put money on Le Tissier scoring if he'd been the one to take the next England penalty. In the event the player selected to step into the spotlight in the feverishly tense atmosphere was David Batty, who had never previously taken a penalty. Batty's spot-kick was saved by Carlos Roa and England were out of the World Cup.

The trend in modern football is for players to move clubs in search of fortune and fame. Le Tissier bucked that trend and was atypical, not just of footballers but of people in general, in that he found something early in life which made him content, and also allowed him to make other people happy. Having found it and recognised it, he stayed with it. It might be called by some a lack of ambition but to me it was knowing that he had something of value and cherishing it.

Throughout his career there was almost constant speculation that Le Tissier would move on from Southampton. I asked him whether, when he saw players like Tim Flowers and Alan Shearer leaving the Saints and going on to win things at Blackburn, he was tempted to make a similar exit. 'Not really, I'm quite happy where I am. Obviously those two felt that they could be happier somewhere else and they've made the move and it's worked out fantastic for them. That doesn't mean that if I did it that it would work out the same for me. I'm quite happy where I am and don't intend to leave.'

I had read that Le Tissier would consider leaving Southampton to enhance his England prospects. He had been left out of the latest squad at the time we met but even that hadn't made him think again about asking for a move. 'No not at this moment in time it hasn't. I still believe that if I'm playing to the best of my ability I'd like to think the England manager wouldn't be able to leave me out so as from the start of next season that's what I've got to try and do.'

Not long before Le Tissier retired from professional football, Southampton moved from The Dell to St Mary's. The final competitive match at The Dell was played on 19 May 2001, against Arsenal. In a 'you couldn't make it up' scenario Le Tissier, on as a late substitute, scored in the 89th minute with a spectacular left-footed volley from outside the penalty area to give the Saints a 3-2 win. It was the last goal ever scored at The Dell.

It was Southampton supporters who had the final word on Le Tissier's career. He retired at the end of the 2001/02 season and in June 2002 over 32,000 people turned up at St Mary's for a testimonial match between Southampton and a side of England all-stars.

Matt Le Tissier wasn't the first gifted individual to be overlooked by England. A few months before meeting Le Tissier I'd had lunch with one from a previous generation.

*

If James Bond had been a footballer, he would have been Rodney Marsh.

Marsh was born on 11 October 1944 in Hatfield, Hertfordshire. He played for Fulham (twice), Queens Park Rangers, Manchester City, Tampa Bay Rowdies and England (nine times, scoring once). He made his first Fulham debut in 1963 before making the short move across west London to QPR, then in Division Three, for £15,000 in March 1966. He made an instant impact at Loftus Road; in his first full season with the club he scored 44 goals including 30 in the league. QPR were Division Three champions in 1966/67 and won the League Cup that season, coming back from 2-0 down to beat First Division West Bromwich Albion 3-2 in the final. Marsh scored the equaliser with a low angled drive into the far corner of the net after a run from the halfway line. It was the first time the League Cup final had been played at Wembley. The following year, QPR were promoted to Division One, although they were relegated after one season. In 1971, with QPR still in Division Two, Alf Ramsey gave Marsh his England debut against Switzerland.

Not long afterwards, in March 1972, Malcolm Allison signed Marsh for Manchester City for a then club record £200,000. At the time City were five points clear at the top of the table and on course to win the title but by the end of the season they had slipped to fourth place. In 1972/73 Marsh became a crowd favourite, scoring 19 goals. After playing in the City side which lost the 1974 League Cup final to Wolverhampton Wanderers, Marsh left the club not long into the 1974/75 season. In 1975 Marsh headed for the United States to play for Tampa Bay Rowdies before returning to England in 1976/77 for a brief spell at Fulham where he played alongside George Best and Bobby Moore. He went back to Tampa Bay in 1977 and retired in 1979.

I saw Marsh play a couple of times during his career. The first was under lights at Loftus Road in November 1969 as Queens Park Rangers beat Watford 2-1. Marsh took over the game, which turned into a personal duel between himself and Watford goalkeeper Mike Walker. Despite his brilliance, Marsh didn't score as Walker managed to keep him out. The performance captivated me and I watched entranced again some five years later one of the few games in which Marsh, Best and Moore all started for Fulham, a 2-0 win at Luton. I recall Marsh and Best playing a one-two in their own penalty area. Both those games were watched by crowds of 19,000-odd and it was clear that Marsh was a player who gave people what they wanted.

Just before Christmas 1994 I was invited to sit at Capital Gold Sport's table at a sportswriters' awards dinner. I didn't know who would be in our party and I was in for a big surprise. As I arrived I saw some Capital boys standing around drinking in a group of football people. As I drew closer I recognised Frank McLintock, the ex-Spurs full-back Gary Stevens, the then Crystal Palace manager Alan Smith, Alan Mullery, and – oh, fuck me, that's only Rodney Marsh. They'd all done some punditry recently for Capital Gold Sport and had been invited as a thank you.

The dinner itself was top notch. It was one of those dos where you get waited on hand and foot. I didn't even have to pick up the bottle of wine on the table to refill my glass – there was someone there to top it up before it was even empty and to brush the crumbs off the tablecloth between courses. But it was the company which made the evening a joy. The mood was relaxed and the banter flowed as freely as the wine. At one point someone said that they would love it if for just one day every league manager swapped places with the chairman of their club. Quick as a flash, Alan Mullery responded, 'If you did that there'd be 92 sackings.'

At the time Smith's Palace were in the top flight and battling against the odds. He told us that no Palace director had been present at their recent game at Anfield, which had ended in a 0-0 draw, and afterwards chairman Ron Noades had phoned him to say, 'It's a shame you couldn't have pushed on a bit in the second half.'

But it was Marsh who was the main attraction at the event and when he walked across the room to the stage to draw the raffle an affectionate chant spontaneously went up of 'Rodneeeee, Rodneeeee!' I wished I could have had more time to talk to him and when I asked him if we he would like to meet up for lunch some time he agreed. It took some time to arrange because he was flitting between the States and England at the time and when something came up he phoned to cancel, which left me wondering whether it would ever happen. But he was as good as his word and he phoned again after he got back from the States. We arranged to meet in an Italian restaurant in Wimbledon.

We met on a Monday, which made it all the sweeter. On many people's least favourite day of the week, when the world was returning to work after the weekend, I was on my way to have lunch with Rodney Marsh.

He'd done a Best and Marsh roadshow the previous evening. 'It's great fun,' Rodney told me laughing, 'when he turns up.' The food was fine but I can't remember what I ate. We weren't there for the food or drink, we were there to talk football. It was for me to set the agenda and Rodney responded generously, readily giving me his thoughts.

Rodney was a footballer who pleased both aesthetically and as an entertainer. On top of that he had an acute appreciation of players cut from the same cloth as himself as I found out during our lunch.

I wanted to make the most of our time together and it wasn't long before we found ourselves focussing on a subject that has always interested me: whether football can be considered an art form. Rodney told me, 'Well, I think when you're talking about people like George Best and Stan Bowles, and [Paul] Gascoigne and [Eric] Cantona, and people like that, then you're talking about footballers that are genuinely creative, artistic people playing in a sport that generally isn't thought of as being artistic, but certainly players like that are yes.'

It was 1995, not long after Cantona had controversially launched himself at Matthew Simmons, the spectator in the Selhurst Park crowd at a Crystal Palace v Manchester United game who had made a remark which had offended and upset the Frenchman. Some people had called for Cantona to be banned for life as a punishment and I asked Rodney what he thought of them. 'Well the first thing I would say is that the reason that Cantona is such a successful player is because he's such a creative, artistic, philosophical type of a person and I'd put him in the same category as musicians and artists that are you know unique and what I would say to these people that make me sick actually when they come out and say things like "he should be banned for life", I would say to those people, well, until you've been there, until you're in that position of being creative and what goes along with being creative is the emotion of the event and the sensitivity of being creative then you can't judge people that easily because they don't live life on the same terms as we do. They're creative geniuses like you know Beethoven and Mozart and Rembrandt and Van Gogh, they've all got their own you know niche of life in their creative geniuses and that's why Cantona makes £15,000 a week and other people make 250 quid a week.' He was laughing as he finished the sentence and I formed the impression that although Marsh could talk about serious subjects he didn't take himself too seriously.

Cantona was serving an eight-month ban from football at the time and I asked Rodney whether he thought that the forward needed support from other people. He replied, 'Well I'm not sure about that, I think like Paul Gascoigne and certainly when I played it was people like Stan Bowles and as I said earlier George Best, I think they're insular. Creative people are insular and they don't really need endorsement from other people. I mean it's always nice to have that but certainly people that have condemned him right off the bat I would say to those people, until you've been in that position be thankful that you've had the opportunity to see probably one of the greatest players to play in this country for the last 20 years and be thankful that you've had the opportunity to see Eric Cantona play.'

I had the impression that as a player Rodney had come into contact with people who maybe tried to stifle his natural creative instincts, so I asked him whether that did really happen. 'It did all the time, and I didn't care because I didn't respect the people that were telling me those things, you know football in my opinion is for the players and for the supporters, it's not for hierarchy, it's not for the media, it certainly isn't for the media, it's not even for managers, it's for players and supporters. I felt my role in football was to entertain the fans and that's what I did, I think I did it very, very successfully. I also won some things with QPR and Manchester City, played for England a few times and really enjoyed my career so yes I was an entertainer first but the people that were against my creative entertainment philosophy I didn't used to bother with because I didn't respect them and I couldn't be bothered with them.'

I asked Rodney what it was that people enjoyed most about watching him play, and he surprised me with his answer. 'Well I still get people today come up to me and say, "We saw you with George Best and Bobby Moore at Fulham, and wasn't it great in those days and how much you enjoyed it and you were smiling and scoring great goals and dribbling and shooting and passing," it's in my soul, that's the way I play, I just play to love the game and I love scoring goals, I love scoring great goals, I love winning although winning was never number one as a player for me, which is a contradiction in terms sometimes I think, now that's changed, now winning to me is everything since I've become a coach in America and a manager and of course chief executive of Tampa Bay Rowdies it goes from being an entertainment art form to being win at all costs and that's something I have to wrestle with on a day to day basis because sometimes you come up against a Rodney Marsh now I'm the manager, I come up against a Rodney Marsh it's sometimes difficult to swallow.'

Football is a team game played by individuals. What is more important – the team or the individual? It's a conundrum, and there is probably no right or wrong answer. It depends upon what the team is and who the individuals are. A team can be successful without an outstanding individual superstar, but then again a successful team can be built around one brilliant individual, an obvious example being the Argentina side which revolved around Diego Maradona and won the 1986 World Cup in Mexico. The Matt Le Tissier Southampton side which time and again avoided relegation is another example. I asked Rodney how important the superstar is, and whether the role of the ten at Southampton was to support Le Tissier, and for his view on the whole 'football as a team game' debate.

'Do you know that's a very good question, because over the years I've had this conversation with all sorts of people, all the way from the top at the moment with Terry Venables to George Best and everybody in between. My view is slightly different than the norm, and that is that everybody believes that you have to have a team first, right, my point of view is that over the years every great team has had a great individual, every great team, and if you look at the ultimate of that of great teams is Brazil. Brazil have won the World Cup more than any other team in history, the ultimate prize in football is to win the World Cup, I think they've only not qualified once ever in the history of the World Cup, so Brazil by those standards are the best team in the world, for years they had Pelé who was an individual, complete individual, and was also a great team player but was an individual first, all the way to today with Romário who by his own admission is a greedy, selfish player, right, still they go on to win the World Cup final, so I think that it's critical to have a superstar, gifted, individual genius player, it's critical.'

Euro 96 was still a year away and I asked Rodney, who was closer to Terry Venables than most, how he thought England would get on. 'I think Terry Venables will bring success to England but you have to qualify what success is, don't you. I think England, and Terry Venables, is in with a great chance of winning the European Championships. I think that especially as we haven't got to qualify, and we're playing at home, that Terry will put a team on the field that is going to be very competitive and won't give too much away. Getting back to the original point, that's his trademark. Over the years Terry Venables has put together teams that play as teams, with great tactics, great coaching and great management. But you'd find it hard to look at Terry Venables teams and look at an individual creative genius in any of the teams Terry's had, including Barcelona. The first thing he did when he got to Barcelona was to get rid of Maradona. I think you'd find it hard over the years to find a Terry Venables team that had that type player in it. That's why I'm delighted to see him trying to play Matthew Le Tissier.'

Mention of Le Tissier was an interesting development which I leapt on, perhaps going slightly overboard by asking, 'Do you think he should build the team round him?'

'Well that's a little bit premature to say that but you see when I was talking about qualification in terms of qualifying England success, England will be successful but relatively. When you get to the highest level you have to have somebody that will unlock the game, you have to have that, whether it's Romário or [Hristo] Stoichkov or [Gheorghe] Hagi or you know [Roberto] Baggio or whoever you want to talk about. World-class teams at the highest level have somebody that can unlock the game by a touch of genius. Baggio's a great example. Do we have that in England? We have the best striker in Shearer, we have David Platt, top midfield player, are they the type of player that can unlock a zero-zero game by a stroke of genius, probably not. Matthew Le Tissier is as close to having that skill, that genius that can unlock a game as anybody in this country, so I would love to see him have the opportunity to do that, yeah.'

I was warming to the conversation and I asked Rodney to expand on his thoughts on people having misconceptions about footballers. 'Well that's always been the case, I mean, and to get back to your original point Simon, when we talk about some of the people making these sweeping judgements about banning people for life you know you've got to look at Eric Cantona who borders on being a genius and it's what we all want to see in a player and when you do that you look at the emotional side of his character, you look at the creative, artistic side of his character, you know, and it's the same as Gascoigne, very emotional player, when he was crying in the World Cup, when England got knocked out, you don't sort of, you can't imagine as an example Carlton Palmer being a painter. Good player, but he's not that creative genius, and until you've been there, in that position you know your point is there are creative, intelligent people in the game as footballers and I think the other side to the coin is you have to be tolerant of their behaviour sometimes because they are geniuses, and the same thing you praise them for I don't think you can condemn them for, so your point is well taken, yeah you're right.'

I couldn't have had a conversation with Rodney without mentioning Queens Park Rangers and he gave me an assessment of his contribution to the club's recent history. 'Well I think the number ten tradition started with Rodney Marsh, certainly, and the fact that in the seven years that I was there we won the League Cup final, we won the Third Division championship, we won promotion the next year to the First Division, I scored 44 goals in one season, was the leading scorer for five consecutive years, the crowds went from 4,000 to 22,000 and they built a £6m stand, so that was the start of the number ten QPR success story and it went on with Roy Wegerle, Tony Currie, Stan Bowles, Simon Stainrod wore number ten and it was a tradition that was formed of number tens at QPR.'

At that point I introduced the subject of Manchester City to the proceedings by asking Rodney how he compared his time at QPR with what happened up at Maine Road. 'Well Man City was a fascinating experience because when I went there they were five points clear in the First Division and lost the championship and it was my fault they lost the championship so I always found that to be a big cloud that hung over my career, because that's when people started to say that I put entertaining the fans before winning and if they hadn't signed me they would have won the championship. That's possibly true but the crowds went from 30,000 to 55,000 people when I went there so I think the fans enjoyed it and I don't think the fans blamed me.'

I found his candour disarming; Rodney's answer was a showstopper and I thanked him for his time before making my way home thinking to myself that as a conversationalist Rodney was as engaging and entertaining as he had been as a player.

*

I agree with Rodney; football is many things including an art form, but for me the twist is that footballers do not consciously create art, they do it unconsciously which only adds to the beauty. As far as I know no player, not even Eric Cantona, has gone on to the pitch at 3pm on a Saturday thinking, 'I'm an artist and I'm going to paint a picture today, I'm going to run elegantly and beautifully and move with balletic poise.' Their aim is to win a football match but the byproduct of that endeavour – the movement, the shapes, the colours, the patterns – is undeniably artistic. Footballers, like artists, are to different degrees creative, imaginative and technically proficient and unselfconsciously they produce an aesthetic spectacle. A great game flows like a sparkling river for its duration.

There has to be more to watching football than seeing which team of 11 people can get an inflated leather sphere into a space bordered by three pieces of wood or metal the most times in 90-plus minutes. I couldn't have watched the number of matches I have in my life if that was all it entailed. Football creates a beauty all of its own which transcends the physical contest in a way that no other sport, even the ones I really enjoy watching like squash, tennis and snooker, does. This artistic element for me lifts football above all other forms of sporting contest.

I believe that football as an artistic spectacle would be further enhanced if its more creative players were properly protected. Due to the threat they pose, inevitably these players become a target for destructive opposition players. I sometimes think that turning football into a non-contact sport would be an interesting experiment because it would make the game cleaner, but that is probably going too far at this stage.

It is currently too easy though for players to gain an unfair advantage. Players are very quick to recognise when an opposition team has the possibility to launch a dangerous attack, often a counterattack, and they will cynically and deliberately take a player out to prevent this happening. It's known as a 'tactical foul' and the cost is a yellow card or, if a goalscoring opportunity has been prevented, a red card. It's called 'taking one for the team' and it is seen as a virtue by many in the game but to the supporter of a team whose player has been fouled or to someone who is a lover of the game in general and wants to see it flow freely it is frustrating. Clearly because it happens so often simply issuing a card is an insufficient deterrent. Sometimes a player will not only make a challenge which stops a promising attack, they will commit a foul on an opponent who just happens to be the other team's best player which forces them to leave the field of play and not return. I have seen these things happen with my own eyes too often and they tarnish the game as a spectacle.

Imagine Picasso sitting at his easel painting *Guernica* and some maniac rushes in with a chainsaw and tries to chop off his arms. There was a comparable scenario in 1966 when Pelé was ruthlessly kicked by opponents in Brazil's World Cup group games to the extent that he vowed never to play in the competition again. Thankfully for the world of football he changed his mind and turned up in Mexico in 1970 to create some of the most beautiful images ever seen on a football pitch.

10

Towards the end of my first season with Capital Gold Sport, on Sunday, 22 March 1992 I went to Highbury to get a post-match interview with George Graham. The game was between Arsenal, who had won the title the previous season, and Leeds United. Arsenal went into the game in sixth place, their chances of retaining the championship all but gone. Leeds were in top spot at the time and went on to win the final old Division One title by four points from Manchester United. Leeds earned a useful point that afternoon with a 1-1 draw, Lee Chapman opening the scoring for the away side before Paul Merson equalised.

As it was Highbury and a Sunday a lot of the top journalists were there, including the excellent Brian Glanville, well known for his love of Italian football. He got excited when the results of the Serie A matches played that day started filtering through to the Highbury press room, hopping from one foot to the other and exclaiming things like, 'Fiorentina got a 0-0 draw at Udinese, and they didn't even play *catenaccio!*'

The post-match press conference, featuring Howard Wilkinson and George Graham, was held in a small theatre and was a beauty. To say the least it was tetchy. The tone was set when first Wilkinson walked in, sat down and stared at the press as though he loathed them all, daring someone to say something. The opening question, when it eventually came, was a classic. Someone asked, 'Were you disappointed when Arsenal equalised?' Wilkinson replied with a straight face and without hesitation, 'No, I was delighted.'

I didn't get involved in the questioning. My main task was to conduct a one-on-one post-match interview with George Graham, the type of interview I would do regularly and without any problem with other managers. I followed George out of the press room after he'd given his press conference and he agreed to do a piece. I'd never interviewed George before but I had been told by Dave Victor that he could be a little difficult. It was generally accepted that Arsenal were out of the running for the title, and there was a fascinating tussle going on between Leeds and Manchester United for top spot. I asked George what I thought was a straightforward, reasonable question, 'Who do you think will win the league?' I figured that if he didn't want to plump for one of the two contenders, he could evade the question and say something safe and non-committal like, 'Well, they're both good sides, Leeds are strong here, Manchester United have these qualities, I think that it's going to be very close.' Something like that could have been played on air by Capital Gold Sport. The response I got was a terse, 'I don't answer questions like that.' I don't know what sort of answer I would have got if I'd asked George a difficult question.

There were probably all sorts of reasons George responded as he did. I guess he was disappointed that Arsenal hadn't beaten Leeds, that they weren't in contention to retain the title, and that I hadn't asked him a question about his own club. He probably had a nice Sunday dinner waiting for him at home and didn't want to be delayed answering questions he didn't want to have to think about which were being asked by a reporter he hadn't met before. I never interviewed George again.

I was back at Highbury just over six months later, on 5 October 1993. It was a League Cup second round second leg match between Arsenal and Huddersfield Town. Arsenal were effectively already through as they'd won 5-0 away from home in the first leg (an Ian Wright hat-trick, one each from Kevin Campbell and Paul Merson). The second leg was something of a formality but the game turned out to be interesting anyway because Iain Dunn scored in the first half for Huddersfield to give them a 1-0 lead they took into the interval. Arsenal certainly didn't want to lose at Highbury to a Division Two side. They stepped up the pace in the second half and equalised through Alan Smith, the game ending 1-1.

Neil Warnock was manager of Huddersfield at the time and I discovered that he could be a bit of a comedian. At the post-match press conference someone asked him what he'd said to the players at half-time. He replied, 'I told the goalscorer, "You've really gone and done it now. We'll get fucking murdered in the second half. The best thing we could do is sneak out of the changing room, lock the door, get on the bus and go home."'

Arsenal didn't win either of the domestic cups in the 1993/94 season but they were triumphant in Europe. On 4 May 1994 Alan Smith scored as they beat Parma 1-0 in Copenhagen in the final of the European Cup Winners' Cup. I'd worked as third man a couple of months earlier on a super-charged European night at Highbury. Torino and Arsenal had drawn 0-0 in Italy in the first leg of their quarter-final, then Arsenal squeezed through 1-0 on aggregate thanks to a Tony Adams goal in the second leg. Frank McLintock was the Capital Gold Sport pundit that night. I was due to do a piece at half-time and would need to use his headphones. When I told him this he said to me, 'I'll keep them warm for you until half-time.'

I don't know why but unintentionally I developed a bit of a habit of upsetting the top people at Highbury. Some years later I was sitting at home on a Sunday morning when the phone rang. It was Capital Gold Sport commentator Dominic Johnson asking me what I was doing that day. The previous day I'd covered Watford's 3-2 home defeat to Sunderland in the Premier League. I was knackered and I was looking forward to doing nothing. Capital were covering the game at Highbury that afternoon between Arsenal and Derby County and they needed an extra body to help, doing reports for a club phone line. Normally I wouldn't have thought twice. The chance to go to and watch Arsenal and be paid for it would have had me accepting excitedly straight away. I did say 'yes' but only to help Capital out and it was a weary body and mind which I dragged up to north London. On top of that, because of the short notice there was no chance to do any preparation.

The game in question was played on 28 November 1999. Arsenal had signed Thierry Henry from Juventus for £10.5m in August 1999. Henry played up front in his youth but at Monaco, under Arsène Wenger, and at Juventus he played on the wing. When Henry joined Arsenal, Wenger started playing him as a striker again. Before the Derby game Henry had started eight times but had only scored once, in Arsenal's 1-0 away win over Southampton on 18 September. Some were questioning whether Henry would make it as a striker.

It was against Derby that Henry finally broke through, scoring twice in a 2-1 win. It was in that game that Henry and Bergkamp looked a really effective partnership for the first time.

I was too far gone to fully appreciate the significance of it all at the time and to do the occasion justice. My reports were flat and lifeless and because of my tiredness I must have sounded disinterested to the listener.

Sometime previously I'd been among a group of journalists which had been given an informative tour of the new North Bank stand by Arsenal vice-chairman David Dein. I wouldn't have expected an important, busy man like him to be listening in to my full-time report on Arsenal v Derby but he was. I was packing away my broadcasting equipment, relieved that I could finally go home and relax, when an agitated Arsenal press officer came rushing into the press box. He told me that Dein wasn't impressed with what he had heard and that my report must be replaced with something else as soon as possible.

On another day I was in a fit state to fully appreciate the beauty of Arsenal's play. On their way to lifting the FA Cup in 2002 Arsenal had a 4-2 third-round win at Watford and played the best football I had ever seen at Vicarage Road up to that point. The Arsenal side featured the likes of Ashley Cole, Patrick Vieira, Sol Campbell, Martin Keown, Freddie Ljungberg, Kanu, Thierry Henry and Robert Pires, all playing at or near the top of their game. The speed of thought and movement of the Arsenal players was breathtaking. They moved the ball so quickly that if you switched off for a second you missed an incisive pass. There are sometimes seemingly insignificant moments in a game which make an indelible impression, and one occurred in this tie. The ball was loose in midfield; Gary Fisken and Vieira both went for it. The relative starting positions of the two players made Fisken the 70-30 favourite to win the ball, until Vieira stretched out a long leg and nicked it away from the startled Watford player. It must be almost impossible to play against that.

Football reporters as well as players need to be quick thinking and after that match, I was outwitted by a BBC Radio 5 Live reporter. The pair of us were waiting for Arsène Wenger to finish an interview so that we could talk to him. We would both be interviewing him individually and we both wanted to go first. That was the way to get the best interview and it also meant that you could get your work on air before your rival. As I stood there deliberating about how to get in first, the 5 Live man smiled at me and asked politely, 'Do you mind if I go first?' He'd done me up like a kipper. Of course I minded but I couldn't say so and I replied meekly, smiling back, 'No, please do.'

*

I had a ball in the 1991/92 season, my first at Capital Gold Sport, and I didn't want it to end so I found a way of extending it by one day.

During the season I'd covered a few Barnet matches and it was a fun gig. Having taken a long time to reach the Football League there was no way that Barry Fry was going to compromise on the attacking football which had got them there. After the 7-4 defeat at home to Crewe Alexandra in their first match in Division Four there were only ten goals in their next game, a 5-5 draw at home to Brentford in the League Cup. There followed a run of three league wins, which included a 6-0 victory at Lincoln City. Andy Pape in goal, Gary Poole, Mick Bodley and David Howell at the back, Roger Willis and Paul Showler in midfield and Mark Carter and Gary Bull up front were all regulars in a team which scored 81 league goals, winning 4-1 at York City on the final day of the season to finish seventh and qualify for the play-offs. Bull, the cousin of Wolves legend Steve Bull, played all 42 league games and scored 20 goals.

I'd really enjoyed watching them play and I was intrigued to find out how they would get on in the play-offs. I faced the prospect of a summer without football and to get in one more game I went to Underhill for the first leg of the Barnet v Blackpool play-off semi-final. The match was played on a Sunday, the day after Liverpool beat Sunderland 2-0 in the FA Cup final.

Capital Gold Sport were not on air that day but they arranged a press pass and said that if I was going I may as well get some post-match interviews. Barnet played well and beat Blackpool 1-0 through a Mark Carter goal in front of 5,629 people, leaving them with a decent chance of reaching the play-off final. Everyone at Underhill was pleased with the outcome of the match, apart from one man – chairman Stan Flashman.

Fry was always ebullient after a Barnet win; chirpy, wisecracking, great value as far as the press were concerned. He would usually emerge from the dressing room quickly to speak to reporters. With Underhill being small it didn't take very long to get from one part of the ground to another anyway. After the win over Blackpool, Fry took longer than usual to appear and when he did arrive he seemed strangely somber and subdued. His opening words to the waiting journalists stunned us, 'My team were shit, crap and a disgrace, the chairman's words not mine. I've been sacked and Edwin Stein will be in charge of the team for the away leg on Wednesday.' After that short statement Fry walked off towards the club house, pursued by a group of bemused journalists eager to find out more.

Stories had been circulating during the season that the relationship between Fry and Flashman was tempestuous and had become strained but this was the first time that one of their rows had spilled out into the public domain. While Fry was talking more about what had happened I noticed Flashman come out of the boardroom and thought I'd take the opportunity to talk to the main protagonist in the post-match story.

I'd never met Flashman before. I introduced myself and asked him if he would do an interview for Capital Gold Sport. He agreed, and in an attempt to set the parameters for the interview before we started I asked if he would mind talking about 'the Barry Fry situation'. He asked, 'What's that?' As I switched on my tape recorder I said, 'According to Barry Fry he's been sacked.' Flashman's reaction was sudden, violent and totally unexpected. He yanked the microphone from me and whacked me over the hand with it while screaming, 'I'm not going to talk to you unless you ask fucking sensible questions!' I concluded that was the end of the interview, the shortest I'd ever conducted. My immediate instinct was one of self-preservation; he was a massive guy, he must have been at least 20st and he was enraged. We were only about ten yards from the nearest bystander but I wasn't sure anyone else was watching what was taking place. I thought that I might about to be on the receiving end of a kicking so in an attempt to calm him down I apologised, grabbed my microphone back and scurried to the safety of the nearest journalist who'd only been vaguely aware of what had been happening.

The incident was unreal; it was like something out of a cartoon. It made good audio and Capital Gold Sport ran the story on the eve of the return leg at

Bloomfield Road along the lines of, 'Twenty-four hours before the most important match in Barnet's history this is what is happening at the club.' They played my 'interview' with Stan, bleeping out the expletive.

Fry was in charge for the second leg at Blackpool as Flashman reinstated him the day after the first leg. Altogether Flashman sacked and reinstated Fry eight times.

Barnet lost the second leg 2-0 to go out 2-1 on aggregate, but their second season in the Football League turned out to be even more successful than the first. Gary Phillips replaced Andy Pape in goal, Richard Huxford came in for Gary Poole at right-back and Dave Barnett was the regular number five instead of David Howell, but the nucleus of the side remained the same. The languid Kenny Lowe and the diminutive, energetic Derek Payne in midfield started more games than they had the previous season but it was again Gary Bull and Mark Carter who scored the goals. This time Bull actually missed a league game, starting 41 out of 42. He scored 17 league goals and Carter 11 as Barnet gained automatic promotion with a third-placed finish. I was in the press box for the game which secured promotion, a 1-1 draw at home to Lincoln City on 1 May 1993, Mick Bodley scoring for Barnet. By that time Fry had unsurprisingly left Underhill, of his own volition, and had been replaced as manager by Edwin Stein. I was sprayed with champagne as the Barnet players celebrated after the game.

It was beautiful to witness the unbridled joy of footballers who had achieved their goal. All the hard work, the training, the ups and downs of the season had borne fruit and proved worthwhile.

I didn't get close to that type of celebration too often but on one occasion I found myself inside a dressing room after a moment of triumph. That came after a non-league club, Wycombe Wanderers, had won promotion to the Football League. Wycombe were not really on Capital Gold Sport's radar but I was sent anyway to get post-match interviews on Thursday, 15 April 1993. Wycombe beat Runcorn 5-1, a victory which included a solo Steve Guppy goal where he received the ball from the goalkeeper's throw out just outside his own penalty area, ran the length of the pitch and scored with a low shot.

It was my first trip to Adams Park and something was clearly happening.

Wycombe were formed in 1887. They won the FA Amateur Cup, Isthmian League titles, the FA Trophy and knocked league sides out of the FA Cup but it was over 100 years before they were able to make that huge leap into the Football League. Martin O'Neill took over as manager in February 1990. He built slowly and steadily as Wycombe finished 1989/90 in mid-table and in fifth place the following season. In 1991/92 Wycombe finished with 94 points, won 30 games and were in the title race until the final Saturday when Colchester United claimed promotion on goal difference.

The club started 1992/93 as favourites for the Conference title and won it by 15 points. After the Runcorn game I went into the Wycombe dressing room to get interviews. I wasn't familiar with the players and it was even more difficult recognising them without any clothes on when they didn't have numbers on their backs. One person I had no problem recognising was Martin O'Neill. He was elated but when I asked him how the achievement compared with winning things as a player he told me that for him managing didn't come close to playing football.

At the time, the excellent commentator Alan Parry was a director at Wycombe and he captured the euphoria of the moment. I said to Alan, 'At this rate you'll be playing AC Milan in the final of the Champions League in a few years' time.' He replied, 'I'd rather play Barcelona.'

11

When I hitchhiked from Coimbra to Rome in May 1977 I arrived at my destination a few days before Liverpool played Borussia Mönchengladbach at the Stadio Olimpico in the final of the European Cup. I had no trouble getting a couple of tickets and Jimmy and I watched Liverpool win the competition for the very first time with a 3-1 victory. Kevin Keegan gave World Cup winner Berti Vogts a difficult evening and in the 82nd minute the German brought down Keegan to concede a penalty which Phil Neal put away for Liverpool's third goal.

Keegan was born on 14 February 1951 in Armthorpe, near Doncaster. After being rejected by Doncaster Rovers he was taken on by Scunthorpe United. In May 1971, following 120 appearances for Scunthorpe, Liverpool paid £35,000 for him and on 14 August 1971 he scored at Anfield against Nottingham Forest, 12 minutes into his debut.

By the time of the 1977 European Cup final victory Keegan had won the league championship three times, the UEFA Cup twice and the FA Cup once. But Keegan was very much his own man and in the first of several unpredictable moves after 323 appearances and 100 goals he left Liverpool for Hamburg SV for £500,000. His judgement proved to be spot on; Hamburg won the Bundesliga title for the first time in their history in 1978/79, Keegan was nicknamed 'Mighty Mouse' by the fans after the cartoon superhero, and he was European Footballer of the Year in 1978 and 1979.

In February 1980 Keegan made another surprise move, this time returning to England to play for Southampton, where Lawrie McMenemy was manager. The team, which also included Alan Ball, Phil Boyer, Mick Channon and Charlie George, clicked. Keegan spent two full seasons at The Dell. In the first, 1980/81, Southampton came sixth, then their highest league finish. In 1981/82 they were one place lower. In that second season Keegan scored 26 of Southampton's 72 goals and was voted the PFA Players' Player of the Year.

Just before the start of the 1982/83 season Keegan was on the move again, signing for Division Two Newcastle United for £100,000. During his two seasons at St James' Park Keegan built up what was to become an enduring rapport with the Newcastle fans. He played 78 times for the club, scoring 48 goals, and with Peter Beardsley, Chris Waddle and Terry McDermott also in the side he helped them to win promotion in 1984.

Keegan retired at the end of the 1983/84 season, going into exile in Spain with his family for eight years before making a dramatic return to St James' Park. On 5 February 1992 Newcastle manager Ossie Ardiles was sacked and was replaced by Keegan. Newcastle were 23rd in Division One at the time. They went on to avoid relegation and finish 20th.

In the following season, 1992/93, Newcastle won Division One by eight points after starting the season with 11 straight wins. Victory number nine in that run, 2-1 at Brentford, came on 4 October 1992 and I was at Griffin Park to witness it. I was looking forward to seeing Newcastle play and I wasn't disappointed. The work rate and commitment of the players, typified by Lee Clark who played every league game that season, was phenomenal. They had other good players, like the goalscorers that day, David Kelly and Gavin Peacock, and others such as Rob Lee, Barry Venison and John Beresford.

Capital Gold Sport asked me to get a post-match interview with Keegan, coming during Graham Taylor's time as England manager. Taylor had endured crass reporting during the 1992 European Championship finals in Sweden. England had crashed out at the group stage, drawing 0-0 with Denmark and France and losing 2-1 to Sweden in Stockholm in their group matches. In the final fixture against Sweden, Taylor had brought off Gary Lineker, at the time one goal short of equalling Bobby Charlton's record of 49 goals for England.

The following day one newspaper headline read 'Swedes 2 Turnips 1'. The same newspaper also published a photo showing Taylor's head superimposed on to a turnip. You might think that this was the idea of a particularly vindictive teenager on work experience but it was actually a 'proper journalist' who dreamed it up. An intelligent six-year-old would have found the photo juvenile and offensive. It felt puerile and unnecessary but more than that it was dehumanising and it was far from the truth. Whatever failings Taylor had as England manager, he was a diamond human being, but it seems that some newspapers don't necessarily see it as their job to portray a truthful picture of a person, and that poisonous stories sell papers.

Taylor had done so much for Watford and had brought so much pleasure to the lives of its supporters. In combination with Elton John as chairman, who backed him financially, in his ten years as manager between 1977 and 1987 Taylor galvanised not just the club but the whole town and community. On a journey which before it started was dubbed by local cartoonist Terry Challis 'The Impossible Dream', he took Watford from Division Four to runners-up in Division One in 1982/83, to the third round of the UEFA Cup in 1983/84 and an FA Cup final defeat to Everton in 1984. He built a hardworking, disciplined side that without the ball pressed the opposition and with the ball played exciting, attacking football in which wingers played a prominent role. In his ten seasons in charge Taylor saw his side score 692 league goals.

In 1983 Taylor ran the London Marathon to raise money to build a family terrace at Vicarage Road.

In November 1972 centre-forward Ross Jenkins had joined Watford for £35,000 from Crystal Palace. In the pre-Taylor era I was regularly taken to Watford by a great old boy called Stan who had a season ticket in the Rous Stand. Before Taylor became manager, Stan used to despair of Jenkins, 'Six foot four and he can't head a ball.' Jenkins played in a 1-0 defeat at Darlington on 30 August 1975 which left Watford bottom of Division Four. When Taylor arrived Jenkins was transformed and he went with the club all the way to Division One. During the journey in 1978/79 he scored 29 goals in Division Three to finish the season as the leading scorer in the Football League.

Watford's style of play wasn't generally appreciated by the press but if say a football supporter had received a phone call on a Saturday morning from a friend who asked, 'I've got a spare ticket for a game today, do you fancy going?' and the friend had told the fan that the home side would play 4-4-2 and that their starting line-up would include Pat Rice, Steve Sims, Wilf Rostron, Kenny Jackett, Luther Blissett and wingers Nigel Callaghan and John Barnes, there is a good chance that the supporter would have eagerly accepted the offer of the ticket. If the day in question had been Saturday, 14 May 1983, the final day of the 1982/83 season, the friends would have seen Blissett and Martin Patching score for Watford as Taylor's side beat that season's champions, Liverpool, 2-1 at Vicarage Road in front of 27,173 people to clinch second spot in Division One. The Liverpool line-up that day included Bruce Grobbelaar, Phil Neal, Alan Kennedy, Mark Lawrenson, Phil Thompson, Alan Hansen, Kenny Dalglish, Sammy Lee, Craig Johnston and Graeme Souness. If one of the friends had placed a pre-season each way bet at the odds available, 50/1, on Watford to win Division One they would have been able to use the winnings to have chicken in a basket on a night out at the town's popular nightclub Baileys after the match.

As England prepared for their 1994 World Cup qualifiers, they lost a friendly 1-0 to Spain in Santander on 9 September 1992 and Taylor came under more pressure. Capital Gold Sport decided to run a campaign in support of Taylor in an attempt to persuade the public to back him and as part of that I was asked to interview Keegan.

My encounter with Keegan after Newcastle's win at Brentford in October 1992 convinced me that it was not possible for me to get a proper impression of someone unless I met them in person. I'd always admired Keegan as a player but I'd had reservations and my view of him had been coloured by the belief that his success had been based more on hard work than flair and natural ability. As soon as Keegan entered the Griffin Park press room any negative preconceptions I had of him as a person were blown away. I realised immediately that I was in the presence of a truly inspirational figure and it became apparent in a flash why he was so revered and adored by Newcastle supporters and players. He radiated sincerity, positivity and humility.

I still carried an image in my head of a hardworking footballer with permed hair who had made the most of his talents and achieved a lot as a player. When he started talking it became clear that there was so much more to him than that, and when he spoke about the Brentford game and what was happening at

Newcastle the press hung on every word in a way I hadn't seen them do for any other manager. After he'd finished his post-match analysis I introduced myself and asked him if he would do a piece about Taylor. He was initially reluctant as he was suspicious that we might be doing a hatchet job. When I explained that we were running a campaign in support of Taylor he immediately relented and agreed to be interviewed.

As we made our way to the press box we talked about the current Newcastle side and Keegan said to me, 'I've got a very good team here.' Keegan had played under Bill Shankly and he told me that one of Shankly's sayings had been, 'If you tell a player often enough that he is tired then eventually he will believe it and become tired.' Keegan was applying the same simple but effective philosophy at Newcastle to convince the players that they could be world-beaters.

Football managers tend to stick up for each other. There is a bond between them borne of a shared experience of doing a job which carries extraordinary pressure and often intense criticism from media and supporters. Kevin did just that when he talked to me about Graham, saying, 'He was the right man for the job a year ago, he's the right man for the job now.' It was a great soundbite and, after England had started their 1994 World Cup qualifying campaign with a 1-1 draw at home to Norway on 14 October 1992, Capital Gold Sport used it in the build-up to the home World Cup qualifier against Turkey, to be played the following month, urging England supporters, 'Don't taunt Taylor, let's stuff Turkey.'

England did beat Turkey, Paul Gascoigne scoring twice in a 4-0 win at Wembley on 18 November 1992.

*

A few days after that England win I was presented with a big opportunity. It was the first season of the Premier League and my second at Capital Gold Sport. I'd covered my first top-flight game, Southampton v Crystal Palace, the previous season but that had been played in midweek. On 21 November 1992 Chelsea were away to Everton in a Premier League fixture to be played on a Saturday and I was given the game to cover. The Saturday show on Capital Gold Sport was the big one. Midweek programmes were important but football in midweek is kind of tagged on to the end of a working day. Saturday was still traditionally the big football day when most people were off work and the whole day could be given over to football.

Capital Gold Sport covered all the league clubs in the London area but there was no denying they concentrated on the Premier League. It was inevitable because the majority of the listeners supported Premier League clubs. Unless they were attached to a Football League club, all the Capital Gold Sport reporters wanted to cover Premier League games. They made the biggest headlines, it was where the best players were playing and it was where you could watch the highest standard of football. I knew that others at Capital would be listening a little more keenly than usual to my reports to see how I handled the demands of reporting on a Premier League fixture.

Covering a big club like Chelsea brought with it a certain responsibility. There would be a few thousand Chelsea fans at Goodison Park but many of those who stayed behind would be following the game on Capital Gold Sport.

After arriving at a ground, particularly one I had never worked at before, there would always be a period of anxiety as I located my seat in the press box, set up my equipment and then established a connection to the studio. Once I knew that the line was working I would relax a little, go and have a cup of tea and start really looking forward to the game and to giving my reports. On this occasion the line at Goodison Park wasn't working and the two engineers who started trying to fix it at about two o'clock wouldn't get it working until about two hours later, which meant that I wasn't able to give my first report on Everton v Chelsea until half-time. I sat in the press box for the whole of the first half mute, like a fishmonger without any fish, unable to tell the Chelsea fans who were listening that Robert Fleck had put them ahead just before half-time.

Fleck's was the only goal of the game and it was the result of the day on Capital Gold Sport. Chelsea were recovering after a slow start to the season and their win moved them up to seventh in the Premier League. Everton were in decline after hitting the heights in the 1980s and only the brilliant Peter Beardsley shone for them.

After the game I went in search of an interview and found Andy Townsend, a key figure in the Chelsea midfield that season. Townsend agreed to be interviewed and I asked him if he would go up to the press box with me. 'Where's the press box?' asked Townsend. Just at that moment Beardsley came walking along the corridor towards us and heard Townsend's question. He instantly sized up the situation and, without breaking his stride as he passed us, he said to Townsend before I could reply, 'It's only just up there,' nodding his head in the direction of the press box, convincing Townsend to go with me to do the interview.

As soon as JP saw me the next time I bumped into him in the studio after my Goodison gig he jokingly said to me with a laugh, 'He's just like Inspector Gadget.' It was a reference to the cartoon police inspector who has high-tech gadgets which he doesn't know how to use. It stuck and that's how I got the nickname at Capital Gold Sport of 'Inspector Gadget' which was shortened to 'Gadget', or just 'Gadge'.

12

Wimbledon had a decent run in the League Cup in the 1993/94 season and I covered a couple of their ties.

I never went abroad as a football reporter. The nearest I got was a trip to Hereford for Wimbledon's second round first leg League Cup match that season at Edgar Street. The drive into the depths of Herefordshire, through the Cotswolds and then along the bendy, hilly road between Ross-on-Wye and Hereford was spectacular. On the way I saw a hoarding advertising a ploughing competition and I wondered how the Capital Gold Sport team would fancy commentating on that. I suppose the winner of the competition would be the person ploughing the straightest furrow.

Formed in 1924, Hereford United were elected to Division Four in 1972. For years they had built up a reputation as a giant-killing non-league side. They appeared in the first round of the FA Cup for 17 consecutive seasons between 1956 and 1972. In 1972 they achieved one of the most celebrated upsets of all time in the English game when they beat Newcastle United 2-1 at home in the third round of the FA Cup. In so doing they became the first non-league club in 23 years to knock a Division One side out of the competition.

Hereford were one of the most isolated clubs in the league and visiting Edgar Street was like going to the club that time forgot. I turned up and made contact with Ted Woodriff, a local press man. Within minutes of my arrival he had begun talking about the win over Newcastle, which had happened over 20 years previously.

At Capital Gold Sport we had recently been issued with new-fangled, high-tech, state-of-the-art reporter phones. I had taken one with me and I asked Ted where I could plug it in. It turned out that the phones used in the Hereford press box were connected to their sockets by metal jack-plugs, which had gone out of use in most places years previously. Ted told me, 'It would have cost £250 to have the press box converted and anyway there hasn't been much demand for phones since the win over Newcastle.'

My reporter phone rendered unusable, Ted sorted me out with a phone line and I wandered off to get a cup of tea. I started chatting with one of the stewards and I asked him who Hereford's best players were. 'We haven't got any,' he replied. 'We nearly went out of the league last year and any good players we get, we sell.'

A tone of gentle self-deprecation prevailed in the press box as well. After about 20 minutes, during which time Hereford had one shot comfortably saved, a local journalist asked, 'Do you think they've weathered our storm now?'

At half-time I drank tea from a china cup in a small theatre behind the main stand, feeling as though I was in some sort of surreal play. Wimbledon won 1-0 through a first-half Andy Clarke goal. After the match someone asked Vinnie Jones for an interview but he declined, saying, 'Nah, I'm dying for a pint,' before heading off to knock back a Guinness.

A few months later Wimbledon were at home to Liverpool in a League Cup fourth round replay. I was at Selhurst Park to be third man and before the game I went in search of an interview. I found Vinnie lurking in the depths of the stadium. This time he graciously accepted the request for an interview and went as far as to invite me into the warmth of the changing room area.

While researching the game I'd discovered that, if Wimbledon won, they would be in the fifth round of the League Cup for the first time in their history. Until then their best run had been to the fourth round, a feat they had also managed in 1979/80, 1983/84 and 1988/89. I knew this because it said so in the *Rothmans Football Yearbook 1993/94*.

After the interview, which went fine, I thought I'd make some small talk before departing. Having thanked him for the interview, I said, 'Vinnie, you do know that if you win tonight you will create a record as it will be the first time Wimbledon have reached the fifth round of the League Cup.'

Vinnie didn't reply as expected and said, 'We reached the fifth round last year.'

The previous season, 1992/93, Wimbledon had reached the fifth round of the FA Cup, losing to Tottenham Hotspur, and had been knocked out in the third round of the League Cup. I wasn't sure how to react but decided to stand my ground and I politely pointed out that they had reached the fifth round of the FA Cup not the League Cup the previous season.

Vinnie was having none of it and said, 'No, it wasn't, it was the League Cup.'

I needed a way out. I considered showing Vinnie the *Rothmans* entry but thought better of it. It had gone too far for me to now provide proof that he was mistaken. I had become conscious that several pairs of eyes, including those belonging to a couple of heavily built security guys, were staring at me quite hard. Vinnie would want to get on with his pre-match preparation and I was beginning to waste his valuable time.

I came out with the best closing line I could think of and said, 'Well, that's what it says in the *Rothmans* but I guess even the *Rothmans* makes mistakes.' With that I turned and hurried back to the sanctuary of the press room.

The game ended Wimbledon 2 (Dean Holdsworth, Robbie Earle) Liverpool 2 (Neil Ruddock, Hans Segers o.g.) after extra time. Wimbledon won 4-3 on penalties to reach the fifth round of the League Cup for the first time in their history.

I saw Jones in action again a few months later, in February 1994. This time his Wimbledon side were overwhelmed by a classic Manchester United performance. On the way to winning the FA Cup in 1994 United beat Wimbledon 3-0 (Eric Cantona, Paul Ince, Denis Irwin) in the fifth round, in front of 27,511 people at Selhurst Park. The Cantona goal was exquisite, an arcing volley from just outside the box over the head of Hans Segers, one of the best goals I saw that season. The United line up that day was unforgettable: Peter Schmeichel; Paul Parker, Steve Bruce, Gary Pallister, Denis Irwin; Andrei Kanchelskis, Paul Ince, Roy Keane, Ryan Giggs; Eric Cantona, Mark Hughes. What a team that was. Joe Kinnear summed it up when he said after the game, 'They were dangerous from our corners,' and he was right. Schmeichel would come and catch a Wimbledon corner and throw the ball either to Kanchelskis on the right or Giggs on the left. Whichever one got the ball would hare down the flank with devastating pace and within seconds, before Wimbledon had a chance to recover, United would be down the other end threatening the Dons' goal.

The post-match press conference was the first time I came into contact with Sir Alex Ferguson. When I saw him my first thought was, 'You've got to admire this man for the team he's put together.' During the game Jones had been booked for a foul on Cantona. When asked about the incident by a journalist, Ferguson replied, 'I don't think it's worth reporting, you'll only feed his ego.'

I only ever covered one game at the Theatre of Dreams and that was between Manchester United and Wimbledon in the Premier League on 17 October 1998. United had just announced plans to increase the capacity at Old Trafford, which already provided sumptuous surroundings in which to watch a match, from 56,000 to 68,000 and in my preview I said, 'Other Premier League clubs will be wondering just how much bigger Manchester United are going to get.'

The match ended Manchester United 5 (Andy Cole 2, Ryan Giggs, David Beckham, Dwight Yorke) Wimbledon 1 (Jason Euell). At the time United had yet to hit top gear and were in second place behind the surprise early leaders Aston Villa. Wimbledon didn't play badly but still lost heavily. Beckham's consistently accurate crossing stood out and I liked the way central defenders Wes Brown and Jaap Stam ran with the ball out of defence, drawing opposition players towards them and only passing when they were pressed.

Of course Roy Keane ran the midfield that day as he so often did but I never warmed to him because I didn't care for the way he played the game. In those football magazines for kids, they used to have a feature where players would answer questions about themselves. One of the favourite questions was, 'If you hadn't been a footballer what would you have been?' If Roy hadn't been a footballer I think he might have been some sort of hitman and I'm sure he would have been very effective.

After the game Fergie's press conference in a mini-theatre was fun. Even though Manchester United had won handsomely I decided not to risk asking a question in case it wasn't to the great man's liking. I got the impression that Ferguson's press conferences were conducted on a bit of a knife edge and I didn't want to be responsible for asking the wrong question and causing the man to walk out, which would have meant that other journalists would have missed out on the quotes they needed to write their reports.

Manchester United won the Premier League that season, by one point from Arsenal – the first of three successive title wins – and completed their famous treble by winning the FA Cup and Champions League as well.

*

Steve Parsons came from a different part of the vibrant and diverse football spectrum.

Without any football reporting, the time between the end of one season and the start of the next tended to drag, but the summer of 1994 was enlivened by a chance encounter. I'd moved away from North Kensington but was still drawn back to the area. On one visit I bumped into some old mates in a pub and we started chatting. One guy, who I hadn't met before, got interested when I told him that I was a football reporter. It turned out that he was an ex-player and he wasn't happy with the media because of the way they reported the 'Crazy Gang' story. What he objected to was that players such as Vinnie Jones, Dennis Wise and John Fashanu had been credited with founding the Crazy Gang when it had been him and his mate who had come up with the name some time before those players even joined the club.

I was more than ready to sit down and listen to his story. His name was Steve Parsons and he played for Wimbledon in the 1970s. He was at Plough Lane at the start of Wimbledon's life in the Football League in 1977. The camaraderie and unique sense of spirit which eventually helped Wimbledon to win the FA Cup in 1988 had begun to develop in his time at the club. Steve had joined the Dons from Isthmian League side Walton and Hersham. 'I went there for a month's trial after which they signed me as a pro. I was there for two and a half years. It was just after they were elected to the Football League and were in the Fourth Division. Dave Bassett was playing at the time, Allen Batsford was manager and Dario Gradi joined as coach. Then Batsford got the sack, Gradi took over as manager, and Harry [Bassett] stopped playing and became assistant manager.'

It was then that the Crazy Gang nickname was coined. 'There was me, Wally Downes, Tommy Cunningham, and Steve Perkins. The name originated in 1978. Basically, it came from the original Crazy Gang. Me and Wally used to go and watch films of them at my mum's house. This was the Crazy Gang of the late '30s and '40s. They were Flanagan and Allen, Norton and Gold and Nervo and Knox. We took our name from them because they used to do bizarre things on stage and screen while we used to do crazy things on the football field and when we used to travel away. That's where we got the name from. This Crazy Gang image they've got, it was us who started it back in 1978/79. Me and Wally, we started the original Crazy Gang at Wimbledon. I don't think anyone down there now would know who the original Crazy Gang are.'

'Crazy Gang' wasn't the only nickname to come from that era. 'Dave Beasant came from Edgware Town. Dario signed him, after Harry used to go and watch him. Dave used to come in by motorbike. When he left his helmet in the changing room we used to fill it with mud, water or whatever. He got his nickname from my dad who saw him come in one day after a game and straight away said "Lurch," after the big, tall butler in *The Addams Family* who used to answer the door and say, "You rang?" That's all we used to give him, "You rang, Lurch?"'

The craziness came to the fore on away trips. 'If we were playing away up north on a Saturday we used to travel up on a Friday afternoon. We used to lock people in their rooms, set the fire alarms off, wake people up at three or four in the morning with early morning calls. Just basically having a right laugh. The four of us – me, Wally, Tommy and Steve were the main ones behind it all.

'On my 21st we played away, we travelled up by train. Dario went to watch a player and Harry was in charge. We've gone up, won 2-1, I scored a goal and on the train home we were having a laugh, singing and everything. As we were approaching Watford station me and Wally got hold of Harry, got his shoes off, a brand new pair apparently, and threw them out of the window. You should have seen him at Euston station walking around bare-footed. What a laugh. We had to run away me and Wally. A couple of days later we had to give him the money for a new pair of shoes.

'We had a very, very good team spirit. We were in the Fourth Division and were made up of players who had been rejected by other clubs, people who couldn't get in the first team and came down to Wimbledon. They'd realise they'd got a second chance and they grabbed it.'

There was a strong sense of unity in the side. 'If someone got into trouble we were all going to get into trouble, nobody was going to be left by themselves. If there was a ruck, or whatever, then everybody was involved. Not that there were any big rucks but people stood up for each other, seven or eight at a time. You could tell that other clubs didn't have our sort of spirit. Some individuals would just keep themselves to themselves, but at Wimbledon we were all together.'

Another of the reasons for Wimbledon's success was the influence and guidance of Sam Hammam. It was the Crazy Gang who were responsible for Hammam being invited to join the board after a typically Wimbledonesque initiation ceremony.

'Sam tried for Chelsea but Ken Bates wouldn't have him, so he came down to Wimbledon. Ron Noades said it was up to the players – if they accept you then you can join the board. He spent about a week with us, we were messing about, throwing him everywhere, throwing mud at him and kicking balls in his face. He loved it. At the end of the week Dario asked us what we thought of him and it was the Crazy Gang who said, "Yeah, we'll have him on the board, we'll have him at Wimbledon." So Ron Noades said, "If they're happy with you, you can be on the board." That's how it came about. We used to have a right funny time with him and he just used to laugh.'

The spirit combined with the coaching of Dario Gradi led to success and promotion from Division Four in 1978/79. 'Dario always wanted to play football. We got promoted from the Fourth to the Third. The night we went up was absolute madness. We were up until eight in the morning, we went up to the directors' bar, started throwing peanuts and everything, just having an absolute laugh. The following month we went to Benidorm as a reward for getting promoted. There was a tennis tournament for the players which lasted five days. These people playing tennis were really serious while me, Tommy and Wally were just messing about. Anyway, after a couple of days we'd spent the prize money. The two guys who played the final came back to find us laughing when they asked where the money was. We just kept on laughing. The geezer who'd won didn't know what was going on.'

Wimbledon didn't last long in Division Three. 'Unfortunately we came straight back down and then I left the club because Orient were interested in me. Dario said it would be a good move for me and I took his advice, though I wish I hadn't as I would have liked to have been part of what happened at Wimbledon.'

Playing for Orient, Steve suffered a broken leg that finished his career at the age of 23. The end came at Grimsby in a grotesque incident which was a bizarre mixture of glamour and horror. Steve's last act as a professional footballer was to play a one-two with Stan Bowles. He explained what happened after he had laid the ball off, 'A guy came in very late and he just smashed my leg to pieces. The guy came from the side and I didn't see him. Within seconds I was lying on the ground and I felt this pain in my leg. As I could move my toes I thought I was all right, but as I picked up my thigh my leg was limp from the knee down. I lay down and the pain hit me. My leg was put in a bag which was inflated but then I was left outside the ground for 25 minutes. As the Grimsby supporters walked past me they spat at me, and called me a southerner, Cockney whatever, which I didn't appreciate. It took me a year and a half to get over it. I had operations on my left leg, on my toes and all that, but I still ran with a limp. They said I wasn't fit enough to stand up to that standard of football, and to train every day. So I had to drop out of football.'

It's all glamour, football.

I saw Steve play in a park game once and even with a limp through his natural ability he ran the game.

13

In the summer of 1995 I took a call from JP, who asked me, 'Would you like to cover Watford home and away from next season?' By now I was covering Watford regularly so this wouldn't involve a huge change but JP was suggesting that the arrangement be formalised. I would officially be Capital Gold Sport's Watford reporter. I couldn't think of a bigger honour and I accepted with delight.

Also, by becoming the Watford reporter I would have continuity and certainty. In the Capital Gold Sport studio there was an A4 page-a-day diary in which were written, as soon as they were released, the fixtures involving Capital's clubs for the whole of the forthcoming season. As and when it was decided who would be covering a game, the initials of the reporter allocated were entered next to the fixture in the diary. I would find out which games I'd been given by going through the diary. I used to love coming back late at night from a trip up north, going back to the studio, opening the diary and seeing 'SM' next to a string of fixtures stretching far into the future. By agreeing to JP's suggestion and becoming the regular Watford reporter I was guaranteeing that 'SM' would be written next to just about every Hornets fixture for the foreseeable future.

Apart from my affiliation making it a dream gig, Watford were a really good club to cover – just the right size, friendly and accessible. I sometimes found it difficult to gain access to the players at some of the bigger clubs, who could be a little remote and occasionally unwilling to engage. When Watford hosted one of the big London clubs in a pre-season friendly, I would try to get post-match interviews but the big stars were often reluctant to talk and some would just refuse to do interviews. Maybe I was wearing the wrong aftershave. The best refusal I had was from Gary Doherty of Tottenham Hotspur. I asked him for an interview after a Watford v Spurs pre-season friendly and he declined saying that he was 'too tired'. After a game against Chelsea, Marcel Desailly just told me straight, 'I don't talk to the press.'

On the other hand, I always found the Watford managers and players ready to talk. Steve Perryman had resigned in July 1993 and in the same month Glenn Roeder succeeded him. Glenn was superb with me, a top man. I interviewed him at Vicarage Road soon after he'd been appointed. It was at the pre-season press day and I was the last to speak to him. He'd done all his other interviews by the side of the pitch but when I asked Glenn for some of his time he said, 'Let's go to my office.' I'd never been in a manager's office before and I felt like I'd been invited into some sort of inner sanctum as he sat behind his desk and I relaxed into a comfortable chair opposite.

Glenn had taken over after Watford had finished the 1992/93 season in 16th place. In July 1992 Perryman had bought Paul Furlong from Coventry City for £250,000; in his first season Furlong had been Watford's top scorer with 22 goals. Inevitably he was being linked with a move to a bigger club and the question when Glenn took over as manager was whether Furlong would be sold. I asked Glenn and he answered that he'd learned from Tommy Docherty that 'every player has his price'. In the end Furlong stayed for another season, at the end of which he was again top scorer, this time with 19 goals. In May 1994 we found out what Furlong's price was as Chelsea took him back to the top flight for £2.3m. Watford used the money to build a new stand at the Rookery End.

In 1993/94 Glenn, like Perryman before him, faced something of a relegation battle. In March 1994 a run of three defeats saw Watford in 23rd place so Glenn acted decisively, making several signings which all came off and brought about a revival. Tommy Mooney arrived on loan from Southend United, Colin Foster was acquired from West Ham for £80,000, Keith Millen came in from Brentford for £65,000 to play alongside Foster, and Dennis Bailey was brought in on loan from QPR. Foster had been a regular in Billy Bonds' West Ham side that had won promotion to Division One in 1990/91 and had played in the 1991 FA Cup semi-final defeat to Nottingham Forest. He moved to Watford after a few seasons disrupted by injury and in his six games in 1993/94 the Hornets only conceded one goal.

On New Year's Day in 1992 Bailey had scored a hat-trick for QPR in a famous 4-1 win over Manchester United at Old Trafford, but then he fell behind Gary Penrice and Bradley Allen in the pecking order at Loftus Road. In three games in a row in 1993/94 he came on as a substitute for Watford and scored. After four wins and a draw from the last five matches Watford finished in 19th place, three points above the relegation zone. One of those five wins was by 3-0 at home to Southend, with Mooney scoring against the club from which he was on loan.

The following season, 1994/95, turned out to be Watford's best since they'd finished fourth under Steve Harrison in 1988/89. The side revolved around Craig Ramage, a talented, flamboyant, attacking midfield player bought for £90,000 from Derby County in February 1994. He had been capped by England at under-21 level while at Derby, where injuries had held him back. In 1994/95 he played in all but two of Watford's league games, scoring nine goals.

In goal Kevin Miller, who had been bought by Glenn in August 1994 for £260,000 from Birmingham City, showed the sort of form which was later in his career to bring him to the verge of an England cap. Like Ramage, Miller made 44 league starts. In front of Miller were David Holdsworth and Colin Foster, who made 38 and 34 appearances respectively. In midfield the work rate of Andy Hessenthaler (43 starts) was complemented by the skill of Gary Porter (41 starts), who had been at Watford since 1980. But for me Ramage had made the side tick and had been more responsible than any other player for the seventh-placed finish.

I made my way to cover Watford's first game of 1995/96, at home to Sheffield United, hoping for an even better campaign. In my first season as Capital Gold Sport's Watford reporter I imagined covering a glorious promotion campaign in which Craig Ramage featured prominently, but as a reporter you don't write the script – you read it. The bubble of optimism burst even before the first game had kicked off. On my arrival at Vicarage Road for the visit of Sheffield United I was delighted to see that the cover of the matchday programme featured a photograph of Ramage next to the words, 'Craig Ramage – Up and Running for 1995/96'. That was exactly what I wanted to see, my favourite player on the cover with a positive headline.

When I arrived at Vicarage Road the stewards were always already in place and ready for a chat and a laugh as I made my way in. As well as being good people they were a great source of inside information which one in particular, Mark, was happy to impart. One of his areas of responsibility was the home dressing room and he would know the Watford line-up by which shirts had been hung up ready to be worn by the players. The shirts of those starting were in one part of the dressing room, while those of the substitutes were in another. On this particular day, 12 August 1995, Mark dropped a bombshell by telling me that Ramage, although not injured, had not been selected to play. Ramage may have been 'Up and Running for 1995/96' but he was not running fast enough for the manager's liking. Apparently he had reported back for training overweight and had not reached the required level of fitness during pre-season training to warrant a place in the side to face Sheffield United. Watford won 2-1 but something was missing.

The next Saturday I was at the McAlpine Stadium to see Watford play Huddersfield Town. Ruud Gullit had created a stir by signing for Chelsea in the summer and on 19 August 1995 he made his debut at Stamford Bridge against Everton. JP described the Chelsea fans wearing dreadlock wigs at the match to celebrate the arrival of a great player. I seemed to be a long way away from the colour and vibrancy of the picture JP was painting. In my considered report, after seeing Huddersfield beat Watford 1-0 through a Ronnie Jepson goal, I said, 'There was not a dreadlock in sight at the McAlpine Stadium.'

I met a new face in the press box that day. Nick London had started working for BBC Three Counties, the local radio station which covered Watford. Nick and I immediately hit it off. He was a striking character with a completely shaven head and because it was a hot day he had turned up at the McAlpine wearing shorts. Hilariously, they nearly didn't let him into the press box because this broke their dress code.

Nick went on to become a commentator for BBC Radio London, which meant that he got to work with a pundit, an ex-footballer, and we sometimes travelled together to Watford away matches. On one occasion we had Gary O'Reilly in the car. Gary had an interesting career; he started at Spurs but because of the strength of the squad he wasn't getting enough games. He moved to Brighton & Hove Albion in 1984 and started playing regularly alongside players such as

Jimmy Case, Eric Young, Danny Wilson and Frank Worthington, making 97 appearances.

Gary once told us that just after Christmas 1986, when he had been out for a few drinks in Brighton, he was called into the office of the manager at the time, Alan Mullery. Gary assumed that Mullery had found out about his gallivanting and he expected to be fined. Mullery told Gary that because of the financial difficulties Brighton were having at the time they needed to raise £40,000 quickly or there wouldn't be enough money to pay the wages. Gary's immediate reaction was to think, 'I'm expecting a fine but £40,000 seems a little excessive just for going out for a drink.'

Mullery then revealed the real reason behind the meeting. Brighton had received an offer of £40,000 from Crystal Palace for Gary, which they wanted to accept, and Mullery asked Gary whether or not he was happy to go. Gary said 'yes' and it turned out to be a great move. Palace were promoted to the top flight in 1988/89 and reached the FA Cup final in 1990. In the run to the final Gary scored in the tumultuous 4-3 semi-final win over Liverpool. He then scored in the 3-3 draw with Manchester United in the first game in the final itself.

Another of Nick's pundits was Iain Dowie. The three of us travelled together to cover a midweek 2-0 Watford win at Sheffield United in October 2001. Iain had already had a brief experience of being a manager. After ending his playing days at QPR he'd been player-manager of the reserve side and he'd been caretaker manager at Rangers for a while in the autumn of 1998 between the dismissal of Ray Harford and the re-appointment of Gerry Francis.

He was desperate to get his career as a manager going properly and on the way to Bramall Lane he talked about how much he wanted to get back into a management position. He said that he would take just about any job, he just wanted someone to give him a chance. At the time Sheffield Wednesday were about £20m in debt and teetering on the brink of relegation to the third tier of English football. I asked Iain whether that was a job he would take if he was offered it. 'Absolutely, without doubt,' was his response. In the event he didn't have to wait long before being offered the job of assistant manager at Oldham Athletic. He took it and, when Mick Wadsworth was axed, he became the boss at Boundary Park.

*

Watford followed up the defeat at Huddersfield by losing their next two matches. The slow start saw them in a relegation place in early September and they didn't win again until 9 September when Ramage, playing his second game of the season, scored twice in a 3-0 victory over Stoke City. Andy Hessenthaler had been injured in late August and was out for just over two months. The season was on the slide and there was to be no repeat of the confident, assured performances of the previous year.

A few days after the win over Stoke there was a midweek home game against Crystal Palace and JP came to Vicarage Road to commentate with Alan Mullery as his pundit. I'd been telling everyone at Capital Gold Sport that Watford were going to achieve great things that season and I was somewhat embarrassed that they saw a sterile 0-0 draw. I somehow felt responsible that JP and Mullery hadn't seen a good game and I apologised.

After a 4-2 defeat at Ipswich the following Saturday, in which Watford had been outplayed by a good footballing side and had defended poorly, I wrote a downbeat final report. As sometimes happened Glenn Roeder came up to the press box to do an interview after the game and he was standing nearby as I waited to give my report on air. I decided that I didn't want Glenn to hear me giving such a gloomy verdict so I hurriedly re-wrote it to give it a more positive slant.

Watford were outplayed again about a month later at Sunderland. It was the only time I ever heard the Roker Roar. It was a strange sound, unlike anything I had ever heard in a football ground; it was more like a howl than a roar, beginning quietly when Sunderland started to build an attack and gathering in momentum and growing in volume as they moved the ball downfield, reaching a crescendo if there was an attempt on goal. Despite Sunderland having most of the possession and plenty of attempts on goal, Watford nicked a 1-1 draw.

The day after the match I picked up *The Observer*, turned to the sports pages and saw that there was a report on the Sunderland v Watford game. I liked to read reports of matches I'd covered to see how they compared with my own description and it was always nice when there was a report on one of my games in a quality broadsheet. The report began, 'As the man who shouts professionally for a London radio station said, "There was more than an element of fantasy about the scoreline."' That was the opening line of my considered report. The journalist writing for *The Observer* had nicked my line and used it at the start of his report. I took it as a compliment and I felt that somehow he was giving me an identity. I was now 'The Man Who Shouts'.

For me the main reason for Watford's decline in 1995/96 was that Craig Ramage wasn't able to recapture his form of the previous season. Something must have happened between him and Glenn in the summer. In between his double against Stoke and a 4-0 defeat at Crystal Palace on 17 February 1996, Ramage scored only twice.

I'd always enjoyed going to Glenn's post-match press conferences. I once walked in after he'd started talking, carrying my big blue bag of radio equipment and he greeted me with, 'Where are you going, fishing?' Yes, Glenn, fishing for quotes.

By the time of the Palace game, which Watford went into rooted to the foot of the table, I'd stopped going to Glenn's press conferences. He'd retained his dignity but I felt that he had run out of explanations for what was happening and I wasn't confident that he could turn it round. I didn't enjoy watching him suffer. Just before the Palace match he brought big Devon White to the club, an act which smacked of desperation.

As Crystal Palace v Watford was quite a big game for Capital Gold Sport it featured fairly high on the running order and I was given the luxury of a pundit, Alan Mullery. In the build-up Watford had announced that they had given Glenn, who had been working without one, a contract. It seemed a strange move considering the club's position in the league and their loss of form. It turned out that Watford were preparing to sack Glenn and the reason they gave him a contract was so that he didn't have to leave without a pay-off.

The defeat at Selhurst Park proved to be Glenn's last match in charge. It was all about to change at Vicarage Road in a big way.

*

While a club's league position is all-important, the cup competitions can provide an interesting diversion and so it proved in the 1995/96 season before Glenn was sacked. Watford were drawn against Bournemouth, a division below them, in the second round of the League Cup. In the first leg played at Vicarage Road in September 1995 a spirited Bournemouth side took a first-half lead through Steve Jones. Richard Johnson equalised in the second half leaving the tie wide open when I travelled to the south coast for the second leg the following month.

It was my first trip to Dean Court and it proved to be a crazy night. As usual I got to the ground early and having picked up my press pass, I went in search of the press box. It was a weird setup at Dean Court. Instead of one big press box they had several small separate press areas spread out along the back of the main stand. I didn't know where I was supposed to be sitting and there seemed to be fewer people to ask than usual. I needed to get my equipment set up and to make contact with the studio as soon as possible. In these situations, a football reporter has a sort of homing instinct, a bit like a salmon, which kicks in. I managed to find out that I wasn't in any of the mini press boxes in the main stand. I was to sit on my own in a section of the small PA announcer's box behind one of the goals. I'd always been used to reporting from the side of the pitch. It was a first to have to work from behind the goal and a little disconcerting.

Watford had the better chances but couldn't score the goal that would have put them in the lead on aggregate. Bournemouth, with Matt Holland and Steve Robinson in midfield, pushed them all the way. It was goalless after 90 minutes and the game went into extra time. If it had stayed like that until the end of extra time then Bournemouth would have gone through because of the away goal they had scored in the first leg. Then in the last minute of extra time Watford won a corner on the right-hand side, over 100 yards away at the other end of the pitch to where I was sitting. Gerard Lavin took it, in a crowded goalmouth Colin Foster challenged for the ball, Wayne Andrews missed it and someone, it looked like Darren Bazeley, headed the ball in.

It had been a hectic night in the Capital Gold Sport studio. Of our clubs Arsenal, Brentford, Crystal Palace, Fulham and QPR were all playing in League Cup ties as well as Charlton Athletic and Wimbledon who were facing each other. Charlton v Wimbledon turned out to be an exciting match which also went into extra time. The programme, which had been scheduled to finish at 10pm, stayed on air to allow Steve Wilson to continue commentating until the end of the game at The Valley.

The cardinal sin of a football reporter is to get a goalscorer wrong. I was 99.9 per cent certain that Darren Bazeley had headed in the Watford goal, but that wasn't enough. JP used to come up with catchphrases every now and then which he used on air and one of them for a while was, 'Are you sure?!' Once when he was commentating on a game between Manchester City and Spurs at Maine Road, he said something like, 'And they're saying that it's not a very good season for London football. Leyton Orient are going well in Division Three, Brentford are pushing in Division Two, Crystal Palace are chasing promotion from Division One, Arsenal are top of the Premier League and Spurs have just taken the lead at Maine Road, ARE YOU SURE?!'

You had to be sure on Capital Gold Sport.

Pete Simmons was as usual producing the show the night I was at Bournemouth v Watford. He was being helped out by a young assistant called Darren who was still an apprentice but would later become a masterful producer in his own right, so much so that he became known as 'King Darren'. I'd been communicating with Darren and I told him that Watford had scored, but I wasn't absolutely sure who the goalscorer was. I heard Darren convey the message to Pete by saying, 'Watford have scored but he doesn't know who got the goal.' It was near the end of the show and Pete was near the end of his tether. From somewhere over the other side of the studio I heard him explode, 'What do you mean he doesn't know who scored, he's at the fucking match!'

I did a report saying that Watford had scored, without actually giving the name of the goalscorer. So technically I didn't get the name wrong but I didn't get it right either. For that goal I was a zen football reporter. I found out later that it was indeed Bazeley who'd scored, but it was better to be safe than sorry.

On a night when the level of drama increased the longer the game went on, Bournemouth equalised in the fourth minute of time added on at the end of extra time through Marcus Oldbury. The tie would now be decided by a penalty shoot-out.

Just as extra time at The Valley was finishing, Charlton beating Wimbledon 8-7 on aggregate after drawing 3-3 on the night, the shoot-out at Dean Court was beginning. To round off the evening Capital switched to me to commentate on the shoot-out from my position behind the goal.

As Steve Wilson cued me, Bazeley was shooting in off the post past Ian Andrews to make the penalty score 2-1 to Bournemouth. Steve Robinson and Matt Holland had both scored for the home side while Steve 'The Professor' Palmer had missed Watford's first penalty. The penalties were being taken down the other end to where I was sitting which meant that I could easily identify the taker by the number on the back of their shirt when they went up to spot the ball. Adrian Pennock scored next to make it 3-1 before Geoff Pitcher sent Andrews the wrong way to score for Watford.

Kevin Miller made the first of three saves in the shoot-out to keep out Russell Beardsmore and when Tommy Mooney hammered left footed into the roof the net Watford were back in it at 3-3. David Town making it 4-3 to Bournemouth meant that Watford had to score to keep the shoot-out alive. Significantly, Glenn Roeder had decided that the fifth and potentially crucial Watford penalty would be taken by Craig Ramage. It gave me the opportunity to eulogise about Ramage and I said, 'There isn't a cooler player in the Watford side, there couldn't really be a better player to have this responsibility.' Ramage sent Andrews the wrong way for 4-4.

I enjoy penalty shoot-outs. It's said that they're a lottery, but they're not. They're a test. Skill and a lot of nerve are required to score from or save a penalty as the taker and goalkeeper try to outwit each other. After a period of stalemate, it's time to move on to something which will be decisive. The drama of shoot-outs is that they can swing first one way and then the other, which was exactly what happened at Dean Court.

Shoot-outs are tense and exciting, and when they get to sudden death, they become electric. It was getting to Roeder and he strode to the edge of the pitch just before Robert Murray sent Miller the wrong way for 5-4 to Bournemouth. Richard Johnson was a midfield player with a ferocious shot and he blasted the ball in to make it 5-5. Then Miller made his second save as he denied ex-Watford man Mark Morris. If Gerard Lavin could score the next penalty Watford would be through, but he didn't, Andrews saving. Miller was really warming to the shoot-out and he dived away to his left to make a great save from John Bailey. Again, Watford were potentially in a winning position and this time they capitalised, Keith Millen putting the decisive penalty to the left of Andrews.

Watford supporters spilled on to the pitch as they celebrated jubilantly in the pouring rain.

It was time for me to calm down, hand back to the studio and to reflect. It had been an exhilarating night and when I played my commentary back, I was amused by how much 'stepping up' had taken place. To say that a player 'steps up' to take a penalty is one of the English-speaking football reporter's stock clichés. The words 'penalty' and 'steps up' are inextricably linked. I was no exception that night. I used the phrase 'steps up', or a variation of it – 'stepped back,' 'stepped up,' 'stepping up' – on 14 separate occasions in the ten minutes or so the shoot-out lasted!

*

Not long after the Bournemouth v Watford game, King Darren featured in a dream I had about football reporting. I turned up for a match, I don't know where it was played but Spurs were one of the teams involved. My seat in the press box was high up in the main stand. I could only see one half of the pitch as there were tall boards along the touchline blocking my view of the other half. I said down the line to King Darren, who was producing the show, 'Darren, I can only see half the pitch, how am I going to report on the match?' He replied, 'Use your imagination.'

Then an elephant walked across the part of the pitch I could see and the dream ended.

*

The week after losing 4-0 at Crystal Palace on 17 February 1996, Watford played Ipswich Town at home in the league. By the time their players ran on to the pitch for that game there had been big changes at the club.

Graham Taylor's next job after resigning as England manager in November 1993 had come in March 1994 when Sir Jack Hayward made him manager of under-achieving Wolverhampton Wanderers. That season Wolves finished in eighth place in Division One. The following season 1994/95 they finished fourth, their highest league finish since the early 1980s, and they qualified for the play-offs. They lost 3-2 on aggregate to Bolton Wanderers in the semi-final. The 1994/95 season proved to be Taylor's only full one at Molineux. Wolves got off to a poor start in the next campaign, winning four of their first 16 games, and Taylor was fired in November 1995.

Taylor's managerial career and his popularity with the general football public were at an all-time low. There was though always one place he could go and be not just accepted but welcomed with open arms. Just at the right time after sacking Roeder, Watford were looking for a manager, and the magician returned for an encore. The position was bleak – bottom of Division One with 18 games to play – but if anyone could turn it round it was Taylor. He was appointed as caretaker manager until the end of the season with Watford heroes Luther Blissett and Kenny Jackett on the coaching staff.

It took a few weeks for Taylor to improve the team's performances and results but when his influence began to be felt supporters were treated to a thrilling ride.

In the first game following Taylor's return, at home to Ipswich on Saturday, 24 February, playing on adrenaline alone Watford stormed into a 2-0 half-time lead but the Suffolk side's superior quality was apparent in the second half and they won 3-2.

Since he'd sold the club in the late 1980s Elton John's role had diminished, and although he was still life president he no longer had a close involvement in day-to-day affairs. Elton though still took a keen interest and he was dismayed by Watford's decline. He was at the Ipswich game and after the match I saw him hanging around the tunnel area not talking to anyone in particular. No one had said that we couldn't interview Elton and I couldn't see any of 'his people' whose permission I might need to obtain before approaching him, so I just walked up to him and casually asked whether he was OK to talk. Elton was as excited as any Watford supporter that Taylor was back and he readily agreed. He was keen to share his thoughts on the game and the club in general. He was a delight to interview. He was as lucid and as passionate about football as anyone I've come across, and he had strong views about where Watford had gone wrong.

At least Elton had seen Watford score a goal for the first time in a while. 'I saw them score two, nearly three actually, if it hadn't been for the bar,' he said, but he hadn't seen the result he wanted. 'No, I mean first half, you came in at half-time and I thought, well, this could be a really good ending, a great way to start Graham Taylor's new association with the club but the second half was completely different, it looked like a different team out there, it looked as if their legs had gone a bit and once Ipswich scored the early goal, they played magnificently and could have got more than three probably.'

Elton agreed that it was going to take quite a while if Watford were going to climb back up to where they had once been. 'Yeah, there's no instant, magic turnaround here, it's an uphill task to turn a club around, I don't think we had the best of luck and that happens when you're down here, we've only won two games out of 25 and once you're on that sort of a run it's awfully hard to turn it around, but it will get turned around. But that's not taking away from what Ipswich did, they came here, they were 2-0 down at half-time, they probably got a rollicking from their manager, they came out in the second half and they played magnificent stuff, you know, I thought they played brilliantly and any team that does that away from home when you're two down, they've got some fight, we need to get some of that fight in this club now, like that.'

Taylor had talked about a timescale of three years so the message to the fans was that it would take time. Elton agreed, 'Yeah, it's gonna take time, but the fans were great. One of the nice things about today which I enjoyed was that we doubled our gate to about 12,000, they were rowdy, they were noisy and they gave us great support, it was great to see the stadium that noisy again and the Ipswich fans also contributed to that. I enjoyed the game, it was a shame about the result but you can't really complain about it.'

As far as Elton was concerned Watford were not down yet and were going to fight relegation as long as it was mathematically possible to stay up. 'I think the players fought all they could today, I don't think they're as fit as they should be, and some of them are coming back from injury, and Gary Penrice had to come off and he's had flu, but you can't make excuses, the result stands 3-2 and we've got to start working on that.'

Elton had indicated that he was going to get more involved again, so the question was in what way exactly. 'Well, I'll probably be playing centre-forward next week, me and Devon! I'll just be here more, Graham and I, I'll help Graham all I can, and the board, to try and turn things around, we've got a lovely stadium, we just need to get involved with the community much more. Standards have dropped here, and I mean standards have dropped, there are ten players here who live over 60 miles from the club and that's not healthy because they're driving a long way to training and going home, they're tired, we need players who live in the area, to go out into the community, to present prizes, to go to schools. This is a club in Hertfordshire that the people will support and the club's got to give something back to that, and that's what happened the first time Graham was here and that's what needs to be done again and it needs to be done quickly.'

I thanked Elton, told him that it was great to see him back at Watford and legged it to the press box to tell the studio about my scoop. Dave Clark was in that day and I said to him, 'Dave, I've just interviewed the most famous person you've ever had on Capital Gold Sport.' When I told him who it was, he replied laughing, 'I don't think so, we had an interview with Nelson Mandela once.'

Elton may not have been the most famous person to have appeared on the show but, with apologies to Kevin Keegan, he is the best singer I've ever talked to about football.

*

Elton had said that things would be turned around at Watford but that there was no instant fix and he was right on both counts. Watford were relegated to Division Two on 5 May 1996 but they went into the last game of the season with a chance of staying up. As a reporter the last thing I wanted was for the season to die and Watford's efforts to stay up made a story, even though it didn't have a happy ending.

The fight to avoid relegation failed, but the team gave it a real good go. What I particularly liked was that for a spell Watford were banging in goals right, left and centre. Immediately after the Ipswich game there was a run of three games in which Watford didn't score. Then a 2-1 home win over Oldham, in which Craig Ramage scored both goals, was followed by a mad 4-4 draw at West Bromwich Albion. It was one of those games in which it looked as though every attack would end in a goal. Watford were 3-0 down after half an hour and trailed 4-2 with ten minutes remaining but by now Taylor's philosophy, that as long as the game continues you have a chance of scoring a goal, was beginning to take effect and Watford scored twice in the last six minutes.

The goals came in a flood towards the end of the season. Watford played eight matches in April 1996, only failing to score once. There was a 3-3 draw at home to Sunderland then later in the month there were successive home wins over Port Vale (5-2), Reading (4-2) and Grimsby (6-3). Ramage returned to form with 11 goals in the last 14 games to finish the season as leading scorer on 15. Before scoring one of his goals Ramage had eased Tommy Mooney out of the way to make sure he had the opportunity to shoot. Ramage often used to hang out in the tunnel before kick-off and when I saw him before the next Watford home match, I played up to him by telling him that I'd liked the way he'd pushed Mooney out of the way before scoring. Instead of denying it and saying that he'd never do anything as ungentlemanly as push a team-mate out of the way to get a goalscoring opportunity, he said, 'Oh, it was Tommy, was it?' I got the impression that Ramage liked to think he was top man at Watford and for a while he was definitely the most talented and effective player at Vicarage Road. Mooney peaked at a later age than Ramage but once he did, he became a club legend.

Kevin Phillips had been injured in March 1996 and wasn't able to play for nearly a year. In his absence another young striker, David Connolly, came into the side. Connolly scored a hat-trick in his first start of the season, the win over Port Vale. He and Ramage both scored hat-tricks in the victory against Grimsby which meant that the penultimate match of the season, at Norwich, was what football reporters like to call a 'must-win' game. I went to Carrow Road ready to read the last rites on Watford's season but they made it four wins in five with a 2-1 victory. Connolly scored from the penalty spot to take his tally to eight goals in five matches. The winning goal from Gary Porter was a 30-yard screamer into the top corner. Porter had waited until that moment to score what proved to be his only goal of the season.

With Watford in with a chance of staying up, the game at home to Leicester City on the final day was deemed important enough by Capital Gold Sport to send a commentator to cover it. I met up with Steve Wilson and we had breakfast sitting outside a café in Highgate. It was one of those days when we were kidding ourselves. It was early May but not really warm enough to sit outside. The croissants were cold and so was the coffee. Leicester under Martin O'Neill needed a win to be sure of a play-off place and they got it, Muzzy Izzet scoring the only goal of the game.

14

The 1995/96 season ended with relegation to Division Two but the nature of football is such that disappointments are soon forgotten. For Watford, Graham Taylor was back on board, Elton John was involved again and they started 1996/97 among the favourites for promotion. I went to the pre-season press day at a sunny Vicarage Road and talked to just about everyone. Kenny Jackett had taken over as manager with Taylor moving 'upstairs' to become general manager. It was Kenny's first job as manager and he was looking forward to it, aiming for promotion at the end of the season. Kenny was being supported by Luther Blissett who had been given a coaching role in February 1996.

Goalkeeper Kevin Miller was still at the club despite paper talk linking him with a move away and he was expecting a more physical challenge in Division Two.

Craig Ramage was out of contract and leaving his options open, 'I spoke to Grimsby a couple of weeks ago, I think they're keen, I really want First Division football but I'm enjoying it here again with Kenny, Kenny's working with us at the moment, you don't know what's round the corner.' Players wanting to leave was an inevitable consequence of relegation. Craig had no problem with Watford but he wanted to play at a higher level than Division Two, 'There's nothing wrong with the club and everything else, it's all been turned over again, it's looking good for the future but I'm 26 and I think I've got to be looking onwards and trying to get a First Division club or higher.' Craig was waiting on other clubs to come back to him. 'Not just Grimsby, I'm hoping there's a few more in the pipeline but I'm waiting to see what my agent says and all that, so I'm just leaving my options open at the moment, it's still early and I'll see what options I get before the start of the season.' Craig thought that Watford were capable of mounting a promotion challenge. 'Oh yeah they've got plenty of talent here to do that,' he said, but ominously for me, who so enjoyed watching him play, he doubted that he'd be part of it. 'Whether I'm involved or not, I shouldn't think I'd be involved on a week-to-week basis but the players they have got here I think they'll do the job very good and get Watford into it.'

Robert Page, on the other hand, had signed a new three-year contract and had been made club captain. He was as pleased as he could be considering Watford had just been relegated, 'Things are looking up for myself, being appointed club captain and signing a new contract I couldn't be happier at the moment, the only disappointing thing is obviously the club got relegated last season but we've just got to get on with it now and hopefully get promoted back to the First Division next season.' The end to the previous season, which had almost seen Watford avoid relegation, had also engendered optimism for Page, 'We played the last eight or nine games at the end of the season, unfortunately we did end up going down, but we showed a lot of promise during them last few games, we scored a hell of a lot of goals, and hopefully if we can continue with the goals we scored plus the way we started playing at the end of the season, then you never know what's going to happen next season.'

During the summer David Connolly had made his debut for the Republic of Ireland at the age of 18 and had scored two goals in four matches for them. Watford had turned down a seven-figure offer from Wolverhampton Wanderers for Connolly and after the way he had burst on to the scene at the end of the previous season much was expected of him. He'd enjoyed the international experience and had taken it in his stride, 'Obviously it's a step up, I think I coped with it OK, you know. It is definitely a step up, there's more pressure on you to keep the ball, there's more pressure on you to find a pass and if you get a chance you've got to make sure you take it because not many of them come along, whereas maybe in league football you get a few more chances and if you put maybe half of them away then you're doing well, at international level really if you get a chance you've got to stick it away.'

Jackett had been at Watford since joining as a schoolboy in 1976 at the age of 14. He was a key component in midfield during the golden years in the 1980s. After being forced to retire through injury at the age of 28 he'd become a part-time coach, youth team coach, youth team manager, assistant manager, youth team manager again, joint coach and ultimately manager in May 1996. Connolly had joined Watford as a schoolboy at the same age as Kenny. Watford had offered him a new contract but from the answer he gave to my question about that, and the rejected bid from Wolves, you could sense that he would not be around anywhere near as long as Kenny, 'I'm contracted to Watford for another year, I've been here for a number of years and I've always enjoyed it here, I believe Wolves have made an offer, I don't actually know the size of the figure, but I'm a Watford player, I enjoy playing here and I think the coming season will be a good season here. We've got a new manager, I think we'll do very well, it hasn't restricted me internationally so I'm looking forward to things.'

I looked back at the previous season with a downbeat Kevin Phillips, who'd recently suffered several blows. First, he'd seen Glenn Roeder, the man who had brought him back into league football, sacked in mid-February. Then a couple of weeks later, in an away game at Reading, he'd picked up the foot injury which was to prevent him playing for just under a year. The injury meant that he had been unable to contribute to Watford's relegation battle, or to join in the end of season goal spree. While I was convinced that Watford's downfall began with the rift which developed between Roeder and Ramage, Kevin told me that the view of the players was that the number of injuries was the main reason for relegation, 'Yeah, maybe you could say that was a feeling amongst the lads at the beginning of the season when we lost Hessenthaler, lost a couple of others through minor injuries. I think Hessenthaler was the key. The damage was done earlier on in the season simple as that. Since Mr Taylor come things picked up and the side looked very good and we finished the season strong, let's just hope we can start the season like that.'

I'd gone to the press day not intending to talk to Graham Taylor because I wanted to concentrate on the people who would be directly involved in the football in the coming season. As general manager, Graham's input would be more on the administrative side. In a twist which reminded me a little of my meeting with Bobby Moore, after I'd finished talking to Kenny Jackett and the players

Graham came over to me and said 'hello'. I was disarmed by his openness and friendliness and we started chatting. After the initial chat I took the opportunity to turn my tape recorder back on. I'm glad I did because, no matter what position he held, he spoke so much sense and he was so positive.

I asked him how he was enjoying his new role. 'I'm enjoying it very much, what I do know it's very busy. If I wanted to be downstairs, I couldn't be anyhow because there's so much coming in. A football club behind the scenes there's so much going on and understandably supporters are not always aware of that, and quite rightly so, the main thing that they want to see is a successful football team. That's now Kenny Jackett's and Luther Blissett's responsibility, not mine.'

Things had been going well over the summer from Graham's perspective. 'From a season ticket point of view, they've gone excellently. We were relegated last season, everybody knows that but two or three weeks before the season starts, we're well past the number of season tickets that we had for the whole of last season so that means that our income has held up and that in itself is a very, very good sign because it shows that there is a nucleus of support here that very much wants the club to get back to some of its old ways.

'We've not actually as a relegated club sat back and sort of held our head in our hands. We've invested in the refurbishment of the Rous Stand, all of the boxes which has cost us something like over £200,000, we've renovated all of the dressing room area for the players so that they themselves can come in, because I do think that is important, if players say "hey, hold on, something's happening here", their changing facilities, their training facilities, I felt were not really what a professional football club should be, so we've invested into that. Obviously, supporters don't see that, they're just two or three sort of instances that I'm talking about. But I think generally what we're trying to convey is that it's not a question of depression simply because we've been relegated. That's a fact and what we've got to do now is to get ourselves on the way back and to do that I think you've got to create an air of optimism, you've got to be positive, and you've got to make sure that you believe that things are turning, that we've now bottomed out and we're going to go again. Now we know that's all talk, but at least you've got to try to do something and give that base for all concerned with the club, and we've been trying to do that in the summer.'

Taylor was back and it seemed obvious to me that there was a connection between his return and season ticket sales being up, despite relegation. I put this thought to him and suggested that he might be too modest to agree. The views expressed about Taylor in the media have been more polarised than those on just about any other manager. His answer to my question reassured me that he was clever enough not to fall into the trap of believing his own publicity, good or bad. 'Well, because of the last time we were here we were successful, then people obviously associate with that but I've been taking great pains and I'll say it again this is a new era, it's about Kenny Jackett being the team manager, it's about Luther Blissett assisting him, it's about setting up the youth situation, it's about a completely new era of which I happen to be the general manager. Now you can't look back and you can't turn round and say it is going to be as it was because that doesn't happen. But there is still no reason why in the small way that I can, from whatever position I'm in, try to sort of give that positive attitude, give that belief, that this club can in fact and will in fact improve upon its present status. Whether we can ever get back to challenging the Newcastles, the Manchester Uniteds and the Liverpools, that would be a miracle, that would be a football miracle. People thought it was last time but I think everybody knows now that the gap is so, so wide and we're not just talking about Alan Shearer's recent transfer move [a world-record £15m from Blackburn Rovers to Newcastle United in the summer of 1996], we're talking about every aspect of it. But I think that's what makes it so exciting, that's the challenge because that's what we were able to do before, you know we were able to have a go and give it a real go and I hope now that that's what will happen again.'

As Graham had said, football had greatly changed since the 1980s when Watford regularly finished in the top half of the top flight and I wondered whether he thought it was still possible for a club the size of the Hornets to compete at that level without a substantial outlay of money. 'Well, I mean you can stay in there, I mean Wimbledon, Southampton, a few clubs you could name stay in there, whether they can make an impact, I mean I think what Wimbledon have done over the years is absolutely tremendous but they've always done it, almost always, on what you would call a positive transfer account, they've always had players that they've been able to sell on and I'm sure their supporters there accept that. I mean if you went back and if you counted, you looked at all the Wimbledon players playing for various other clubs you'd say you might have a potential championship winning side there so they have stayed in there but their supporters have understood from the word go with Wimbledon that they're going to have to sell players to sort of make sure that they can stay there. But then making sure that they've stayed there they've actually bought in players and they've brought their own.

'Whether you can actually go up now and make a big impact and hold that impact I think is very much open to debate, we've just seen the television agree a £750m five-year deal with the Premier League clubs and therefore I can't see why people are surprised there's a £15m transfer. But if you think that we're talking about a television deal with Sky now with the Nationwide clubs, we'll get £300,000 out of that as a Second Division club. That is substantially more than Second Division clubs have ever had in the past but if you compare it with the millions of pounds that each Premier League club is going to get then what does £300,000 buy you now as a player?'

I had to ask Graham about David Connolly. It was obvious that the club rated him very highly because of the bid for him that they'd turned down and because they'd offered him a new contract. But in the relationship between the player and the club it became clear from Graham's response where the power really lay. 'Of course, it's true at a club like this that every player has his price and anybody that won't accept that or doesn't believe it are living in cloud cuckoo land. The point is this, that we're talking about a young boy that has burst on to the scene, he's only played eight games at the first team level, eight I think as substitute. People say he's the prize asset, he's become a prize asset because one club has made a bid for him which we've turned down at this moment but I mean I can't guarantee that we would never sell David. We've offered David a three-year contract, he's chosen not to sign that, this was before all of these situations were arising, so it isn't as if we weren't trying to keep the player here before all of this came along. David went out as an 18 year old and played for the Republic of Ireland in the summer and did extremely well, scored some goals, has come back, has got himself an agent which as I was saying earlier is the sort of name of the game now for everything and so our hands are tied in many respects, we can only sort of try our very best to keep our players and then if big offers do come across you've got to weigh it up.

'David's only got one year left on his contract so if he chooses not to sign another contract for us, what option do we have? You know, if somebody could say to us, "Look, we know how you could sort of get David Connolly into a room and we know how you could put a pen in his hand and we know how you can actually force him to sign his name on that contract," tell us how to do it, I'll tell you if it's possible and we'll do it. But we've tried all of those kind of things and at the moment we have turned down a seven-figure offer from a club and I think that should show the supporters that you know we're not going to just give up on players or we're not going to sell players at first shout but I can't say that it means we won't sell players. We lost over £1m last season, I mean it's as simple as that.'

Watford were clearly in a very difficult position. If they were to sell Connolly while he was under contract, they would get more than if they sold him after his existing contract had expired, for a fee determined by a tribunal. Graham continued, 'And there's a difference as you well know between a transfer fee and a compensation fee, but there is the other fact that David could stay and he can go abroad if he got a club abroad and we'd get nothing. So, there's so many things, it's a much wider and fuller picture sometimes than you know is aware and when this first broke you know I got a few letters from supporters saying we shouldn't be doing this, once you'd spoken to one or two, I think they saw that hold on a minute, it's not quite as straightforward as people are saying.

'The days when clubs can keep players like a John Barnes as we did for six years are gone, and I'm sorry to have to say this, that's a fact of life, that's what we have to deal with and I hope that some of the experience that I have I can bring that to help, I think the biggest thing is supporters won't always agree and I don't expect them to, but if you try to explain things to them as fully as you can without breaking confidences I think the majority of supporters then while they might not like it they accept it more and understand it more and all I would try to do as I did previously and all I will try always to do with the Watford supporters is tell them the truth as I see it without breaking confidences obviously and sometimes you do have to keep quiet and you can't say anything. But I mean in this particular case that's what we're really talking about with David, we would very much like him to stay, there is only a certain amount that we could afford to pay David, I mean anybody would know that, but if at the end of the day the boy wants to leave and a club comes in and offers the kind of money that makes it sort of impossible to turn down then obviously David is going to leave.'

I asked Graham how far he thought Connolly could go as a player and whether he could become a long-term established Republic of Ireland international. Graham answered, 'I haven't got a clue, I mean we're talking about a boy that's played eight first team games, he's scored his goals, he's got a goalscoring record. I think it would be most wrong of me, I've seen this said so oftentimes about young players, you know all the marvellous, wonderful things that they're capable of doing, supposed to be, and what they will become and after six months you never hear of them again. Now I think it would be most unwise of me to even hazard a guess or to say publicly what I think David is or isn't capable of doing. What I do know is that with just eight games under his belt and he's had this international appearance it's a great start for an 18-year-old boy. Where it will go who knows, it depends on so many outside factors as well, not just the boy himself, not just the club, what advice he listens to, what decisions he makes, does he stay fit, is he going to be injury-free? There's so many factors come into it, it's almost an impossible question to answer.'

We finished the chat on a jovial note when I asked Graham what his involvement would be in the playing side at Watford. 'I'm there as a person to smile to myself when I'm watching on a Saturday and I'm watching Kenny bouncing up and down on the touchline and Luther squirming on the seat, I'm the person that's just going to smile to myself, "I know what you're going through, fellas."'

*

Exactly one year after that pre-season press day, I was back at Vicarage Road talking to Graham Taylor, Watford manager. He'd decided to put himself through the wringer once more.

Watford had finished 1996/97 13th in Division Two. The season never took off. For Kenny Jackett the goal of promotion in his first campaign as manager proved unattainable. In the previous season, a thrilling roller-coaster ride which had ended in relegation, Watford had scored 62 league goals, more than Sunderland who had gone up as champions. In 1996/97 they couldn't find the cutting edge to win matches and drew 19 out of their 46 fixtures, more than any other side in Division Two. Connolly suffered from injury and loss of form, didn't build on his sensational end to the previous season, and ended with two league goals from 13 appearances. He ended up getting the move he wanted when he joined Feyenoord on 1 August 1997 and at one point he was the highest-paid player in Dutch football. As Graham feared, Watford did not receive anything from the move.

Craig Ramage didn't get his transfer before the start of the season but, as he'd expected, he wasn't really involved at Watford. He was also injured some of the time and spent a month on loan at Peterborough in early 1997. Kevin Phillips returned to the side in late February 1997 and managed four league goals from 16 appearances. On the same day that Connolly signed for Feyenoord, Ramage joined Bradford City, then in Division One.

Tommy Mooney was beginning to emerge as Watford's most inspirational player and ended the season as leading scorer with 13 league goals from 37 appearances.

Jackett didn't receive the necessary financial support from owner Jack Petchey. With goalscoring a problem the manager had wanted £200,000 to bring in Barry Hayles, who'd scored 34 goals in Stevenage's 1995/96 Conference title-winning side. The money wasn't forthcoming and Hayles ended up having a successful goalscoring career in league football after moving to Bristol Rovers for £250,000 in 1997. Petchey wasn't a popular owner at Watford. On 15 March 1994, the night I'd sat in the press box watching Arsenal beat Torino, Watford had lost 3-0 at home to Grimsby Town in front of 5,109 people. At the end of the game some die-hard supporters had vented their frustration by storming the directors' box in a protest at the way Petchey was running the club.

The highlight of the 1996/97 season came off the pitch. The penultimate game of the season was at home to Bury on the last Saturday in April. Two days previously Watford had lost 2-0 at home to Chesterfield to effectively end any chance of qualifying for the play-offs. When I arrived at the ground for the Bury game, I got wind that something was happening, that some major announcement was imminent. As kick-off approached I left my seat in the press box and made my way downstairs to the press room area. Just as I entered the press room a neatly typed official Watford press release headed 'Elton's Coming Home' was being handed out stating that a consortium headed by Elton John was buying the club from Jack Petchey. Elton had sold to Petchey and now he was involved in buying the Hornets back. Elton had told me over a year previously that he wasn't happy with the way Watford had slid, and now he was doing something positive about it. Elton, the only owner who had been genuinely popular with Watford fans since I'd started following the club in the late 1960s, was returning to the helm. On top of that Graham Taylor was to become manager again. The dream combination, of flamboyant multimillionaire pop star and son of a Lincolnshire sports journalist, was back. Most of all, Graham Taylor the magician was returning and the audience was ready for some more magic.

I had to get back to the press box to tell the studio what was going on. On the way I ran into Graham and asked him for an interview. It was not the time or place. There was so much pandemonium and he was so much in demand that he declined. It was the only time Graham ever refused an interview when I asked him for one. I hurried on my way and made it back to the press box. By then everyone in there knew what was happening and it was frantic.

At Capital Gold Sport a running order was prepared for the hour between 2pm, when the show went on air, and 3pm when games kicked off. Every second was accounted for and it was not often that we deviated from the running order. Very occasionally big news would break in the first hour of the show, and this was one such instance. Steve Wilson cued me by saying, 'Simon Michaelson, big news at Vicarage Road.' I responded, 'Steve, news doesn't get much bigger around these parts,' and went on to tell the listeners about the return of Elton and Graham.

A year previously Leicester City had got what they needed to secure a play-off place, and their supporters had celebrated at Vicarage Road. In a goalless draw Bury got the point they required for promotion to Division One and it was again away fans who were celebrating at the Vic. But this time the Watford faithful went home with good reason to dream about a golden tomorrow.

*

So Graham, what do you mean you're returning as manager, are you crazy or something?

I was able to ask Graham Taylor about his decision at the press day before the start of the 1997/98 season, only of course I did it a little more diplomatically than that. My conclusion was that he was doing it because he loved football and he wanted to be directly involved once more in what he did best.

Graham had been busy since taking over again and hadn't wasted any time getting in new players. 'Yeah, we've signed five new players, we've had a tournament out in Lithuania, and we've had ten days in Finland, so we've been quite active this pre-season.'

However many signings had been made I always wanted to know whether there would be any more, so I asked him. 'Well, there's nothing imminent but I think that there will be more signings, yeah, and the players knew that when they reported back. I mean I told them we'd be looking to sign players, the intention is to try to give this club an opportunity to possibly repeat some of its former successes.'

That was music to my ears, but Graham was always careful not to promise anything he wasn't capable of delivering, or to big things up too much. Football is littered with unfulfilled promises and broken dreams. After he'd been re-appointed, the club hosted a black-tie dinner for local businesses at the Watford Hilton, to which I was invited. The idea was to get businesses on board and to seek their backing. Graham made a speech in which he invoked memories of the glory days but he was careful to stress that he couldn't guarantee a repeat. His message to the businesspeople was, 'We can't promise that we'll be successful but we're going on a journey and we'd like you to come with us.'

When Graham told me that he was going to attempt the incredibly difficult feat of repeating former successes I wondered why he felt he had to do it. I could think of all sorts of reasons for Graham lying low, picking up a decent salary and not diving back into the shark-infested waters of football management. He had achieved so much already and they say you should never go back; his standing was incredibly high among the people of Watford, didn't he feel he was putting his reputation on the line by going back as manager? Wasn't it tempting to continue as general manager? He probably had a cosy life, or was it that he preferred being on the sharp end of things? 'Well I'm a football man, football manager, I'm not really all that bothered about reputations, they're there to be made, they're there to be shot at and other people decide themselves, all I do know is that this club has always had a special part in my life, we're back down in the Second Division now and I think people know me well enough to know that we'll do everything possible to try to get out of the lower divisions as soon as we can. Whether we achieve it or not only time will tell but it's football, it's being involved with football people, and we're trying to improve these players as players and improve their career prospects.'

There was a question I'd been burning to ask Graham for a long time and I felt that now was the time to ask it. He'd been through so much with the England job, so given the success he'd had first time round at Watford did he ever regret, just for a moment, leaving? He answered head on. 'No I don't think that you can do that, I mean certainly I wanted to become the England manager anyhow and even if I had stayed at Watford I would still have wanted to have a go at international management because that was my ambition, my aim, as I hope some of these players that have now joined Watford want to play in the Premier League, be it with Watford or be it with another club, that's what you must be looking for, you must be looking to strive to better yourself and to achieve things, so no I have no regrets about leaving Watford, what was it ten years ago now.' The answer pleased me because the thought that Graham regretted his time as England manager would have been hard to bear.

Graham was back in tandem with Elton John, the pairing people were calling the Dream Team. I asked Graham how important Elton was to Watford. 'I think the club, having had the success it had, and then unfortunately things went a little bit wrong for them, I think it was important that the supporters felt that people who were now owning the club had the feel of the club, they understood what the heartbeat of the club was about, and in the main the supporters here have a great respect for Elton and they trust him and I think that really is what had probably been lost, through nobody else's fault previously. I mean it was a very hard act to follow in '87 when we left and then probably two years later Elton had left and I don't envy anybody having to try to follow that sort of measure of success, but I think that the supporters lost a little bit of trust in some of the things that happened and I think that has returned now with Elton returning as the chairman.'

I told Graham that I thought he was absolutely right. I'd been there for the Bury game when Graham had stood on the pitch and the announcement had been made to the crowd that he and Elton were back and the roar was unbelievable. I told Graham that players played on the pitch and he picked the team and it was relatively easy to see what was happening. Elton was a backroom man and supporters couldn't see what he was doing. I asked Graham what his actual influence would be. 'Well, it will be very similar to what it was previously. What he is very good at, he lets people manage and he lets people get on with their jobs and you know some people say, "Oh you're very fortunate having Elton John or various people," what you have to do, you have to produce the goods because you can't blame your directors. There's a lot of people in my game you know, they make excuses and they say "oh if I could have bought that fella, I didn't have the money" or "this director didn't" or "it wasn't this" or "it wasn't that". You don't have those excuses at Watford because when Elton's there you're allowed to do your job, you're allowed to manage and it's the same with the players, you play, you're here to perform, you're here to get results. So there's a great freedom but there's also a responsibility with that as well, but also as a sort of public performer himself he knows what's expected, he knows that you have bad days, and he also knows that when you don't feel so well you've still got to go out there and perform, so there's an empathy between him and the players in the sense that he understands you know what performing at your best means but he also understands, he can also see those players that don't do that, that actually don't, you know if you don't feel like it, you don't perform, you can't have that, so he's very, very good.'

One of the biggest changes in football since Graham had last been Watford manager, and the club had challenged Liverpool for the title, was the amount of money that was in the game. It was astronomical and going up all the time. I asked him whether he really felt that Watford could compete on the same footing as some of the massive clubs. 'Well at the present time we've got no chance whatsoever to do that. I mean people will see at the present time that I've bought five players in and I haven't spent £800,000. Now £800,000 is still a lot of money but for five players, now you can understand, how can you compete with that? You can't, but we're not in that league at the moment, we're not in the Premier League, we'll never be a big club and people misunderstand me sometimes when I say that, we were not a big club previously but we could compete with the big boys so even if we were to get back in the Premier League, we'll never be a Manchester United, we'll never be a Newcastle, we'll never be a Liverpool and I don't think we really want to be, but what we'd like to do, we'd like to be in there snapping at their heels now and again, which we did before and we had a period of time doing that, and we enjoyed ourselves doing that. I think that's the biggest thing, and I think the return of Elton particularly means that whatever happens, even if we don't get back into the Premier League we'll enjoy having a go at trying to do that, because we did that previously, everybody enjoyed themselves and that's what we'd like to return to the club here, the fact that you know we want to be ambitious, we want to be successful, but we want to make sure that people do enjoy themselves and don't lose sight of the fact that although there is big business, big money, it is still a game.'

I observed that Graham had bought young players with potential, with an eye on the long term. I asked him whether, when he became manager again, he already had players in mind who he wanted to go out and get. 'Well, I mean, people say I took a year off last year, I mean I didn't take a year off from football because as you say I was the general manager and I learned a lot about football as a business anyhow off the pitch. But it also gave me an opportunity to watch the Second Division, you know the games that Watford played, see some of the opposition players as well, and it gave me an idea, I could take a step back and just look and say "well I think that this is going to be required.". Now the players, the five players that we've signed, Jason Lee is the oldest at 26 at £200,000, the youngest is Chris Day who's only just 22, so when we signed him, he was 21. Micah Hyde is 22, from Cambridge. Peter Kennedy, 23, from Notts County and Dai Thomas from Swansea who's only 20, so you know we've got that bracket in there. I'm not going to turn round and say that these are this kind of player, they're that kind of player, but they're at a nice age, they've got a bit of experience behind them of the lower divisions and hopefully we can now improve them and they can help this club achieve its ambitions and also improve their career prospects as well and if we're doing that then we'll be being successful.'

As usual Graham had been more than generous with his time and I thanked him and told him that I was looking forward to seeing the new players in action.

15

I was now firmly established at Capital Gold Sport as the Watford reporter and I was delighted that I'd found something of value, a niche in which I felt I belonged. It was a position which suited me and in which I felt completely comfortable. I told myself that I honestly didn't think that there was anyone in the world who could have performed the role better than me. I wasn't being boastful, I just thought that I was the right person for the job. I was happily bouncing from one week to the next getting games regularly. King Darren told me that when he was training new reporters, he would tell them to listen to me and use me as an example of how to do the job, which was a nice compliment.

I may have been a smallish fish in a big pool but I knew how to swim, and I wasn't just reporting on Watford matches. Towards the end of the 1996/97 season, I was given Derby County v Spurs to cover in the Premier League, on 22 March 1997. It was the third-ranked match of the day on the show. The top game, being covered by JP of course, was Middlesbrough v Chelsea at the Riverside. Steve Wilson was covering Coventry City v West Ham at Highfield Road. On my way to Derby's old Baseball Ground home, I called in at the studio to pick up a tape recorder. I happened to see the day's running order and next to it was JP's intro to the show, which he always prepared in advance and typed out.

I read it and gulped. Whereas normally I heard JP's intro through headphones at a noisy ground when I was preoccupied with my game, on my own in the quiet of the studio I could study his words and properly take them in and digest them. It was a time when the foreign revolution had taken hold at Stamford Bridge, and Middlesbrough had one or two foreign stars themselves. I knew that JP was excited by watching the great players from overseas in the Premier League, and he was able to communicate that excitement brilliantly. In his intro he talked of 'names like Di Matteo, Zola and Juninho dripping deliciously from our lips'. If that didn't get the listeners' juices flowing then nothing would. The thing with JP was that he meant it, it wasn't an act. He got a huge buzz from watching sublime football, and uttering lines like that was how he articulated his appreciation.

Just before half-time at Derby I got to do a bit of commentary. JP's half-time at the Riverside had come first, so Steve picked up and started commentating from Highfield Road. Then Steve's whistle blew and they came over to the Baseball Ground where the game was still going on. I wasn't sure whether to just give a report so they could go on to someone else, or to start commentating. I decided to start commentating; someone would tell me to stop if necessary. I only had a few minutes but there was nothing happening on the pitch and I had to fill. Spurs were awarded a free kick just outside the Derby box and before he took it Teddy Sheringham wanted the wall back a full ten yards, and to give his central defenders time to get into the penalty area. As Teddy stood there with his hands on his hips waiting everything kind of went into slow motion.

After the game I interviewed John Scales, who'd played at the back for a Spurs side which had been beaten 4-2. During the interview as Scales explained away the defeat, I don't know why but I thought to myself, 'This is unreal, I'm talking to a footballer who's being paid £40,000 for a week's work, which culminated in him losing a football match, and I'm getting paid just a tiny fraction of that to interview him.' Not that it really mattered to me.

*

One of the Spurs goalscorers in the defeat at Derby was Ronny Rosenthal. The next time I saw Rocket Ronny play he was wearing the yellow of Watford.

I decided that the theme song to Watford's 1997/98 season should be 'Moving On Up' by M People. Watford were not out of the top two all season. In his first spell in charge Graham Taylor won eight and lost two of his first ten league matches, and the second time round his record was seven wins, two draws and one defeat. There were major contributions from the new players. Watford opened the campaign with a win over Burnley at Vicarage Road, Jason Lee scoring the only goal. The first scorer in the next match, a 2-0 win at Carlisle, was Peter Kennedy, a player plucked by Graham from Notts County reserves who went on to win 18 international caps for Northern Ireland. He was one of many who benefitted from playing under Graham, who always encouraged his players to have a go at goal. Playing on the left side of a four-man midfield Kennedy, or 'The President' as he became known, had a fierce shot, was a good, accurate crosser of the ball and was potent from free kicks.

Before moving to Watford, Micah Hyde had made his mark at Cambridge United and had captained the side. He scored his first league goal for the Hornets in a 2-1 win over Wycombe Wanderers in early September 1997. I appreciated the play of Micah because he was the sort of midfield player I'd aspired to be – busy, always involved, passing and then supporting a team-mate, accurate rather than spectacular, not a prolific goalscorer but he would weigh in with a few every season. I met him shortly after he joined Watford and he described his game by saying, 'I wouldn't say I'm a goalscoring, attacking midfielder, I like to say I'm an attacking midfielder. I like to score the odd goal here and there but my game isn't really to score goals from midfield, my game is to attack and join the attack and keep the attack going.' He shared the vision of Graham and knew exactly the direction in which he wanted to head. 'Yeah, if you look around the ground and the facilities they've got here it really is a First Division club, should be pushing for Premier League, not a Second Division club pushing for First Division. While I'm here, and we're in the Second Division at the moment, my objective and the club's objective is to push towards the First Division and then hopefully on to the Premier League.' Like Kennedy, Micah won international honours while at Watford. Altogether he played 17 times for Jamaica.

Of the early acquisitions made by Graham, the most spectacular was Ronny Rosenthal on a free from Spurs. He signed the day after the win over Burnley. Unlike those seeking to establish themselves in the game, the Rocket already had an impressive and diverse CV. He was coming towards the end of his career and was an Israel international with 60 caps. Ronny had started out at Macabi Haifa in 1980 and with them he won the Israeli Premier Division in 1983/84 and 1984/85.

From 1986 to 1988 he played for Club Brugge where he won the Belgian Premier Division in 1987/88. In the four years he spent with Liverpool between 1990 and 1994 he won the Division One title in 1989/90. The three and a half years at Spurs which followed did not yield any trophies and in his final season there he only started four league games. The invitation to join Watford came at the right time. He was 33 when he signed but with all that top-level experience, he was always likely to cause big problems for Division Two defences. So it proved as he scored eight league goals in 25 appearances. One of them, a joyous romp through a bemused Blackpool defence, was the best individual goal of the season for Watford.

The last of the first ten games of the season was an astounding 4-0 victory at Luton Town. It was amazing on several levels. Watford and Luton are big rivals and have been since the 19th century. I first became aware of the rivalry in the 1968/69 season when, as both clubs went for promotion from Division Three, it deepened. Watford ended up as champions, two places and three points ahead of Luton, who missed out but went up the following season.

Luton were the more successful side in the 1970s. They had already had five seasons in the top flight, between 1955 and 1960, before they played in Division One again in 1974/75. In 1981/82 the rivalry intensified further when Watford and Luton found themselves both striving for promotion once again, this time the prize being a place in Division One. On this occasion they both made it, Luton finishing as champions eight points clear of second-placed Watford. The clubs both played in Division One for the next six seasons, before Watford were relegated. There were some monumental matches between them during that time, none finer than the third round FA Cup tie in 1983/84. The sides drew 2-2 at Kenilworth Road after Luton had raced into a 2-0 lead. The replay at Vicarage Road was played under lights and both sets of players were inspired. This time Watford went two goals ahead, leading 3-1, before Luton scored twice to force extra time. A goal from Mo Johnston in extra time was enough to settle it in Watford's favour.

Luton lasted in Division One for another three seasons before they were relegated in 1991/92 and joined Watford in the second tier (called Division One, with the old Division One having been renamed the Premier League). Seemingly joined at the hip, after four seasons in Division One the two clubs were relegated together in 1995/96 and both stayed in Division Two the following season. They had contrasting starts to the 1997/98 season and on 4 October 1987 Watford emphasised how far they had come in a short space of time under Graham Taylor when they stormed into a 4-0 lead at Kenilworth Road inside 30 minutes. The goalscorers were Richard Johnson, Dai Thomas (in for the suspended Jason Lee) and Peter Kennedy who knocked in two, one with each foot. There was no further goalscoring as Watford recorded their first win over Luton for ten years. Lennie Lawrence, John Moore and the rest of the home bench received terrible stick from their own supporters in the main stand. I'm convinced that was the reason the club decided to move the dug-outs to the other side of the pitch, so that they were located in front of the docile corporate boxes.

It was taking off at Vicarage Road and those first ten games set the tone for the season. Previously it had been enough for me just to be able to cover games involving Watford, now I was covering games which meant something in a season which could have promotion as its outcome.

A fascinating tussle developed at the top of Division Two between Watford and Bristol City. It was made poignant because Bristol City manager John Ward and Graham were friends of long standing. Ward joined his first club, Lincoln City, in 1970 when Taylor was still also a player at the Sincil Bank club. He was top scorer when Lincoln won the Division Four championship in 1975/76 with Taylor as manager. He stayed at Lincoln until July 1979 when Taylor took him to Watford for £15,000. Ward wasn't a major player at Vicarage Road and in May 1982 at the age of 31 he took on a coaching role. Just over three years later he became Taylor's assistant and held that position until Taylor resigned in May 1987. Ward followed Taylor to Villa Park and was assistant manager there for three years from January 1988. During Taylor's time as England manager Ward worked as an England B and under-21 coach and under-21 manager. By the 1997/98 season Ward was at his third club as a manager in his own right.

The first meeting between Watford and Bristol City in 1997/98 was at Vicarage Road on 13 December 1997. Watford went into the game as leaders, a position they'd held for over three months, while City were second and had been for more than a month. It was a classic, cagey top-of-the-table affair, with both sides playing good football but not producing too many chances. The status quo was preserved after a 1-1 draw, Gifton Noel-Williams scoring five minutes from the end after Shaun Goater had given City the lead.

I found myself reporting on some terrific matches, including a 3-2 home win over Bristol Rovers on 28 February 1998. Before the game Watford hadn't won for four league matches, their longest winless run of the entire season. Rovers were pushing for a play-off place themselves and under Ian Holloway were a very lively side. With a front two of Barry Hayles and Jamie Cureton for most of the season and an attacking style of play Rovers ended 1997/98 as leading scorers in Division Two with 70 goals. The game at Vicarage Road was a tremendous cut-and-thrust affair. Watford took a two-goal lead into half-time through Rocket Ronny and Noel-Williams but a second-half comeback saw Tom White and Cureton draw Rovers level. Cureton's equaliser came nine minutes from the end and with the clock running down I had my full-time report ready saying that the game had ended 2-2 and that Watford's winless run had extended to five league matches.

Then came one of the pivotal moments of Watford's season. In his first spell Taylor had signed winger Wilf Rostron for £150,000 from Sunderland in October 1979. In an inspired move Taylor converted Rostron into a highly effective attacking full-back. Glenn Roeder had signed Tommy Mooney as a striker in 1997/98 and in a similar move, Taylor played Mooney in a defensive role, usually on the left side of three centre-backs. Even though he was playing at the back, Mooney didn't lose his attacking instinct and he ended the season with a very useful six league goals. One came in the 88th minute against Bristol Rovers. Charging upfield, Mooney collected the ball inside a crowded Rovers penalty box with the away side determined to cling on to their point. More through sheer willpower than anything else, Mooney forced his way past several desperate challenges and emerged with the ball on his left foot at an acute angle to the goal. When his shot almost unbelievably hit the net to clinch the 3-2 win it was a real sign that Watford's promotion challenge had meaning. I hastily rewrote my full-time report and joyfully relayed the news.

Just under a month later there was another clear indication that Watford were in great shape. It was 21 March 1998 and marked my only visit to Boundary Park. Oldham Athletic were not doing brilliantly in the league but they were formidable at home and had only lost once there all season. Watford started well, Darren Bazeley curling in a shot from outside the box in the eighth minute to give them a 1-0 lead. During the week Oldham manager Neil Warnock had brought in one of his favourite players, Adrian Littlejohn, from Plymouth Argyle and he equalised in the 53rd minute. Watford restored their lead eight minutes later but it was the source and manner of the goal which left me amazed.

Nigel Gibbs joined Watford as a schoolboy in May 1981 and made the right-back position his own once he'd established himself in the side. Between 1983 and 2002 he scored five goals in 407 league appearances. I'd never seen him score and had very rarely seen him in a shooting position. Then with the score 1-1 at Oldham, Nigel moved forward with the ball, played it to Jason Lee, collected the return and smacked in the most delicious shot from just outside the box. Where it came from, I don't know. Watford were held to a 2-2 draw when Oldham equalised through Mark Allott deep into time added on but they were back on top of Division Two, having been displaced the previous Saturday.

When Graham did an interview at the Capital Gold Sport point after the game glowing with admiration, I asked him, 'How do you do it?' I don't know what I expected him to say, whether he might reveal all his secrets or something. I should have known that magicians never do that. All he said in reply was, 'We haven't done anything yet.' I thought, 'You must be kidding, you've transformed an average Second Division side into one that's playing great football, is scoring great goals and is surely on course for the club's first promotion since the last time you were manager. You've somehow influenced Nigel Gibbs to score at Boundary Park with a shot from outside the box. You can't tell me that you haven't done anything.' Of course, it was the old manager's trick of 'keeping your feet on the ground and not getting carried away, we haven't actually won anything yet'. I would never have made a manager, one win and I would have thought I was Bertie Big Bollocks.

Promotion came shortly after that draw at Boundary Park, and was confirmed with the Easter fixtures. On Saturday, 13 April 1998 Watford were at home to Wrexham knowing that a win would be enough to send them up. The match itself was too tense to be enjoyable. Nothing else mattered expect getting the three points and, with Watford playing with little fluency it was a scruffy goal, the only one of the game, which won it. It came early, in the ninth minute, which meant that there was a fair amount of hanging on to do. Jason Lee ended the season with ten league goals, one behind leading scorer Peter Kennedy. Apart from his goals he made a valuable contribution, leading the line well. Going into the Wrexham game he hadn't scored since 1 November 1997, over five months previously. But he popped one in when it mattered, his cross shot deflecting in off a Wrexham defender to settle the biggest match involving Watford in many a year.

Two days later, on Easter Monday, the fixture mattered as well. It was the second meeting of the season of the top two in Division Two, Watford and Bristol City. With both sides already up, City having been promoted on Good Friday, the prize being pursued was the title. City had regained top spot just over a week previously and the game ended the same way as the first meeting at Vicarage Road. This time it was Watford who took the lead, Lee scoring in the 64th minute, but Rob Edwards equalised four minutes later. After the game there was a touching exchange between the two managers. John Ward came into the press room when Graham was in full flow. Someone asked whether Taylor and Ward, being such good friends, kept in touch. Taylor responded, 'I haven't contacted John for ages. I haven't spoken to him since they went top.'

'So Graham,' I thought, 'you only ring when you're winning.'

16

Even at a successful football club it will never be possible to keep everyone happy. This was true of Watford as they closed in on the Division Two title. In November 1996 Kenny Jackett had signed Stuart Slater from Ipswich Town on a free transfer. Stuart had first come to my attention, and that of the general football public, as a West Ham player in the early 1990s. In particular he'd hit the headlines when he played brilliantly and scored his side's second goal with a 20-yard shot when West Ham beat Everton in the sixth round of the FA Cup in 1990/91. During the 1997/98 season I used to have a drink in the players' bar at Vicarage Road after home games and I was introduced to Stuart. He was such an open, friendly guy. Everyone liked him and wanted him to do well. It seemed that he was a friend of everyone at the club, and had time for anyone.

As a kid like so many I'd wanted to become a professional footballer. For a while, encouraged by a junior school headmaster who mistook my enthusiasm for ability, I actually believed that it might happen. Reality eventually set in and when I found myself unable to get into the first team in the third year of secondary school, I realised that maybe my future lay elsewhere. It didn't stop me wondering what it would have been like to have been a footballer and Stuart generously gave me an insight into how it had been for him.

Stuart loved being a professional footballer. He felt that he really was 'living the dream', but he had a difficult time at Watford because for the most part he didn't fit into Graham Taylor's plans. Despite that, and despite the injuries he suffered, he had an overwhelming gratitude for the life he'd been given.

Stuart told me, 'From a very early age you read, you listen, you hear and it's everybody's schoolboy dream to become a footballer.' To have achieved it was 'a great, great feeling'. But there was a flipside and on the day we talked he told me that he was 'probably at the lowest point of my whole professional career and having seen some very highs in my professional career I am at my bottom point and I tell you what, to not be wanted at this minute in time, I'm not wanted at Watford Football Club, it's not a nice feeling. People think it's really, really glamorous even still to be training for a club but I may be contradicting myself but I'm just saying that as a personal point of view now, that you know it's still a great life, you get up at ten o'clock, you train until one, but when you're not wanted at a club it's the worst feeling ever in a professional footballer's career, in my career. You go into training, you can do as much as you want in the training to try and impress but it still won't get you anywhere. It's like banging your head on a brick wall and getting nowhere. So I'm just waiting at this moment in time just to try and get myself a lift and get some enthusiasm, to get a new sort of lease of life in football. But at this moment in time, for the last year, since I've really known that I've been out of the team it's not all what it's made out to be.'

Stuart felt that he wasn't rated by Taylor, but he was very popular with Watford fans and he told me that was important to him. 'It gives me a big buzz knowing that the supporters are on my side and are with me, they've seen very little of me over the last eight months but you know I still see people in the street and they come up to me say, "How come you're not playing?" and, "How come you're not being given a chance? Whenever you've played you've entertained and you've produced moments that you know we have for our memories," and you know that's a great, great buzz that you get but you know sometimes other players will be content with not being liked by the fans but being liked by the manager because at the end of the day the manager dictates your life, your family's life and if you're liked by him then you're going to be a part of the club especially Watford for a long period of time.'

Stuart told me about his early football memories and about how he had developed the dribbling skills which characterised his game as a professional. 'Yeah well, I started kicking a ball about when I was three, four, whenever, I mean my mum and dad were different class to be fair. If it weren't for me dad I wouldn't be where I am now. He took so much time to teach me to learn, I remember in and out of cones when I was four, five years of age, we used to go to the field, put these big metal cones up and go in and out of them, dribbling, and we used to do that for hours and hours and hours upon end and me dad's dedication towards me to just playing football was awesome but my first sort of memory of playing was when I was about seven when we played in a five-a-side competition and I was playing a year above meself so all the other lads were eight and a lot bigger and stronger than me but my skill was in evidence then. We won the trophy and I won man of the match and I remember us getting you know carried about you know winning the trophy from my parents and having our photos taken with me having man of the match with my first ever medal so you know that was my first memory.'

Stuart recollected the point at which he'd realised that he not only had a chance of playing football and enjoying it but of also making a living out of it. 'I think, I was playing for a Sunday side called Langham Lions and another person, Roy Knightsbridge, if it weren't for him and my dad I would have been nowhere, their support for me was awesome. But we were playing for this team called Langham Lions and Jason Dozzell was playing, obviously he was at Ipswich and Tottenham and now at Colchester as we speak. He was so tall then, he was 6ft 2in at an age of about 11 that he was attracting all sorts of scouts because he was scoring goals for fun, he was just so much stronger than anybody else and fortunately for me scouts came and watched him and I was playing and they were asking about me and they were amazed that I was a year younger playing with him doing so well so it was probably around the age of 11, 12, I was training with Ipswich at the time but there was other clubs like West Ham, Arsenal, all of them wanting to take me on and sign me as a schoolboy, but then you know then the dream was starting to become more real. Obviously, there was still a lot of hard work still to be done and I wasn't taking anything for granted but at the age of 11 or 12 when you start training with professional clubs you think "phew, this is what I want to be". When I signed schoolboy forms for West Ham, it was a decision between West Ham and Ipswich, you know then I knew that there was a good chance because obviously I had been promised apprenticeship if I'd signed schoolboy forms, so they were the first times.'

Stuart's decision to join West Ham was soundly based. 'Well I always thought it was so easy at Ipswich, it was sort of on my doorstep, but if I didn't make the grade at Ipswich it would be a struggle to make it anywhere else because having been at West Ham and joined West Ham there was so many London clubs at that age, 16, 17, 18, if you got released then even at a youth team you know you're known, you're well known about because as I said London's got so many clubs whereas Ipswich you know you're out in the back of beyond so the attraction to go to West Ham was always a pull on going and then when you see the likes of Trevor Brooking and Alan Devonshire.

'I'd been training with them when I was a schoolboy in my summer holidays you know and they'd looked after you so well and put up with me and you know to actually train with them at that age you know was an unbelievable experience and you know I would never forget that. You knew that they were pushing you and trying to make a career for you by training with them and playing with them.'

If ever a club was based on tradition, it's West Ham and, having joined them, in time Stuart became acutely aware of the significance of pulling on the famous claret and blue shirt. 'Yeah, at that time, I was an Ipswich supporter to be fair, I mean it was strange how it went, I've just given my reasons why I did go to West Ham, but you know I'd followed Ipswich for a long, long time up until 12 as a season ticket holder so I knew the Ipswich players inside out whereas when I came to West Ham you know it took me about a year to know the tradition and the history of the club, what some players had achieved, Bobby Moore, Martin Peters and Geoff Hurst and it took me a while to settle in but then as soon as I knew it, it was like some players that they've had and as you said the tradition that they've got playing wise to put on that shirt and to know that so many other better players, well top, top-class players have put it on, it was an amazing feeling.'

Stuart played the best football of his career in his early days at West Ham. 'In the last year of John Lyall, then Lou Macari took over, and then Billy Bonds, there was an era for three years, three seasons where I couldn't do anything wrong. Even if I thought I had a bad game I still got nine out of ten in the paper, you know it was just one of them where for two or three years I was at the top flight of my career, I was flying, I had that pace where I could get by people and was entertaining and you know people were saying so many good things and as I said I had good games, really, really good games, but had, obviously you weren't human if you didn't have below par games, but even if I had a below-par game people were raving about it so there was that stage where I was 19 to 22 where it just all happened and I was injury-free and I played about 130 games on the spin without getting injured and you know they were the years and everyone keeps coming up to me even now when we played, West Ham played Everton in the quarter-finals of the FA Cup and that's when Sky was just starting and we won 2-1 and I got the winner and had a purple game there and got us into the semi-final and people always remember that. I've got a lot of other memories when I played a lot better than that, but that's the one people always remember.'

Injury as much as anything else restricted Stuart to nine starts and five substitute appearances in Watford's 1997/98 promotion season. Fifteen days after the draw at Ashton Gate, Watford had a midweek home game against Bournemouth. With the title in sight it was a big occasion and Vicarage Road was in party mood for the last home match of the season. For the first time in a while there were celebrations in the home sections of the ground at the end of a season rather than the away end. Watford started well but before they could score Bournemouth took the lead, Mark Stein firing in a 14th-minute free kick. One of Taylor's strengths as a manager was to make decisive substitutions and with Bournemouth still 1-0 ahead at half-time, he brought on Stuart for Alon Hazan. Stuart had one of his most effective halves for Watford and was instrumental in turning the game round. In the 47th minute Jason Lee scored his third important goal in four matches when he headed in Darren Bazeley's cross. Stuart wasn't involved in that goal but he did have a hand in the winner in the 69th minute. After Lee had headed a cross down, Stuart prodded the ball against the post and Gifton Noel-Williams was there to turn in the rebound.

Four days later I was at Craven Cottage on the day when the destiny of the Division Two championship would be decided. With Fulham needing results to go their way if they were to qualify for the play-offs, it was a day to be savoured. Before the game I bumped into Stuart inside the ground. He'd played against Bournemouth with painkilling injections and, having done so well, he was hoping to be involved in the climax, but he wasn't even on the bench. Stuart was despondent. I told him that the following season I would be running a football prediction competition and invited him to take part. I told him he'd have to predict where teams would finish in 1998/99 and said that if he wanted to he could put Watford down on his entry form to get promoted. He declined the invitation, adding, 'The way I feel at the moment I'd put Watford down to get relegated.' It was an understandable reaction.

Fulham were on the way up as well as Watford. After finishing 17th in Division Three in 1995/96 they were promoted under Micky Adams the following season. Mohamed Al-Fayed bought the club in the summer of 1997 and a few games into 1997/98 he appointed Ray Wilkins as manager and Kevin Keegan as chief operating officer. They attracted good players to the club and in the Fulham side to face Watford were Maik Taylor, Paul Peschisolido, Paul Bracewell, Chris Coleman and Peter Beardsley. The following season, 1998/99, with Keegan as manager and many of the same players, Fulham took Division Two by storm, winning the championship with 101 points. However, 2 May 1998 was a little too early for them and they had yet to properly gel and Watford knew that one more big game would bring their first title in 20 years. Noel-Williams gave the Hornets a 35th-minute lead when he turned in a Micah Hyde cross, and it stayed that way until half-time. The news at the break was that after three goals in the first ten minutes at Deepdale, Preston North End were leading Bristol City 2-1. It was all looking good for Watford.

Fulham showed their class at the start of the second half and in the 61st minute Beardsley fired in an equaliser from the edge of the box. The championship hung in the balance. You couldn't get a more contrasting player to the aesthetically pleasing Beardsley than Jason Lee but it was the sometimes maligned centre-forward who won the day, scoring the winner in the 71st minute. Bazeley crossed deep to the far post, Hazan nodded down and Lee sent a shot just inside the post. It wasn't a particularly well-struck shot but it didn't matter. Lee had come alive again when it mattered, scoring four crucial goals in the last five league matches of Watford's season. When news arrived that Preston had beaten Bristol City 2-1 the triumph was confirmed. Watford had won the title on the last day by three points.

It felt like there couldn't be a better time and place to win it than on a sunny May afternoon on the banks of the River Thames.

*

The 1997/98 season was a great one thanks to Watford's title win but a game I'd covered on 10 January 1998 also made a huge impression on me. I got a call from the Capital Gold Sport studio during the week to tell me that I would be covering Liverpool v Wimbledon the following Saturday. It would be the first time I'd ever covered a match at Anfield and it was an awesome prospect. By that time, I'd worked at Highbury, White Hart Lane, Stamford Bridge, Upton Park, Roker Park and other great and historic grounds but this was somehow different and in the days leading up to the game I found myself lying awake at night thinking about it.

After Bill Shankly had walked through the Anfield gates in 1959 to become manager of a club languishing in Division Two, he had declared his intention to turn Liverpool into a 'bastion of invincibility' and to my mind that's pretty much what they were for a couple of decades. Between 1971/72 and 1990/91 Liverpool finished outside the top three in Division One in just one season, 1980/81. They created a dynasty and during that period appointed managers from within the club. Bob Paisley, Joe Fagan and Kenny Dalglish followed Shankly and were all steeped in the Liverpool way and were able to almost seamlessly continue the winning tradition. The full force of what Liverpool had been, the embodiment of consistency and excellence, hit me as I thought about covering a game at Anfield and made my head spin. Liverpool's had been a collective triumph; of course there had been amazing players like Ian Rush, John Barnes and Kenny Dalglish and many more but no one individual player or manager had dominated. It had been a supreme team effort.

Working at Anfield seemed to me to be on another level. The sense of awe I felt was akin to being told with a few days' notice that I had been nominated to interview God on behalf of the whole of humanity and that I could ask anything I liked. 'Thank you for speaking to us, God, I won't take up too much of your time. Some brilliant scientific minds have developed plausible theories about how the universe was created and about evolution and we have an understanding of what exists in space beyond the confines of Mother Earth. But in one way we are walking in the dark and life is a complete mystery. Can you explain please why You created the universe and everything in it, and why You created a human race that has so far proved itself to be so dysfunctional, that is of course assuming that what we call "reality" is "real" and that what we are experiencing is "really" happening and is not all a dream?'

Liverpool had a decent team at the time and players like Michael Owen, Robbie Fowler and Paul Ince all played in a comfortable 2-0 win over Wimbledon. Steve McManaman was particularly impressive in his penultimate season at Anfield before his move to Real Madrid. Jamie Redknapp's two goals gave the Reds their fifth successive league win in a season in which they finished third in the Premier League.

When I arrived at Anfield I was struck by the number of Scandinavian Liverpool supporters going to the game, possibly influenced by the presence of Norway international Øyvind Leonhardsen in the home team. Making my way to the press box inside the ground I passed the trophy room. Many of the grounds I visited as a reporter didn't have a trophy room. Anfield definitely did and it contained a huge glass cabinet bulging with the gleaming trophies Liverpool had won down the years.

Once in the press box, as I was setting up my equipment, I noticed former Leeds United midfielder Johnny Giles sitting a few seats away and I decided to engage him in conversation. Once we'd exchanged greetings, I told him that I was currently reading Brian Clough's autobiography. Johnny responded by giving his opinion on Clough which was slightly less than complimentary and was a bit of a conversation-stopper.

17

During the summer after Watford's promotion to Division One I went to a Star Trek convention where I had a chat with Mr Spock. Inevitably before long we started talking about football. Mr Spock had an interesting perspective on the game and he told me that he found it highly illogical that supporters celebrate when their club returns to a division that it had left only a couple of years previously. I explained that football is a game of emotion and that fans acknowledge every positive development at their club however big or small. They celebrate when their team wins a corner during a game let alone gets promoted. I told Mr Spock that when a club is relegated there is no guarantee that it will return to the higher division. The bigger the club the more likely it is that it will return but even then no one knows – if it even happens – how long it will take. So, when it does happen, the event is to be celebrated.

The supporters of some clubs will think that a promotion from the third to the second tier of English football is the first step in a two-part journey and that their 'rightful place' is in the top flight. In the summer of 1998 Watford fans were not thinking like that at all. Until then Watford had spent six seasons in the top flight and the general consensus was that their 'rightful place' was about tenth in Division One.

In the summer of 1998 Watford supporters may have day dreamed about promotion to the Premier League while lying on the beach sunbathing, but there was no expectation whatsoever that if it arrived at all it would happen the next season. Graham Taylor had other ideas and went searching for players of a similar mind.

The squad would clearly need to be strengthened to compete in Division One – the question was how Taylor would go about it. During the early part of the summer stories began to circulate that he was looking to make a purchase from Carlisle United. Watford had done the double over Carlisle in the 1997/98 promotion season, winning 2-0 at Brunton Park and 2-1 at Vicarage Road. At the end of the season Carlisle had finished in 23rd place and had been relegated. Ian Stevens had scored in the game at Watford and had finished the season as Carlisle's leading scorer with 17 goals. Stevens was Carlisle's best-known player and when I heard the transfer rumours about Watford being interested in a member of their squad, I assumed that it was probably him. In the end two players did make the move from Carlisle to Watford, but Stevens wasn't one of them.

The two players were Nick Wright and Allan Smart. Wright had started his career at Derby County in August 1994 as a trainee. He made no appearances for the Rams before going to Carlisle on loan in November 1997 and then signing permanently in February 1998. In 1997/98 he made 25 league appearances, scoring five goals. Smart had been in the game a little longer than Wright. The Scot had started at Inverness Caledonian Thistle in August 1993 and had moved to Preston North End about 15 months later. He'd gone on loan to Carlisle and Northampton Town before signing permanently for Carlisle in October 1996. In 1997/98 Smart had made 16 league appearances, scoring six goals. Watford paid £100,000 for each player.

These were not signings to get my pulse racing. Either Taylor was having a laugh or he was better able to see a player's potential than me.

I got the opportunity to 'gauge the mood of the squad' at the press day before the start of the 1998/99 season. It was good to be able to reflect with Peter Kennedy on the previous campaign, which had gone so well for him and for Watford. 'Yeah, it was a great season personally for myself but also for the team and obviously for the club as a whole. Obviously, this season's going to be very difficult but you know you never know what could happen you know, obviously going into a new league and playing better teams but hopefully the gaffer will get us organised and we'll perform to our best and hopefully we'll get the results.'

Peter had played in the last seven games of the previous season but had then undergone an operation. He was hoping to stay injury-free in 1998/99, and also to win his first cap for Northern Ireland, which he'd been tantalisingly close to doing previously.

We touched on the subject of the Premier League and Peter's response seemed to suggest that while playing there was an ambition, he didn't think that it was on the immediate horizon. 'I think nowadays that's even every kid's dream, and whatever you know, so I mean definitely I'd love to play in the Premier League someday, hopefully with Watford.'

I always really enjoyed talking to club captain Robert Page at press days. He was still on a high from the 1997/98 success, having played 41 league games, and he interestingly revealed that Watford's aim before the start of the season had been to win the Division Two title. 'Yeah, that's right, everybody done ever so well last year, got what we wanted, we set out at the start of last season to win the Second Division, to go up as champions and we got it so everybody was pleased with that. We've had a nice break, I think we're in our third week of pre-season now, everybody's fighting fit, the new lads have settled in pretty well, and we're looking forward and we can't wait for the season to start.'

Robert was looking forward to testing himself at a higher level and the prospect of playing in Division One didn't hold any fears for him. 'No not at all, I think you don't know how good you are yourself as a player, and as a team, until you play against higher standards as you go up into the higher divisions, so obviously Watford Football Club just got promoted to the First Division, that's not it, we want success, we want good cup runs, we want you know promotion again, we want to get into the big league, we want to get into the big time so that's what our aim is.' You couldn't have had a clearer statement of intent than that.

Robert was confident that the players would be able to cope with the higher standard of football. 'Well obviously like you said the standard's going to be a lot higher but you know I've said all along the lads we've got at the club are capable of playing in the First Division anyway so it shouldn't be a problem to us and I think the lads we've got here are such a good bunch I think they'll rise to the challenge.'

It was inspiring listening to Robert but new signing Smart knocked me out. He seemed so sure of what he was doing, and that the move he'd made would prove to be a good one. Football reporters always like talking to new signings – a new face, it's a way of introducing them to supporters – and there is a set of stock questions that will be posed. Why did you make the move, what attracted you to the club, how far do you think the club can go, etc. I bowled all of these questions to Allan and he smashed every one of them for six, with an attitude that said, 'How dare you question my belief?'

An enquiry as to how the move to Watford came about was met by, 'Well originally I was speaking to Northampton Town and everything had been sort of, well, discussed and agreed and I was due to sign on the Monday and over the weekend the chairman came back to me from Carlisle and said that Watford were interested and obviously I came down and spoke to Mr Taylor and everything went smoothly from there really.'

Sometimes a manager might have to sell a club to a potential new signing. There was no question of that when Allan moved from Carlisle to Watford. Taylor didn't have to be particularly persuasive to get Allan to sign. 'He didn't really have to say a lot to be honest, the fact that he's obviously been an England manager and the fact that he rated me enough to bring me down and he wanted to sign me was enough for me. He didn't have to sell the club in any way, shape or form, and I was absolutely delighted when he asked me to sign.'

Allan hadn't been at Watford for very long but he'd already formed a positive impression of the club. 'It's been a good experience, very, very organised and the discipline throughout the club is there and everybody can see that, and I think if you've got your shop in order off the park and everybody's sort of pushing in the general direction, I think it can only mean positive things for the club.'

Allan gave me an idea of the type of player Watford had acquired. 'I'd like to think that I try to link up with my midfield players and people behind me and I'd like to think I get my fair share of goals and I have done in the past so fingers crossed that I can keep doing that.'

Allan hadn't set a target for the number of goals he wanted to score in the forthcoming season. 'Never set any targets really because then you're obviously, you can put a number on things but it's just a hypothetical kind of thing, I just want to try and play as well as I can and get as many as I can.'

Allan had no doubt that he would be able to cope with playing at a higher level than he had previously. 'Well, everybody at the club is stepping up if you want to look at it like that, the whole club is stepping up a division, so I don't see why I should be any different from anybody else at this club. If I wasn't confident, I don't think I should be here to be honest with you.'

It was clear that Allan had a burning desire to play in the Premier League and I was amazed at how achievable he thought getting there was, 'Oh without a doubt, that's right. We've got to take everything one step at a time, the old clichés come out, you know the first game against Portsmouth that's where we've got to start and we've got to start well, and take every game and if we play well in every game well the Premier League's just round the corner.'

Taylor also brought in central defender Dean Yates on a free transfer from Derby. Having dropped down from the Premier League to move to Vicarage Road at the end of his Pride Park contract, Dean had set his sights on getting back there with Watford. 'Oh definitely, I mean everybody knows that is the best place to play and you know I've certainly not finished playing there, I want to get back in there again and you know the manager and the club do as well.'

It wasn't to be for Dean. He started the 1998/99 season as a first-choice centre-back but after only ten games he sustained an injury which ended his career.

I couldn't help wondering, after all he'd done in football at Watford and elsewhere, how hungry Graham Taylor was to get back to the top fight. He turned the question on its head by pointing out that, with the sands of time slipping through his fingers, he wouldn't have many more opportunities to achieve the feat. 'Well, I think very much so because as every year goes on it's less of a year, if you can understand that, I mean I'm not a manager just starting out on my career, I think I'm starting now something like about my 28th, 29th year as a manager, never mind as a you know player before that and so I'd very much like to get back into the Premier League and also take Watford back there.'

One of the main talking points at any club during the summer is the players brought in by the manager, particularly at a club which was promoted the previous season and will be playing at a higher level with the increased income which results from promotion. The players brought into Watford by Taylor that summer had not been big-name, big-money signings and he seemed to have his own philosophy when it came to bringing players in. 'This club has never spent big money, people think it has and they think it should. It doesn't guarantee anything. For a club Watford's size spending two, three, four million pounds on one player I think will

THE MAN WHO SHOUTS

upset a lot of things. This club over the years even when previously it was in the Premier League, it developed its players, developed its own players and the level of that player either brought us up to the Premier League or if at the time we don't move on they themselves move on because of their individual ability, and it's recognising where you are in the structure of football and it's silly for Watford to say, "Oh we are this club that can spend five, ten million pounds on players," because we're not and there's too many clubs are spending money that they don't have.'

The summer signings which had most taken me by surprise had been Wright and Smart and I wondered whether it gave Graham more satisfaction to sign a player someone's never heard of for £100,000 from Carlisle and turning them into a player than buying a ready-made one. 'Well, I think it gives most managers and coaches if they get out on to the field and work with players it gives them great pleasure to see the development of those players but the players themselves must have that inbuilt enthusiasm to want to do it. Now I still believe this and I think it's been shown by the signing of Micah Hyde and Peter Kennedy as an example, there are still players in the lower divisions, or the Third Division, who given the right break along the line can in fact improve their own level of performance as well as say Watford's, and I think they are there and they just need that opportunity.'

Graham gave me an assessment of each of Watford's four summer signings – Michel Ngonge completed the group. 'Well, if we take Dean, who's now 30 years of age, great age and should know what centre-back play is all about, he's played in the Premier League, has played in the First Division. Ngonge, Michel, is different, Michel will interest the Watford supporters. Who is he, where's he from? Well, he's from Samsunspor in Turkey, but I think what they'll like about him is his willingness to work for the team when out of possession and the supporters like forwards who do that, that if it isn't just right for them, they work to get it right and that has a great enthusiasm, that enthusiasm usually spreads through the team, so that's what I see in Michel. In Allan Smart and Nicky Wright, who I've bought from Carlisle, these are 21, 22-year-olds, very much in the sort of Micah Hyde and Peter Kennedy thing. I think both these players with the right kind of support and the right kind of encouragement can develop into good players and consequently help Watford try to achieve their targets.'

As so often happened under Graham, Watford made a good start to the season. Jason Lee scored his only goal of the season when he got an 84th-minute winner in a 2-1 opening-day victory at Portsmouth. This was followed up by another two victories, the second by 4-1 at Bristol City. Watford went on to score four goals in a game on another three occasions before Christmas that season. The next time was the following month and another 4-1 away win, this time at Swindon Town. The County Ground was in tumult at the end of the game with the home fans demanding the sacking of Steve McMahon. For long periods of the game Watford didn't play any better than Swindon, who took the lead in the 29th minute through George Ndah and when they were 4-1 down hit the bar and post with Alec Chamberlain in goal beaten. But the pre-season sense of belief which had been in the air at the press day was firmly rooted in the Watford camp. The side developed an ability not to crumble under pressure and to take the opportunities it created. Goals from two of the summer signings, Smart (2) and Wright, and one from Alon Hazan, turned the score around. The game was a good illustration of Taylor's ability to read a game and make decisive changes which others would not have even contemplated. Wright capped an industrious first-half display by scoring his first goal for the club in the 44th minute to put Watford 2-1 up. A few minutes later Taylor was telling him – and Ngonge – that they would not be taking any part in the second half as they were being replaced by Hazan and Gifton Noel-Williams. Within five minutes of coming on Hazan had put Watford 3-1 up.

The third time Watford scored four goals in a game was in a 4-2 home win over Crewe Alexandra in late November, and it propelled them into second place in Division One.

Three weeks later, exactly halfway through the season, another side from the north-west, Stockport County, conceded four goals at Vicarage Road as they lost by the same score as Crewe. With Watford third in the table, it was a good time to take stock and after the game I spoke to Kennedy, Smart and Noel-Williams.

At last Peter had won his first cap for Northern Ireland, against Moldova. I congratulated him and he told me that he was chuffed to have it, 'Yeah, thanks very much, I'm delighted to get a cap, over in Ireland there's been a lot of speculation over the last year and a half. I'm just delighted to get the first cap, I really enjoyed it, hopefully there's a few more to come.'

Peter agreed that the cap was not just a reflection of the way he'd been playing that season but the Watford side as a whole. 'Yeah, I think with us coming from the Second Division a lot people maybe expected us to struggle a bit, but now we've played half the games and we're still up there, we're playing really well and we're confident, we're playing well as a unit, at the minute everything's going well and everybody's smiling.'

Peter put the brakes on though when I asked whether it was too early to discuss the possibility of promotion. 'Yeah, I think so you know, I mean the way we look at it now is to just get enough points to say we're not going to get relegated, you know, so that's the starting point but the longer it goes on obviously we'll start thinking about it, you know, so you show how good a team you are when that stage comes.'

Taylor had been at the Stockport game following an absence of a few weeks due to illness. Even from his sick bed he'd managed to communicate with the players, as Peter explained, 'The gaffer's a lot better, he's been watching the videos at home and sending us faxes and letting us know who's been doing good and who's been doing bad. It's good to see him back and him being back hopefully it will give us another wee kick going into the Christmas period.'

It was great to talk to Smart and to find that his pre-season optimism was still very much alive. It seemed that the first half of the season had only reinforced his belief that he could make it to the Premier League with Watford. He'd started all but three of the first 23 league matches and had scored six goals, but that only told part of the story. His game was not just about scoring goals but about dropping deep and linking up with the midfield players, and about working hard.

Allan agreed that his Watford career had gone amazingly well so far. 'Yeah, I'm absolutely delighted with the start that I've had, and it's all about playing really, and it's just the main thing to stay in the team from week to week, so I'm delighted with the start that I've made personally but also as a team I think we've started very well.'

Allan was happy with the role which he'd been given within the team. 'Yeah, of course, yeah, the basis of the team is just hard work anyway, there's no prima donnas or anything like that in the team. We set our stall out early to work hard and I'm happy to be a part of that.'

One of Allan's influences was Kenny Dalglish and you could see that in the way he played. Did he think his role in the team was just to score goals? 'No not really, there's boys in the divisions that's banging in goals for fun, two and three times a game, you know. I've only got a handful of goals really in comparison to them but I try to link in with my team-mates as much as I can and try to sort of create things, that's what I try to do anyway.'

Four months into the season and Allan was still adamant about where his ambitions lay. 'Yeah, I'd like to play in the Premier League with Watford to be honest, that's an ideal world, that's what I want to do and that's what we're striving to achieve this season.'

In interviews I did for Capital Gold Sport, they liked me to have one eye on the future and to get players talking about forthcoming fixtures, to provide clips which could be used when those games were being previewed. Watford had been drawn away to Tottenham Hotspur in the third round of the FA Cup and it was when I asked Allan about that game that his ebullience and joy at the way things were going at Watford really bubbled over. 'The confidence is growing in the team, and you don't lose confidence when you're playing the way we're playing, you know and we're working so hard on the training field and it's paying off, we're steamrollering teams here.'

On 30 November 1996 Gifton Noel-Williams had scored in the 69th minute of a 2-2 home draw with Blackpool. Born on 21 January 1980, when he scored against Blackpool Gifton was 16 years and 314 days old. I know because I sat in the press box and quickly worked it out before reporting that Gifton had become Watford's youngest ever goalscorer. Gifton scored again the following week and finished the 1996/97 season with two league goals. He then played an important part in the 1997/98 Division Two championship season, scoring seven league goals in 27 starts. In 1998/99 he didn't get his first league start until 29 September, but he took his opportunity by scoring in a 1-1 home draw with Sheffield United. Up to and including the Stockport game Gifton had managed eight goals from 12 starts. As he'd scored twice against Stockport, Gifton was the player the press all wanted to interview.

Still young, he was beginning to make a name for himself. 'I'm only trying you know, all I can do is my best and I've been fortunate thank God, that God's given me the ability and I could get two goals today.'

Like everyone else at Watford, Gifton was sure of the direction in which the club was moving. 'For Watford, for the club, for the town, it's on the up you know and that's all we can do really is keep going because we're on the up and up, we've come from the Second to the First and even hopefully we could even get to the Premier League you know, we've just to keep on going the way we're going and thank God hopefully we don't get any slips and we should be there.'

Gifton shared Smart's vision of how far Watford could go. 'You know I think we can go all the way to the Premier League, you know once we get there it will be hard and we'll have to buy players and even get a stronger squad but I think we can get to the Premier League, I don't think that's a bigger problem.'

Like most of the squad, Gifton was playing at this level for the first time. 'You know I didn't really know a lot about the First Division before, I'd never played in it in before. It's a new challenge basically and thank God I got the chance through injuries, I got my chance and thank God so far I've took it, I've got to keep on going really.'

After the turn of the year, Watford didn't win in the league in 1999 until 30 January. It was a big win, 2-1 at home to the eventual runaway champions Sunderland, and I wasn't there to cover it. The main Capital Gold Sport game on the day was the London derby at Selhurst Park between Wimbledon and West Ham United, which JP covered. I was asked to forego Watford v Sunderland and cover Spurs' trip to Ewood Park. This time no on-air commentary was required, and I got right on top of the game from the start and conveyed news of a decent 1-1 draw for Spurs.

Watford's victory over Sunderland was a costly one for Gifton. He scored the winning goal but was then taken off injured following a challenge by Paul Butler. With ten league goals Gifton finished as Watford's leading scorer but he didn't play again that season, then managed only one start the following season and never fully recovered from the injury, which left him with arthritis.

Beating Sunderland was followed by a run of one win in eight league games. A miserable 0-0 draw at home to Bury on 20 March 1999 saw the team slip to eighth in the table and it looked as though a season which had earlier promised so much would end without promotion. A top-half finish still looked likely and that would have been acceptable enough for most clubs in their first season at a higher level, but not for Graham Taylor's Watford. Taylor himself never gave up and said that the draw against Bury, who had not won in 1999, could be the most important point of the season.

The catalyst which provided the momentum for a successful push to the top division came on the first Saturday in April, in an extraordinary game at home to Tranmere Rovers. Watford went into the match having not scored a goal in over a month and that didn't change during an uneventful first half. The second half was as stormy as the first had been placid. Tranmere went ahead in the 53rd minute when David Kelly scored after Paul Robinson misplaced a header. Then it was as though all the pent-up anger and frustration engendered by the apparent slide towards mid-table was released. For weeks, since the win over Sunderland, the Watford players had seemed unable to do anything about their plight. They appeared like helpless bystanders at a car crash, as though they were watching themselves in a movie in which they were being played by other people over whom they had no control. In the second half against Tranmere they seemed to collectively decide that enough was enough; they would not be denied their dream even if achieving it meant becoming involved in ugliness and violence.

In the 67th minute at last a Watford goal came, when Kennedy drove in Tommy Mooney's cross for 1-1. During the final 20 minutes an already unpleasant undercurrent became stronger and turned into a flood. Richard Johnson had earlier been booked following an argument with Kenny Irons over a free kick. Then Johnson became the first Watford player to be sent off that season, following a second booking for a heavy challenge on Irons. At the same time Tranmere's Clint Hill was on the ground, seemingly following an off-the-ball clash with Smart. Incensed Tranmere manager John Aldridge encroached on to the pitch to protest at the treatment his players were receiving. The referee hadn't seen Johnson's challenge on Irons and had shown a second yellow card after consultation with a linesman. Johnson left the pitch claiming that he'd won the ball and a furious Taylor confronted the linesman to complain about his role in the sending off. While all this was happening, Aldridge was confronting Watford supporters in the Main Stand.

Then it got even more heated. After John Achterberg in the Tranmere goal had conceded a corner, the linesman who'd initiated Johnson's sending off attracted the referee's attention to a Tranmere foul in the penalty box which no one else had seen. The award of a penalty to Watford led to more mayhem as the Tranmere players, who couldn't believe what was happening, remonstrated. Eventually Kennedy took the penalty, Achterberg saved, and Michel Ngonge put away the rebound. While the referee trotted back to the halfway line expecting that his next act would be to restart the game a mass brawl started in the Tranmere six-yard box. Smart and Kelly were slugging it out and other Tranmere players were continuing to protest to the linesman about the penalty decision. The referee consulted the linesman and Smart was shown a straight red card to become the second Watford player sent off in the match.

Watford's nine men held on for the final few minutes of normal time, and three minutes of added time, to win 2-1. It was all a bit tasty, but crucially the Hornets had won.

The Tranmere game fired a burning arrow which seared through the air and hit its target plum centre.

In seeking an answer to Watford's goalscoring problem, Taylor had brought in Guy Whittingham on loan from Portsmouth. Earlier in his career Whittingham had scored 47 goals in one golden season for Portsmouth – but he didn't manage to find the net for Watford. So Taylor sought the answer from within. Mooney had been used for most of the season as either a centre-back or a substitute. Two days after beating Tranmere, on Easter Monday, Watford were away to Birmingham City. Taylor handed back the number nine shirt to Mooney and he hit the opening goal in a 2-1 win. It was the start of an amazing run of scoring for a player who was to become a Watford legend, with his status recognised by his photograph being hung on the wall in the Vicarage Road press room alongside John Barnes, Luther Blissett and Kenny Jackett.

The following Saturday, fellow promotion-chasers Bolton Wanderers visited for what was billed as the biggest game at Vicarage Road in a decade. Earlier in the season Bolton had been strongly fancied to go up automatically, but they were fading. Even so their starting 11 still contained six players who had cost £1m or more. Watford overwhelmed and outplayed Bolton with a positive, attacking performance. They didn't allow the disappointment of Steve Banks saving Mooney's third-minute penalty to affect them. Watford took the lead in the 24th minute and it was a beauty, Micah Hyde firing into the top corner from outside the box following a Mooney header. Mooney headed in Darren Bazeley's cross just after the restart for number two and that was it. As so often happens in a game of football the losing team gets going when it's behind. Bolton began to create chances but Alec Chamberlain was in the form that contributed so much to Watford's eventual promotion and he saved excellently from Eidur Gudjohnsen and Bob Taylor.

The following week's game at Crewe Alexandra was a huge grin for me. For a start getting to Gresty Road involved a nice easy journey with a short walk from the train station to the ground. Taylor had long had his sights set on promotion and had said before the game, 'There's little point reaching the play-offs and losing.' I always used to enjoy watching Crewe play. They were a small club consistently punching above their weight thanks to the way they developed young players. On the day they played some lovely one-touch football and early in the game Rodney Jack narrowly volleyed over a Mark Rivers cross. But there was a bit of the Corinthian-Casuals about Crewe and if you needed a result, they were usually a good team to play. In the 25th minute Wright played a short pass to Mooney who shot low with his left foot for the only goal of the game.

The tiny Gresty Road press box was cramped and full. I was doing 'off-air' commentary on the game and was overjoyed at the way Watford were playing, which was reflected in the way I was commentating. It was maybe a little over the top for the liking of one person. Mike Vince, who was sitting in front of me commentating for Clubcall, turned round and asked me to keep the noise down. That wasn't going to happen. It was impossible to commentate quietly for Capital Gold Sport anyway and particularly for me on a day when Watford were playing well and winning and were seventh in the table, one position outside the play-off places, with four matches remaining after the Crewe game. Quiet wasn't the Capital Gold Sport house style. I apologised to Mike, saying, 'Sorry Mike, you should have brought ear plugs.' I roared that day and so too did Watford.

By the time Watford played Crystal Palace at Vicarage Road the following Saturday their destiny was back in their own hands, Bolton having lost at Bury the previous evening. An improving Palace side pushed Watford all the way, losing 2-1.

A 2-1 midweek win at Port Vale meant that I found myself sitting in the press box at Barnsley on 1 May 1999 reflecting on a run of six straight Watford victories. Mooney had scored in each of the last five including both goals at Port Vale.

A three-way contest had developed between Wolverhampton Wanderers, Bolton and Watford for the last two play-off places in Division One. Watford's run had transformed them from also-rans into play-off probables. If Mooney scored at Barnsley and Watford won, two club records would be equalled. Mooney would have scored in six consecutive matches and equalled a record shared by Gary Penrice and Johnny Hartburn and Watford would have won seven consecutive Football League matches and equalled a record set under Taylor in 1977/78.

It looked as though a victory was on the cards when Ngonge gave them the lead in a first half during which they hit the woodwork three times, Ngonge twice with a shot and a header and Hyde with a volley. In the second half Barnsley levelled in the 64th minute through Nicky Eaden but three minutes later Mooney, in the form of his life, got the goal which equalled that club goal scoring record to put Watford 2-1 up. It was controversial, Barnsley claiming that Ngonge fouled keeper Tony Bullock when Bazeley crossed. With time running out I wrote my full-time report, 'After seven successive wins Watford need a point on Sunday week to be absolutely sure of a play-off place.' I had to do a re-write when Mark Tinkler equalised for Barnsley in the 89th minute after Scott Jones had thundered a free kick against the bar, 'If Watford beat Grimsby at home on Sunday week they will definitely be in the play-offs.'

I got in promotion mood the following Saturday with a trip to Cambridge United on the final Saturday of the Division Three season. Cambridge and Brentford had already both won promotion and were going head-to-head for the title. A point for Brentford would be enough, and would extend their unbeaten run to 16 games. They hadn't lost since Paul Evans and Scott Partridge had joined the club. Cambridge played with three strikers – John Taylor, Martin Butler and Trevor Benjamin. In a highly charged atmosphere Cambridge were big and direct and Brentford played the more controlled football. It was, as Capital Gold Sport reporter Tom Skippings used to love saying in his reports, 'goalless at the break'. Ironically it was Brentford who got a route-one winner in the second half. Goalkeeper Andy Woodman cleared, Andy Duncan's header was short and Lloyd

Owusu nipped in to score. The experiment of Ron Noades being both chairman and manager had worked and Brentford were presented with the Division Three championship trophy at the ground of their closest rivals for the title.

A day later, a sell-out crowd of 20,303 at Vicarage Road was like a flashback to the 1980s. The game itself was again too tense to be enjoyable but the outcome led to Watford receiving a standing ovation. The crowd saw the home side take a long time to settle but thankfully a goal came just before half-time through a thumping Kennedy volley. That was the end of the scoring as Watford beat both Grimsby and the occasion to reach the play-offs for the first time in ten years.

*

Momentum is such a big factor in sport. When I spoke to Robert Page before the start of the 1999/2000 season, he told me that the Watford players 'knew' as soon as they had qualified for the play-offs that they would go up. Before the start of the season the target had been a top-ten finish; at Christmas that was revised to a play-off place then once that had been achieved promotion could be the only aim. To reach Wembley, though, they had to jump a difficult hurdle and it went to the wire. The following season Premier League Watford played Division One Birmingham City in the third round of the FA Cup. Before the game JP sprung a surprise question on me when he asked me on air which player had missed the decisive penalty in the play-off semi-final shoot out the previous season. Of course I knew it was Chris Holland. To be more accurate, Holland didn't miss; Alec Chamberlain saved to send Watford to Wembley 7-6 on penalties.

Alec once told me, 'I became a goalkeeper because the school goalkeeper broke his leg … I'm sure if I'd stayed out on the field, I wouldn't have been a professional player.'

18

Monday, 31 May 1999 was *the day*. I always get a tingle of anticipation on a matchday; on that day I had the feeling to the nth degree.

In the morning I went for a coffee in Covent Garden and savoured the prospect. Watford v Bolton Wanderers in the Division One play-off final on Bank Holiday Monday. Bolton had been to Wembley many times and in 1923 had beaten West Ham United 2-0 in the first FA Cup final played there. For Watford it was only their second visit. The first, a 2-0 defeat to Everton in the 1984 FA Cup final, still hurt.

Wembley blew me away. During the previous ten years I'd covered many games at many grounds, including Highbury, Stamford Bridge, Anfield and Old Trafford, but Wembley was in a different ballpark. Capital Gold Sport arrived at Wembley mob-handed at about midday. JP was being supported by Billy Bonds, Dominic Johnson, Bill 'do not scratch your eyes' Leslie and myself.

Watford had beaten Bolton at home and away in the league that season but Bolton were still favourites with the bookies (and Billy) to win the game. Bolton were the bigger club, they had recently been in the top division and to many it seemed inevitable that they would return there. They had the better-quality players. For the game at Wembley Bolton had seven players in their starting line-up who had each cost more than £1m. There was Neil Cox (£1.5m from Aston Villa), Robbie Elliott, (£2.5m from Newcastle), Mark Fish (£2m from Lazio), Claus Jensen (£1.6m from Lyngby), Ricardo Gardner (£1m from Harbour View), Per Frandsen and Michael Johansen (both £1.25m from FC Copenhagen). Bo

Hansen, who came on as a sub in the final, cost £1m from Brøndby. Three of the Bolton players – Frandsen (Denmark), Gardner (Jamaica) and Fish (South Africa) had played in the 1998 World Cup finals in France. Eidur Gudjohnsen went on to play at the top level with Chelsea and Barcelona.

Watford's record transfer fee was still the £550,000 paid to AC Milan for Luther Blissett in August 1984. But the certainty felt by the players was shared by the supporters. Just over half the crowd of 70,343 were yellow people and I spoke to some of them. I did a voxpop, which involved asking supporters outside the ground to say a few words about the game. Usually supporters were quite willing to share their thoughts, although occasionally voxpops could be hard going. A few years previously I'd gone to Stamford Bridge to help cover a Monday night game between Chelsea and Manchester City. Chelsea were struggling at the time and my remit was to get the views of supporters on manager Glenn Hoddle who was under pressure. The main question was, 'Do you think Glenn Hoddle is the right man for the job?' I asked one guy who had a cigarette in his mouth. When I put the question to him he looked at me without removing the cigarette and simply nodded his head. A couple of follow-up questions were met with the same response.

The Watford supporters streaming up Wembley Way in the late-May sunshine were a little more articulate and forthcoming and they gave me some great answers which were played on air in the hour before kick-off. Everyone to whom I spoke was confident that Watford would win, not in an arrogant way, but they had a rock-solid confidence and seemed sure that something special was about to happen.

Back inside the ground as I waited for the show to start at 2pm I took in the grandeur of the surroundings. Football reporters are like players in that on matchday they just want to get going. On the day of a big match that feeling is intensified. Music was being played in the ground as part of the build-up. I was sitting next to JP and he said to me, 'They're a good band, the Manic Street Preachers.' I replied, 'This is Oasis.' He smiled; he'd got me, of course it was Oasis and JP knew it. He'd caught me out with a typical wind-up. It was also JP's way of telling me to make sure I was on the ball and ready for the task ahead. Sitting in the press box close to the Royal Box, I was wide awake but the day was already beginning to take on a dream-like quality.

For JP it wasn't 'just another game' exactly because it was Wembley and it was a final, but he had worked at Wembley many times, and at bigger matches, over the years and he had become accustomed to being there, but even so he just couldn't get enough. It was his third play-off final in three days, having commentated on Leyton Orient 0 Scunthorpe United 1 on the Saturday and Manchester City's dramatic 3-1 penalty shoot-out win over Gillingham the previous day. Gillingham v City had finished 2-2 after extra time; all four goals had come in the last ten minutes of normal time. Gillingham went two up then with many City fans having left the ground thinking that their team had lost, Kevin Horlock and Paul Dickov both scored in the dying minutes.

For the next few hours though Watford would be at the centre of JP's world. Usually Watford were a small part of a large canvas but today they were the whole picture. Back in the studio producer John 'Foggy' Curtis put together an hour's radio before kick-off which set the scene. The master stroke was playing 'Get Back' by the Beatles in the opening sequence underneath Graham Taylor saying, 'There are two ways of going to Wembley, you either go just to go or you go to win,' and then JP adding, 'Graham Taylor of Watford back at Wembley for the second time as boss of the Hornets, can he complete a wonderful end to the season, can they make it back into the top flight after 11 years outside the elite?' It was as though Paul McCartney had written the words 'get back to where you once belonged' with Taylor in mind. It was like the greatest pop band the world had ever known was urging Watford to win the game so that Taylor could dine again at the top table.

Bill Leslie, urbane and suave as always, did a live interview with Taylor, the noise and excitement of the occasion audible in the background. The manager again emphasised the purpose of the visit, 'I certainly want the Watford players to actually come here, and obviously we want to win, but I want them to understand that very few people come to Wembley and what is important now is that they deliver the goods.'

Taylor, who knew Wembley well, led his team on to the pitch looking relaxed in his suit with a yellow carnation in his lapel, smiling and joking with his opposite number Colin Todd. Behind Taylor was captain Robert Page, who with his cropped hair managed to look hard even though he was tenderly holding the hand of a mascot as he emerged from the tunnel. Fireworks and thousands of yellow and red balloons enhanced the impression that this was a showpiece event.

JP was at his most expressive as he described the scene, 'A deafening din all around us, what a magnificent atmosphere again these play-offs have produced. No one in European football can understand this, it's an English thing, it's the play-offs, it is spectacularly unique to our game, that whatever the level of football, whether it's FA Vase, FA Trophy, England schoolboys, under-21s, play-offs, Cup finals, England seniors, whenever a game is played here in the home of football, the mecca for players it is a wonderful occasion and today that occasion is given added colour by these gold and red flags and banners of the Watford supporters away to my right hand side, what an occasion this is for the club from north London.'

I had a brief on air exchange with JP just before kick-off when he said to me at the end of the national anthem, 'What does it mean to be a Watford fan here? Every week of the season you hear him covering games for Capital Gold Sportstime, Simon Michaelson, lifelong Hornets supporter, how do you feel Simon?' I replied, 'It's absolutely incredible Jonathan, I've seen Watford this season play at Crewe, I've seen them play at Grimsby, without any disrespect to those clubs this is just incredible this experience, it's not a football match, it's more than that, this is a festival, it's like some sort of celebration of life itself really.' JP then asked me, 'What do you think the score's gonna be Simon?' to which I said, 'Well, having seen the drama of yesterday's match I'm just hoping, because it's my team involved, that it's not going to be a dramatic game like that, I'm hoping for a 1-0 win for Watford with hardly any chances at either end, a very, very boring game, I know neutrals won't want that but I just don't think my heart could stand anything like that Man City game.'

Billy Bonds gave a nice appreciation of Tommy Mooney, 'I tell you what Jonathan, he is a real 110 per center, we talked about the boy the centre-half yesterday Morrison, for Man City, and what effect he's got on their side, I think Mooney's the same type of player. You can play him anywhere, he'll play centre-half, he'll play wing-back, he can play midfield, he's now playing up front scoring goals and he's that type of player, he's a whole 110 per cent man as are the Watford team, I think that's their strength.'

Watford kicked off and the game was under way. Early on Bolton showed how dangerous they could be. There was much talk before the game about the quality of Bolton's creative, attacking central midfield pair, Jensen and Frandsen, and in the second minute Jensen cleverly deceived Richard Johnson, got behind the Watford defence to the dead-ball line inside the penalty area and pulled the ball back. Johnson's central midfield partner Micah Hyde was there to clear.

It wasn't Bolton's intricate passing which led to the first strike on goal in the seventh minute. Instead, it was a clever long ball out of defence by Andy Todd into the path of Bob Taylor. With Page closing him down Taylor shot first time with his right foot from just outside the box. Alec Chamberlain made his first save of the day, diving to collect the ball comfortably.

Bolton were threatening again five minutes later. A probing Elliott pass from the left found the chest of Gudjohnsen on the edge of the box. As Gudjohnsen failed to get the ball under control Page nicked it away, but only to Johansen who shot hard just beyond the far post.

Then after a period of Watford pressure Bolton broke quickly and missed the chance of the half. A Gardner pass from the left found Gudjohnsen running in between Robinson and Page. Again, Gudjohnsen took the ball on his chest, this time he retained possession but had to stretch as he shot with his right foot from about eight yards out. As Chamberlain rushed fruitlessly from his goal the ball spun off the outside of Gudjohnsen's boot about a foot past the post. The incident left Gudjohnsen prone on the floor holding his head in his hands and Chamberlain berating his defenders.

Bolton were looking good going forward but just before the half-hour mark they showed they could cause themselves problems at the back. Watford's game involved pressing the ball and Nick Wright, who did that as well as anyone, caught Todd in possession on the halfway line with Bolton pushed up. A well-timed pass released Michel Ngonge who ran towards the Bolton goal. Robbie Elliott did well to get back and block Ngonge's shot from just inside the box. 'What a game this is turning out to be again here in the play-off finals, stretching wide open,' exclaimed JP.

Just after that Chamberlain's 34-year-old reflexes had to be at their sharpest. A Bolton free kick from just outside the box broke for Gudjohnsen. After a great first touch he shot from eight yards out and Chamberlain dived to push the ball away for a corner. This time he didn't berate his defence because I rather fancy that he was glad to have had the chance to make the save and enjoyed looking good in such a big game.

If 31 May 1999 was the day, in the 38th minute of the game came *the moment.* Peter Kennedy's set-piece deliveries had provided Watford's most potent threat but Bolton had so far managed to defend them successfully. Then Kennedy swung in a corner dangerously to the edge of the six-yard box. Banks in the Bolton goal not having reacted, Todd headed the ball away to a place about eight yards out. The ball was dropping behind the flame-haired Wright and he had to turn towards his own goal to get to it. No one expected Wright to do what he did next. I'd never seen him do anything like it before and I didn't see him do anything close to it ever again. With his back to the goal Wright executed an overhead kick which cleared several Bolton players on its way into the far corner of the net. Neil Cox on the line jumped in an effort to get a header in and looked physically sick as the ball hit the net. Cox joined Watford for £500,000 just over five months later. He must have thought to himself, 'I want to join a club that has players who can do things like that.' It was the type of goal that the Mexican overhead specialist Hugo Sánchez used to score.

JP described it like this, 'Corner ball it is to Watford, their sixth of the game, Kennedy takes it near post, Palmer with a touch, half cleared away, Wright the overhead, it's in, Watford have scored, Nicky Wright with the overhead from eight yards out. Watford have scored at Wembley stadium for the first time, they've taken the lead against Bolton Wanderers, in 1984 they got it wrong, wrong, wrong against Everton, in 1999 they've got it Wright, Wright, Wright and he's Nicked it, it's Watford 1 Bolton 0!'

Billy followed up with, 'Well they've caused 'em problems all afternoon from these set plays, they haven't looked comfortable, but I tell you what I'm just watching it on the replay, and that is a magnificent goal for Wright, overhead bicycle kick into the top corner, great goal, but they have caused 'em problems on these set plays.'

By now JP had seen the replay and added, 'They had three men back on the line, it looped in the end over Neil Cox who couldn't get a header away, what an overhead, right underneath the bar. Michel Ngonge was standing behind the dead-ball line in the goalmouth, he had the sense not to come back on to the field of play, otherwise he would have been offside certainly and Watford are ahead against Bolton Wanderers, well who would have thought this eight weeks ago? Watford heading for the Premier League? Still a long, long way to go.'

During a lull in play JP added a footnote, 'Well he's joined the list of great goalscorers here Nicky Wright, it's his seventh of the season, a year ago he was with struggling Carlisle.'

It was a goal that would have graced any occasion.

Just before the half-time whistle Gudjohnsen again showed his class when he turned Palmer by allowing a Gardner pass to run past him. Again, having made the opportunity for himself, Gudjohnsen missed, curling the ball wide from the edge of the box with his right foot.

Watford were ahead at half-time having not created a clear-cut chance in the first half. Gudjohnsen had failed to take some good opportunities for Bolton. Billy's analysis was, 'It is an open game, both teams looking to get forward. Bolton have had their chances, Gudjohnsen especially, he's had a couple of terrific chances, one very good save from Chamberlain, but it was a really good goal from Wright, an excellent goal and really no more than Watford deserved because they've really, I think you're right, Jonathan, they've outfought them a bit. Bolton we know they want to get the ball down and play and Watford haven't given 'em the chance to do that, their work rate's been terrific.'

JP asked me how I felt at half-time. 'Absolutely incredible, Jonathan, the amazing thing is I don't think Watford have had a really clear goalscoring opportunity yet, because that Wright goal, that wasn't even a half-chance, that wasn't a quarter-chance, that was a fantastic overhead. Gudjohnsen at the other end has had two clear chances, one he stuck wide, the other Chamberlain has saved brilliantly. Chamberlain has been playing like that out of his skin all season, it's fantastic.'

Just before the game restarted JP, having had a chance to collect his thoughts, summed up the first half by saying, 'We said right at the start of the programme, Bonzo, when we talked about the two teams, you look at Bolton the likes of Fish, Johansen, Frandsen, Gudjohnsen, individually they've got to be ranked higher than Watford players but Watford have the spirit, Watford have the unity and they're playing more cohesively as a unit.'

Billy didn't disagree, 'I totally agree with you. I mean let's be honest, Watford, I won't say average players, but not probably the quality that Bolton have got, at the moment though their spirit and their organisation is better than Bolton's at the moment. I think Bolton, really Colin Todd will be in there saying, "Hey come on, we've really got to get hold of this midfield." At the moment Micah Hyde, Johnson, Wright, Kennedy are winning the battles in there, simple as that.'

The second half started, with Watford 45 minutes away from the Premier League. The game continued in a similar vein to the first half and Todd was caught out when he was too slow to play a pass. Ngonge intercepted but the ball ran through to Banks who managed to race out and clear. Gudjohnsen had a header saved, this time comfortably. Elliott made a last-ditch challenge to deflect an Ngonge shot behind.

Having spent most of the first hour frustrating Bolton, Watford began to play themselves. First Wright ran at Elliott on the right-hand side and streaked past him into yards of space. Wright's low pass across the six-yard box wasn't anticipated by either Ngonge or Mooney and Cox cleared. Then Mooney had Watford's first free header of the game as he put Hyde's great cross just wide from eight yards out. With Watford defending in numbers, as they did all game, Bob Taylor was forced to play the ball back to Cox and there was a sense of desperation about his shot, dragged well wide from 30 yards.

When Allan Smart replaced Ngonge in the 75th minute Bolton had a beaten look about them. It just needed someone to finish them off. Wright came close to a second when he was inches away from Mooney's driven cross. 'Great move by Watford again,' said Billy.

Open spaces were beginning to appear in the Bolton defence. Again, Wright broke forward. This time he picked out Kennedy who had the option of shooting or passing to an unmarked Smart. Kennedy blazed a first-time shot wide of the near post with JP screaming, 'Kennedy in on goal to finish it, ooh drives wide, chose to shoot first time, beautiful setup, classical break, the shot was wide.' Billy added, 'Well one minute we've got Gardner running into the box at Watford, and he's put a poor pass on the end of it, he had a great chance, he got in behind. Watford, should have done a better final ball, then all of a sudden we've got Wright galloping at the Bolton lads who've got stretched, he knocked the ball out to Kennedy, it was a fabulous chance and Kennedy's blasted it wide.'

JP summed up the Watford performance so far, 'I don't think you could fault one single Watford player out there today. They've all really put it in, great endeavour, honest performances from all 11, that really typifies the spirit brought about by Graham Taylor's return.'

Again, Bolton were forced to shoot from outside the box as Chamberlain comfortably collected from Frandsen.

Bolton came close for the final time in the 85th minute. Todd played another great long ball out of defence to the edge of the box to Gudjohnsen. Palmer was there but hesitated and as Chamberlain came out to try and deal with the situation, Gudjohnsen knocked the ball goalwards. For a cloudy second it looked as though the ball would go just inside the post but as clarity returned, I could see that it was travelling too slowly and was anyway going just wide. Typically, Page was there just in case to coolly shepherd the ball out of play.

Having stayed in the game until the 89th minute suddenly Bolton were out of it. They lost possession in midfield. A Scott Sellars pass was blocked by Hyde ten yards inside the Watford half. Sellars and Smart challenged for the ball which ran free inside the centre circle. Hyde read the situation brilliantly, strode forward and reached the ball with Todd prevaricating. Hyde then slid a delicate, short pass into the path of Kennedy breaking forward just onside. In a position very similar to the one he'd found himself in a few minutes earlier, Kennedy was again in on goal. This time he was further out but again he had the option of either shooting himself or playing in the unmarked Smart. It was as though he thought, 'I remember what happened the last time when I shot,' and he rolled a ball to Smart which just evaded Todd and Fish who were desperately rushing back to try to put out the fire. This was the moment Smart had been waiting for all season and he was not about to miss. Smart hit the ball first time with the outside of his right foot just inside the post with the assurance of a man who all along had known that he was destined for the Premier League. Smart's team-mates were all a long way behind the play and at first, he was left all alone to celebrate. Probably thinking, 'For fuck's sake, get over here will you,' he appeared to not know what to do and he somewhat comically ran over to the corner flag and dived on it. As the other players arrived, he got up and gestured emotionally to his wife who had found out a month previously that she was pregnant.

With 37,000 Watford supporters going berserk during the build-up to the second goal, JP had to reach a high decibel level to make himself heard, 'Promotion for the second season running is now very much on the cards as they can break away down field, Hyde releases Kennedy, it's two against one, Kennedy's got Smart on the edge of the box, Smart right foot, Watford are heading for the Premier League. Allan Smart finishes Bolton Wanderers off; it's Watford 2 Bolton Wanderers 0, the supersub has sunk Bolton Wanderers with a Smart, Smart finish. Bolton 0 Watford 2 and how the pain will smart for Bolton Wanderers tonight, Watford and Graham Taylor are up surely now. I know we've had a topsy turvy week and Manchester United came back against Bayern in stoppage time and Manchester City did it against Gillingham but surely lightning can't strike thrice and surely Watford are heading up, up and away, beyond their wildest possible dreams on Capital Gold.' It was classic JP and beautiful to hear.

Billy picked up after the long, sustained crescendo, 'Graham Taylor now is just going to his players "concentrate, concentrate", that's all he's telling 'em to do now, but it was a good break from Watford, Bolton overstretched, they found Kennedy down the left side and Kennedy had the common sense to knock Smart in, he saw Smart unmarked in the middle and Smart's blasted it into the back of the net 2-0 and all as I say now Graham Taylor is doing that to his head now, "concentrate lads, don't switch off".'

In the four minutes of added time, during which Watford didn't switch off, JP asked Billy to sum up the afternoon, 'Well, Bolton have got the better players, Jonathan, but what does that matter when you've got spirit like Watford have got, they have worked their socks off, they've battled all afternoon, right from the goalkeeper right through to the front two, Mooney and Ngonge, they've been running back and making tackles, they haven't given Bolton a sniff of the ball and have kept working at them.'

It was lavish praise and came from one of the great battlers of his generation. On the final whistle JP exploded, 'AND THAT'S THE FULL-TIME WHISTLE WHICH SIGNALS THAT WATFORD ARE BACK IN THE PREMIER LEAGUE, BACK IN THE TOP FLIGHT FOR THE FIRST TIME SINCE

1988. GRAHAM TAYLOR'S COACHING STAFF ARE ON THE PITCH AND CELEBRATING, AND WHAT A RETURN TO THE BIG TIME FOR THE LITTLE MAN, SO VILIFIED WHEN HE WAS ENGLAND MANAGER, TO HAVE COME BACK IN THIS STYLE, TO HAVE GUIDED WATFORD TO TWO SUCCESSIVE PROMOTION SEASONS SPEAKS HUGE VOLUMES ABOUT THE MAN WHO THEY DESCRIBE AT VICARAGE ROAD WITH THREE SHORT LETTERS AFTER HIS NAME, "GRAHAM TAYLOR, GOD" THEY SAY AND FOR WATFORD FANS HE HAS ACHIEVED ALMOST DEIFICATION THIS AFTERNOON, WATFORD PROMOTED TO THE PREMIER LEAGUE AND WE'RE BACK IN A COUPLE OF SECONDS TIME TO SEE THEM LIFT THE TROPHY ON CAPITAL GOLD.'

At the end of the game Smart, whose goal had been his first since Boxing Day, cried tears of joy. I have to admit that I was welling up myself as I watched Page lift the trophy which was bedecked in red and gold ribbons, and the players collect their medals, but I thought that it would be unprofessional to break down on the radio and I managed to fight back the tears. Then JP asked, 'What does it mean to you, Simon Michaelson, as a Watford fan, long standing of course?'

It was my moment and I wanted to do it justice. It wasn't easy to sum up what it meant and how I felt. I was sitting in the press box at Wembley, I'd just watched Watford win there for the first time in their history, I would be reporting on them in the Premier League the following season, 37,000 Watford supporters were leaping around ecstatically in the warmth of a late May afternoon under a cloudless blue sky and I'd just been asked by the best football commentator of his generation live on air what it meant to me. Some reporters and commentators think up lines in advance to use in specific scenarios but I hadn't anticipated this moment and hadn't prepared anything so I just said the first thing that came into my head.

I was most pleased for, and wanted to give credit to, Graham Taylor, the family man, the football man who had masterminded the triumph, who had taken over as Watford manager when two seasons previously they'd finished 13th in Division Two, who in his first spell in charge had taken a small club in Hertfordshire to Division One for the first time in their history, who had given the club six seasons in the top flight in the 1980s, who had left to eventually manage England and had been savaged when he hadn't been successful, who had been sacked from his next job at Wolves and had returned to Watford to put his reputation and his neck on the line once again, who had dealt with all the negativity with dignity and stoicism and who had today inspired a Watford side to victory over a famous old club with far more resources and more expensive, talented players. Once more he had touched the lives of thousands and he had enabled a bunch of footballers to experience playing at a higher level than they would ever have done if they hadn't played under him.

Taylor had done it again and I wanted to express my appreciation and gratitude as fully as I could. He'd won promotion with unfancied players, two of them picked up the previous summer for a modest amount from Carlisle United who at the end of the season had been relegated to the bottom tier of English football. I wasn't about to say something like, 'It means a lot, Jonathan,' or, 'I'm over the moon, Jonathan.' Instead, I replied, 'I'd second what Billy said, you've got to remember that the combined transfer fees of those two, Wright and Smart the goalscorers, was £200,000. For me I can really sum it up by saying, Billy I don't know what you think of this, but for me Graham Taylor ranks at this moment alongside Brian Clough, Alex Ferguson, Bill Shankly, some of the greats, that's just the way I feel at the moment.'

It was maybe a slightly outlandish statement but it wasn't meant to be analysed and dissected or even taken literally. It was intended to reflect how I felt in that euphoric moment which was outlandishly good. I also wanted to acknowledge and give thanks for the contribution Taylor had made to my life and to Watford Football Club. Billy understood and he responded, 'Well I'm sure as a Watford supporter you feel that way, obviously I think it's a marvellous achievement what he's done this year. I think he got a lot of stick over the England thing, I don't think anybody deserves that type of treatment that he got and I'm absolutely delighted for him that he's had this success.'

Of course, the boys at Capital found it highly amusing that I'd put Taylor in the same bracket as three all-time great managers – Shankly, the architect of the modern Liverpool, Clough who had been stupendously successful at both Derby County and Nottingham Forest, and Ferguson whose great achievements at Manchester United were sustained over such a long period of time. Along with Taylor these three managers had made the greatest impression on me in my lifetime up to that point.

My comment lodged itself in JP's subconscious and some while later, when I was doing another Watford game with him, he jokingly said to me on air, 'Didn't you think that Watford getting promoted was more important than England winning the World Cup?' I replied, 'Yes Jonathan, I'm afraid I understated it.'

Before he wrapped up the show from Wembley, JP asked, 'Billy, what chance do they have, Watford, of staying up next season, to put things into perspective?' Billy gave a frank answer, 'Er, I don't think any chance whatsoever, Jonathan, and I'm just being totally honest with you, I'm probably saying as much as anyone else would say all round the country and possibly some of the Watford fans, I was talking to some of them up at Port Vale, it's like Graham Taylor said he'd rather get into the Premier League and have the problems there than stay down in this First Division, the expectation would have been higher for them next year because they've had such a good season this year, the expectation would have been high and I think as he said he'd rather get into the Premier League and have all the problems of trying to keep in it next year. But good luck to them, it's a great achievement and I hope I'm proved wrong.'

After the game the Watford players were so overwhelmed that they seemed almost lost for words. Not so Taylor and I was able to listen to him as he expressed his thoughts in the bowels of Wembley.

Taylor wasn't exactly encouraged by the press to wallow in his victory. Football reporters being what they are, they wanted to look ahead and ask about the following season. Their attitude seemed to be, 'Right we've got that game out of the way, that was good, what's next?'

So how would Graham go about creating a side strong enough to at least survive in the Premier League? His answer, 'Well, the thing is today of course, right now isn't the time to be talking about that, what we have to do is, we've got to enjoy this evening, and then we've got a month, just about a month off, well it will be before we start again, and we've got to give that a lot of thought … We're not a big club and it would be very, very silly of me to have to feel that I would spend millions of pounds and thereby in one stroke almost destroy our youth system. Over the years Watford Football Club have produced our own players and we must be very, very careful now as to what steps we actually take, so there's going to be a lot of thinking to do. Obviously we want to stay in the Premier League now that we've got in and that will be our first target to make sure that we can stabilise ourselves. To go into this division now and to expect us to finish runners-up as we did the first time, that's just asking a little bit too much I think.'

The press felt it necessary, even in Taylor's moment of triumph, to remind him that he hadn't succeeded in every job he'd had, and he was asked whether getting promoted to the Premier League wiped out the memories of the dark times he'd experienced. He replied, 'Everything is history, you know as far as I'm concerned today was the most important game in my life because that's what is happening now. I'm a big believer that what has happened you can't change that and it's happened, but in terms of being a manager now for 27 years I just had a bit of a rough time, unfortunately I was right in the middle of the England situation there with the highest profile, and we didn't qualify for the World Cup, I've accepted full responsibility, I mean you have to do that, and I resigned. From that time on I had one full season at Wolverhampton where we reached the play-offs, unfortunately we didn't make it last time, so about a couple of seasons out of 27 years it's not really that bad at all and as I said earlier, what's history is history and you can't alter it, it's all about now and tomorrow.'

*

Management life for Colin Todd was bleak. There had been conjecture even before the final about whether Bolton, if they lost, would be able to keep their talented side together. Seven games into the following season Todd became a victim of Watford's play-off final victory; in September 1999 Bolton sold Per Frandsen to Blackburn Rovers for £1.75m against Todd's wishes and he resigned.

If there had been an Unluckiest Manager of the Season award for the season before the play-off final, 1997/98, Todd would have been streets ahead of his rivals. He had become joint manager at Bolton with Roy McFarland in 1995, taking sole charge in January 1996 when his former defensive partner was sacked. Bolton were relegated from the Premier League at the end of 1995/96 but the following season, 1996/97, they ran away with Division One, finishing 18 points clear of second-placed Barnsley with a team containing the likes of John McGinlay, Nathan Blake and Alan Thompson. So far so good and Todd was on the crest of a wave but the tide turned on 1 September 1997, the day Bolton opened their new Reebok Stadium before playing Everton in front of the TV cameras. The game ended 0-0 but TV replays showed that a Blake header had crossed the line. Bolton took their relegation battle to the final day of the season, when they lost 2-0 at Chelsea to late Gianluca Vialli and Jody Morris goals. The result meant that Bolton were relegated on goal difference, having finished on the same number of points as, but one place behind – of all clubs – Everton.

A year later Todd's misfortune was compounded when he came up against a Watford side on a mission.

19

Going into 1999/2000 I believed that Watford would stay up. I didn't know how it would happen exactly, I just figured that Graham Taylor would somehow work it out. My crazy optimism was shared by the players to whom I spoke before the start of the season.

Allan Smart couldn't wait for the Premier League campaign to start. 'Well that's right it can't come quick enough really, it's only ten days to go now, we're just counting the days off and I'm sure all the boys are looking forward to it.'

So far Taylor had done nothing different compared to the previous pre-season. 'He hasn't really gotten about us yet mentally or anything like that, he's just got on with the training, and we've sort of done it as we did last year. We've had a trip to Isle of Man and Iceland, quite sort of relaxed, but I'm sure this ten days he's gonna be stepping it up and he's gonna be more hands on every day I think.'

What Allan was most looking forward to about the coming season was fulfilling a dream and playing at some of the great stadia. 'Well it's just going you know to the likes of Old Trafford and Highbury and Anfield and places like that. They're places you see on the TV as a young kid and that's the place where you want to play.'

Allan had moved from Carlisle along with Nick Wright to find himself in the Premier League in a very short space of time and I asked him whether he thought he could handle it mentally. 'Well I think the same sort of question was asked of me last year, you know coming from a Third Division side in effect to a First Division side, you know could we handle that? I don't see why not, we've got absolutely nothing to fear, I mean as far as everybody's concerned we're favourites to come down so we can't really do any worse than that.'

The bookies had Watford to finish bottom and I wondered whether the team could use being written off in this way to their advantage. 'Regardless of what we do this year, next year is gonna be our expectation season if you know what I mean, if you know where I'm coming from like. If you sort of finish mid-table people are looking for you to finish above that, if you finish just above the bottom you've got to improve on that, so this year we're getting our benchmark this year, we're pitching in where we think we'll be, I think we'll do OK'.

I asked Allan whether he'd set himself any goals for the coming season. In his first year at Watford he'd been part of a promotion-winning side and had scored in the play-off final at Wembley. Far from congratulating himself though he was not happy with his return of seven league goals from 34 starts. 'Yeah, goals is the main thing, I think. I had a bit of a disappointing season in front of goal last year, it's the worst season I've had, although I would say it's the best season I've had out of the box, linking in with my team and creating things but yeah I've got to start getting on the sheet more often.'

Watford had been promoted to the Premier League but they didn't spend a single penny in the close-season. Three players were signed in three days in July 1999, all on free transfers: Northern Ireland international Mark Williams from Chesterfield, Des Lyttle from Nottingham Forest and Dominic Foley from Wolverhampton Wanderers.

Williams had been attracted to the club by Taylor. 'I think Watford were watching me play sort of last five or ten games. I knew of their interest towards the end of the season and obviously I spoke to a lot of clubs during the summer and Graham Taylor was the one that impressed me the most and I brought my holiday up, come back off my holiday for two days and spoke to him and he impressed me a great deal and that's what swayed me to sign here and obviously with the draw of the Premier League.'

What had Taylor said to convince Mark to join the club? 'He knew a lot about me to start with, which was really good and also I was with him for two or three hours, he didn't try and hide anything you know, he told me everything about the club and he seemed a really, really straight bloke, that's what I liked about him.'

Mark was confident that Watford would stay up and the reason for his confidence was the same as mine. 'Definitely, I've said this all along, that I wouldn't have come here if I thought they were going to get relegated after a year, I spoke to teams in the First Division, good teams in the First Division, you know I would have signed a long-term contract there. I've come here because I think obviously it's going to be difficult this season, I've said before if anyone can keep Watford in the Premier League it will be Graham Taylor.'

I reminded Mark that as a defender he would be going to places like Highbury, Old Trafford and Stamford Bridge and marking players like Dwight Yorke, Dennis Bergkamp, Chris Sutton and others of that calibre. I asked him if he thought he was up to it. 'First of all I've got to get into the team, I've come here, I'm one of 32, 33. Graham Taylor's promised me nothing, you know he's not said that I'm going to be playing, it's up to me to fight for a shirt, but yeah I think definitely I've got a chance, I played in the FA Cup semi-final with Chesterfield, played against some big teams, recently when I made my [Northern Ireland] debut against Germany I marked Oliver Bierhoff, it don't come much bigger than that so there's no point being nervous or scared about it, you've got to look forward to it.'

Mark told me the type of player he was. 'My kind of game is that I'm strong and I might not play well every game but I will give 100 per cent and I think if you're giving 100 per cent then that's half the battle.'

It was a couple of months after the play-off final victory over Bolton at Wembley. Seeing Nick Wright for the first time since he'd scored with that glorious overhead kick put a smile on my face. I imagined that Nick must have not stopped grinning since the goal had gone in. There was only one topic with which we were going to start our conversation and I asked Nick how many times he'd replayed the goal on his video player over the summer. 'Not too many times. I did replay it, the first time I got a copy I replayed it a few times but I went away on holiday with my fiancée and got away from it really and it helped bring myself down to earth because I was on such a high after the game it helped, the break did, but I've watched it once or twice since I came back.'

I asked Nick whether he'd yet been able to work out how he'd done it, or whether he just didn't bother to think about that. 'Well I don't think it's working out, other players attempt goals like that, it's just rare that they do come off and for it to be on such an occasion made it even more rare but I'll attempt them again and maybe not score but it's not something that you can work out how you do, everyone knows how to do an overhead kick it's just whether you use the right technique and get it correct on the day.'

I guessed that it was pure instinct that made him attempt the kick and I asked whether using his instinct was how he liked to play the game. 'I think a lot of football is instinct and you have to react to situations and it was an instinctive reaction. The ball came over from a corner and was headed behind me, there was no one to lay the ball back to for an easier shot so I reacted to try the overhead kick and it couldn't have worked better.'

I could have listened all day to Nick talking about that goal; every nuance and thought he had about it was of interest to me. I suppose I could have listened to his whole life story and taken in everything that had happened to him, and shaped him, and led up to that moment when he struck the ball with such precision and agility at Wembley. But I didn't want to over-egg the pudding and I moved on by suggesting that the whole day at Wembley had given him a taste of the high life and had been a fantastic experience and saying that I guessed he just wanted more of it. 'Yeah it was a great day for everyone at Watford, not just the players, but the fans and everyone associated with the football club. Now we're very hungry for more success and everyone who's doubting us in the Premier League I hope we're going to really surprise because we want more success at this club and I think it's going to be a short time before that happens.'

I asked Nick, if there was one major thing Watford had to do to stay up, what that would be. He replied laughing, 'Get more points than the people who get relegated.' I told him that was a Kenny Dalglish answer. He agreed and when I asked him what they were going to do to get those points he said, 'I think we've just got to build on our strengths from last season. We worked very well as a team, we are one team of 11 players rather than 11 individuals, that's our main strength. The manager's brought in new players who I think he knew would fit in with the players off the pitch as well as fit into the team on it, so I think we've just got to build on it, I don't know whether we'll better our team spirit because it's excellent at the moment but we've got to keep that going and keep the strength of last season.'

Nick agreed that for Watford it was about not having any superstars or any one outstanding individual but working as a team. 'Definitely because the teams with one star, if the star gets injured the team suffers. Most of the players had an injury or suspension during the season and we continued to progress right through. Gifton [Noel-Williams] did very well for us in the early part but he got injured but we still managed to get promoted when he was injured. I think it's great for a team to be able to do that and replace players. It's inevitable that you're going to get injuries so it's important that you can replace players when they do.'

I asked Nick how much of football was psychological, to do with the mind, and suggested that going up to the Premier League it was important for Watford not to be overawed by all the hype. 'It's a very difficult question because it depends what you class as "mind" or, everything comes through your mind really, the way you play your football does, but I think it's important that we don't fear the opposition. We're playing against some of the best players in the world and it seems a strange thing to say but we've not to go into the games with fear, we've got to go into the games excited and it's going to be a great challenge for us but if we go in excited I think we'll perform a lot better than if we go fearing the opposition.'

In terms of what he was looking for from himself, Nick hadn't set a target for the number of goals he wanted to score the following season but he did have an objective. 'I don't set the goals on the amount, I want to score as many goals as I can, I want to definitely beat last season's tally and I think I can do that but not just scoring, I want to make sure that I create more goals and create more chances, just get more consistency to my game, I've had some very good games, some very poor games and it's just making sure that I can balance them out and keep my football to a high standard.'

To finish Nick agreed with me that he and Allan Smart had come a long way in a short space of time. 'Yeah this year's been a dream for us both, we suffered the relegation with Carlisle at the end of last season, which was very disappointing but both got an excellent move to Watford and since we came here things couldn't have gone better for us.'

It was good to talk to Robert Page in triumphant mood. He was probably at the pinnacle of his playing career at that moment. He'd been made captain of Watford at a young age and would now be leading the club into the Premier League after two promotions in successive seasons. 'Yeah it's been a dream come true for myself, Kenny Jackett appointed me club captain when I was 21, I think it was in the Second Division then, which we finished about 15th, 16th, Graham Taylor took over as manager that season, kept me as club captain, that season we got promotion to the First Division and obviously last season was also an achievement in getting promoted to the Premier League, so for myself from a personal point of view it's been a Cinderella story really, it's been a dream come true.'

In telling me what he thought might happen next season Robert, like Nick Wright, stressed the need for Watford to continue to do the things that had got them into the Premier League in the first place. 'What's gonna happen next season, we're gonna do what we've done over the last two seasons, going to give everything we've got, we've not got any individual stars that are gonna run the show, we've got one great set up at Watford, we've got a great bunch of lads, we're all gonna work hard for each other and we're gonna do the best we possibly can to remain in the Premier League and anything above that is going to be a bonus.'

I asked Robert whether he honestly thought they could do it and I found in him the same conviction as everyone else at the club of whom I had asked the same question. 'Yes I do, yeah, otherwise you know I wouldn't be sitting here saying that our aim is to stay in the Premier League this and that, knowing that we're going to get relegated, I wouldn't do that. I don't believe for one minute that we are going to but our aim is to remain in the top flight for as long as we can.'

Robert had won his first cap for Wales in 1997 against Turkey, and on 5 June 1999, only a few days after Watford's play-off final win over Bolton, in his sixth start for his country he'd faced Italy in Bologna in a Euro 2000 qualifier. As a central defender he had been directly up against Christian Vieri and Filippo Inzaghi. Wales had Ryan Giggs, Dean Saunders, Mark Hughes and Gary Speed in their starting line-up but Italy were much too strong and won 4-0 through first-half Vieri, Inzaghi and Paolo Maldini goals, and one just before the end from Enrico Chiesa.

So Robert had recently had a taste of playing against some of the best players in the world, and I wondered what it was like playing against that sort of player and what was needed to counteract them. 'Fitness is a big thing for me, I mean I had to man mark Inzaghi and the biggest thing for me was that the two centre-forwards did not stand still for one second, always moving around you and you're always on your toes thinking "where are they, where are they?" whereas some players in the Premier League do it but you get the odd one which is they just stand still, have a breather and that's when you get your chance to have your breather yourself, whereas that was the big difference for me that they never stood still for a second, for more than a second and you had to be on your toes all the time and follow them everywhere they went on the park so for me the fitness is a big thing.'

I guessed that the midfield players were so good that when Vieri and Inzaghi made that run they would be picked out with a killer ball. 'Yeah that's right they can almost read their mind, it's a case of the left-back, Maldini at the time, say for example Maldini's running out with the ball, he'd have Vieri and Inzaghi practically making the runs before they even know what he's going to do, you know they make his mind up for him so to speak, they've made the runs and then Maldini's just got to look up and see the run and just play it and you know that's one of the big differences as well.'

I always liked to hear Watford players talk appreciatively about Graham Taylor and Robert was quick to acknowledge the manager's impact on his life. 'He's just, basically confidence and you know you have self-belief and he's a big believer in if you enter into a competition what's the point of entering and you know and thinking you're going to be second best, you've got to enter into any competition, not just in football but in any ways of life, knowing that you're going to win, you're going to be successful and if you see yourself being successful you know how can you lose? And for me that's the main thing that's rubbed off on me. I've always been a winner anyway, I don't like to lose in whatever I do but you know it's just all the lads, we all work together and we all go out on to the park knowing that we're going to win and a great example is when we beat Birmingham away knowing that we was gonna go to Wembley to play against Bolton as soon as we won at Birmingham we knew that we were going to be in the Premier League next season because we could not see ourselves losing at Wembley.'

I asked Robert whether the final was the greatest game he'd ever played in. 'I think it's gotta be, yeah, along with I've said earlier along with getting my first full Welsh cap at the Arms Park, playing at Wembley in front of the supporters that we had that day was unbelievable, especially walking up the steps lifting the trophy as well, that's got to be the highlight of my career.'

It was obvious talking to Robert that he took a lot of pride from playing for Wales and clearly playing well in the Premier League would boost his chances of winning more Welsh caps. 'Yeah that's one of my aims as well, to establish myself now in the Welsh set up and become a regular.'

Graham Taylor remarked that the press day at Vicarage Road was crowded with media people because Watford were about to play in the Premier League, 'This particular day I mean it's been a full day for us not just morning it's been morning and afternoon, national press here, players being interviewed, television cameras, radio mikes about the place and tomorrow when I shall see the players I shall ask them, "What had that day, what had press day got to do with beating Wimbledon on August the seventh?" Because the answer is "absolutely nothing". Unless you let it affect you, unless you let all of this affect you and you think "we've arrived, I'm here", then it has something to do with it, but with all due respect to you people here, you're doing your job, we have to respond to that, it's right and proper that we should present ourselves and have a press day but you come to the crunch it's nothing to do with when August the seventh comes, so you have to strip all this hype off it. If I can keep making sure that the players are aware of that and focusing in to what this game is about then who knows what we might be able to achieve? We might just be a bit of a surprise horse and not necessarily be wallowing around in those bottom four or five.'

I loved the idea conveyed by Graham that football is a journey on which you embark that does not have a destination. As soon as you think you've arrived, you're finished. Then I guess life is a bit like that. If you think that you've arrived you either think again, and realise that you don't actually know what your destination is, and you restart the journey with that in mind, or else your journey is effectively over.

Graham had been cautious over the summer, bringing in just the three free signings, and he explained why. 'I'd much rather look at the division first of all and have a feel of you know whatever money I've got to spend where should I spend it, how should I spend it, and I think that's more important at this moment in time than going out and spending it simply because we're in the Premier League.'

In conjunction with the board of directors, Graham had decided that the Watford players who had earned promotion to the Premier League would be given the chance to undertake the next stage of the club's journey. 'I would much rather pay this group of people their increases even though it makes them nowhere near the highest-paid players in the Premier League, I'd rather pay them their increases than to go out and spend substantial amounts in the transfer market and give other players substantially higher money than these players and risk losing the team ethos that has stood us in good stead. This group of players is going to be given a chance to play in the Premier League. If they don't succeed they won't have let me down through not trying, it just will be that they will not have been able to accept that step up and there's no disgrace in that.'

Having managed Watford for six seasons in the top flight in the 1980s, Graham was in a good position to give a view on how football at that level had changed in the intervening period. 'Well I think what's changed more than anything else is that when we went into the First Division as it was then in '82, there may have been four, five world-class players in the Premier League, now there's likely to be something like probably 15 to 20, spread over a number of clubs and I think that has changed. Having said that I think it would be wrong to compare going into the Premier League in 82/83 where we finished runners-up to Liverpool in our first year, I think that's asking too much of us to do that.

'On the same basis as I said earlier if we're saying, "Well look shall we finish fourth from bottom?" I think that's setting your sights too low. What hasn't changed really is, it sounds very simple saying this but I do like to try to keep things simple on the football field is that when the opposition have the ball you've got to do your very, very best to make sure they don't hurt you. When you have the ball you have to do your very, very best to hurt them. In other words they've got the ball or you've got the ball, now that's not changed. Alright when they've got it they might have more skilful players, when you've got it I'll assume that we're more skilful than probably we were 15 years ago, but that basic principle hasn't changed.'

The game against Watford would be Egil Olsen's first in charge of Wimbledon. At the press day a reporter told Graham that everyone would remind him over the next couple of weeks that the last time the pair had been in opposition was when they were both international managers and England and Norway had been in the same qualifying group for the 1994 World Cup. 'I got to know Egil quite well and understandably people relate to this, in fact when I saw the fixture list I said at the time, "Well that's not Watford versus Wimbledon, that's England versus Norway, Graham Taylor versus Egil Olsen," but I mean you live with all of those kind of things.

'He's done a fantastic achievement for Norway, a country of four million people only, being able to get like Jack Charlton got for the Republic of Ireland a club approach, a club atmosphere, it's easier to do that with the smaller countries, establishing a style of play. He said, "This is the style of play that we're doing," and then as I say getting the country to two successive World Cups, magnificent, and anybody that doesn't recognise this, this is what always irritates and annoys me, when people want to pick chunks and pick bits out of people, you know say, "Oh they were very boring in 1994, what a bore, I don't like their style of play." For God's sake hold on a minute, what has this fellow just done for his country? Jack obviously suffered a little bit of that in the early days with the Republic. More difficult for countries that are expected to be successful like England, even though our expectancy has never sort of matched the reality or it's always gone above, the expectancy's always gone above what the reality is, easier for the smaller countries to get that club approach than it is for the countries such as England where you're not only expected to win but you're expected to win in a certain manner and that's more difficult and I'm not too certain what Jack or Egil would have done in the England situation.'

*

I had several reasons for thinking that Watford would stay up. The club had got used to winning over the previous two seasons. Graham Taylor had never suffered a relegation in his managerial career. Watford didn't have anything like the financial resources available to other Premier League clubs and over the summer they didn't spend any money in the transfer market, but I was sure that Graham knew what he was doing and that somehow Watford would find a way of surviving.

20

For me the two biggest thrills at Capital Gold Sport were covering Premier League games and reporting on Watford; now for the first time I got both on the same ticket.

Watford's first game in the Premier League was on Saturday, 7 August 1999 at home to Wimbledon, about whom Graham Taylor had spoken admiringly at the press day. 'Wimbledon have done magnificently. This was a club I think in '77 that got into the league, so they're not even 25 years a league club and they've spent 14 years of them in the Premier League. There's no comparison between Watford's six years even though we were in the top 12 and finished runners-up and Wimbledon's 14 years even though Wimbledon haven't finished high in the league, I mean they've won the FA Cup once for goodness sake, we only got to an FA Cup final. It would be absolutely foolish of me and I wouldn't do it, not to recognise this great achievement by Wimbledon Football Club.'

Ironically the 1999/2000 season proved to be the last for Wimbledon in the top flight as they won only seven games and finished 18th on 33 points.

Wimbledon at home looked like an opportunity for Watford to get off to a winning start. I shouldn't have been, but I was, surprised at the devastating effectiveness of the swift and well-constructed breakaway from which Carl Cort gave the visitors a tenth minute lead. Marcus Gayle sped down the left past two Watford players and crossed the ball. Two Wimbledon players had anticipated and kept up with Gayle's burst and John Hartson touched the ball on to Cort whose finish was too much for Chris Day in goal.

Only seven minutes later, though, I was proclaiming Watford's first goal in the Premier League. Richard Johnson found Tommy Mooney with a pass along the ground, and Mooney delicately flicked the ball into the path of Michel Ngonge who was racing into the box. Dean Blackwell came across to cover and denied a goalscoring opportunity by bringing down Ngonge. A sending off and a penalty, to be taken by the man with the cracking left foot, Peter Kennedy. Neil Sullivan dived to his right and got a foot to the ball which Kennedy fired straight but it wasn't enough to keep it out of the net. 'Watford can win this,' I thought.

But even ten men can score from a free kick and that's what Gayle did just before the half-hour mark, curling his shot over the wall and into the top corner, to put the Dons 2-1 ahead. The irony of the final 20 minutes of the game was that the man who beautifully made Watford's second equaliser then scored an own goal to hand Wimbledon victory. In the 71st minute Richard Johnson clipped the ball over the Wimbledon defence to leave Ngonge with a clear run on goal. As Sullivan came off his line Ngonge lifted the ball over the goalkeeper's head and into the net. 'Watford can win this,' I thought again. Surely they would lay siege to the Wimbledon goal in search of a winner. They didn't and instead in the 78th minute something happened that was so catastrophic it was a while before I was able to properly take in what I had seen. The ball was lofted gently into the Watford box towards Johnson who was under no particular pressure from an opponent. Johnson thought he would deal with the danger by chesting the ball back to Day. At the same time Day decided to come for the ball, not expecting Johnson to do what he did. A basic lack of communication between goalkeeper and midfielder, a Johnson own goal and Watford had lost their first game in the Premier League.

At least Watford were not bottom of the table after the opening match. That position was occupied by their next opponents, the previous season's Division One champions Sunderland, who had been beaten 4-0 at Chelsea on the opening day. Sunderland had run away with Division One, finishing with 105 points, 18 ahead of Bradford City, who finished in second place and were also promoted automatically.

It was a long midweek trip to the Stadium of Light but it was worth it. It was great to see Kevin Phillips in his new habitat; this was the season Phillips scored

30 league goals in 36 games. Four of those goals came against Watford and he got both in a 2-0 win at the Stadium of Light which was a magnificent venue. As I approached, it didn't look that different to other newly constructed grounds I'd been to like Derby County's Pride Park and Middlesbrough's Riverside Stadium. But once inside it came alive, with nearly every home fan wearing a Sunderland shirt. The thought that had gone into the construction of the stadium was such that the back of the work surface I was using was precisely in line with the near touchline. Exactly the right dramatic atmosphere was created when *Carmina Burana* by Carl Orff was played as the teams came out.

So it was two defeats from two games for Watford in their first Premier League season but at least Taylor hadn't lost his sense of humour. Watford's next match was Liverpool away and at the press conference after the Sunderland game he told reporters with a chuckle, 'We'll probably go and win at Anfield now.'

I was covering Wimbledon's 1-1 draw at home to Coventry City on the following Saturday when Watford went to Liverpool and won 1-0, Mooney scoring in the 14th minute against his boyhood club, for a famous victory – the first time the Hornets had ever won at Anfield.

I enjoyed hearing about the result and then moved on to the next game, at home to Bradford the following Saturday. Again Mooney scored in a 1-0 win, the result lifting Watford to ninth in the table and leaving me convinced that they were coming to terms with the Premier League and would be all right. Then three defeats with no goals scored followed, the second of them in a Monday night game at Leicester City. With Dominic Johnson commentating I was third man and was asked before the game to go and get a Watford interview. For obvious reasons players and managers could be reluctant to speak to reporters just before kick-off and I didn't want to disrupt the team's preparations. As Capital Gold Sport's Watford reporter I was expected to do the business and I waited for the Hornets' coach to arrive wondering if I would be able to fulfil my mission. It turned out that Taylor was as usual as good as gold, readily granting my request for an interview. I felt like a hunter-gatherer going off in search of food able to return home and feed his hungry family.

Leicester won 1-0 through a Muzzy Izzet goal, Martin O'Neill after the game accurately describing Emile Heskey as 'unplayable'.

A highlight of Watford's Premier League season came on 18 September 1999 at home to a Chelsea side managed by Gianluca Vialli who would later sit in the hotseat at Vicarage Road. Those three league defeats on the bounce since the win over Bradford saw the team slip to 15th in the table. With Vialli as manager the previous season Chelsea had finished third in the Premier League, their highest league finish since 1970 which had come during the golden era of Osgood, Cooke and Hudson. They came into the Watford game second in the table having conceded only two goals, winning four and drawing one of their first five matches.

Three days earlier Chelsea, in their debut season in the Champions League, had drawn 0-0 at home to AC Milan. Vialli made six changes for Vicarage Road, leaving Frank Lebouef, Dan Petrescu, Gus Poyet and Gianfranco Zola out of the starting line-up, but including two World Cup winners in Marcel Desailly and Didier Deschamps. Three players who struggled to make an impression at Stamford Bridge – Gabriele Ambrosetti and the Danes Jes Høgh and Bjarne Goldbæk – all started. Vialli had dubbed Ambrosetti the 'Italian Ryan Giggs' but he was ineffective against Watford.

By the time of the Chelsea game Watford had shelled out some money for a player by bringing in winger Nordin Wooter for a club-record £950,000 from Real Zaragoza. Wooter made his debut against Chelsea and in the second half went on a mazy run before passing to Paul Robinson who set up Allan Smart, making only his second appearance of the season, to drive the ball past Ed de Goey into the goal at the Rookery End, sending most in the crowd of 21,244 crazy. Smart's goal in the September sunshine revived memories of his clincher at Wembley on a similarly warm day the previous May. It was the first goal Chelsea had conceded that season when Desailly and Deschamps had both been on the pitch.

The win over Chelsea came at a price. Mooney, the match-winner in Watford's two victories before the Chelsea game, was injured shortly after coming on as a substitute and he didn't recover sufficiently to start a match until the final fixture of the season, on 14 May 2000 at home to Coventry City.

Watford's next win wasn't until after Christmas but there was still some fun to be had along the way and the signing of an enigmatic and mysterious Frenchman livened up the season. Xavier Gravelaine didn't stay long at Vicarage Road, but he didn't stay long anywhere. In an 18-year career as a striker he moved clubs 19 times. He had four spells at Paris Saint-Germain and played for France four times in 1992 and 1993. He joined Watford in November 1999 on a free transfer from PSG, signing a contract until the end of the season. For a while it appeared that he might be a catalyst and provide the spark to keep the team in the Premier League. With bulging eyes he had a slightly manic appearance and he played on the edge in a way that reminded me a little of Paolo Di Canio. He was creative and he could play, and right from the off he was in the thick of the action.

Gravelaine made his debut at home to Newcastle United on 20 November 1999 as part of a three-pronged forward line alongside Michel Ngonge and Gifton Noel-Williams. Within half an hour Gravelaine side-footed a chance over and early in the second half his lobbed pass forward led to Ngonge heading Watford in front. Five minutes later Nikos Dabizas shot an equaliser past Alec Chamberlain and it finished 1-1. The match gave me the opportunity to appreciate the sublime all round centre-forward play of England captain Alan Shearer, who in the first half had hit the post with a header.

Watford's game the following Saturday, at home to Sunderland for whom Kevin Phillips was the leading scorer in the Premier League at the time, was engrossing straight from the kick-off. Inside five minutes Gravelaine's pass was controlled on his chest by Ngonge who shot emphatically past Thomas Sørensen to give Watford the lead. There was a lot to admire about the team Peter Reid had built over the previous five years which had won Division One so convincingly the previous season. Sunderland had started 1999/2000 like a house on fire and they came to Vicarage Road in fourth place in the Premier League. They worked hard and moved the ball quickly often with one-touch football which is difficult to counteract because there is so little time to close down and challenge the player in possession. In Niall Quinn and Phillips, Sunderland had a front two who combined brilliantly. As someone who could remember the great Manchester City team of Joe Mercer and Malcolm Allison it was pleasing for me to see Nicky Summerbee wearing the number seven shirt and doing a decent imitation of his dad Mike.

Phillips, who was being touted as a possible partner for Shearer at Euro 2000, scored twice in the first half to put Sunderland ahead, the first a tame shot that had deflected off Robert Page to wrong foot Chamberlain. Phillips' second was a header from a Summerbee cross. In the second half Richard Johnson equalised with a penalty Sunderland were very unhappy about, Stefan Schwarz being booked for dissent, before Quinn set up Gavin McCann for the winner.

A pulsating game ended in controversy when man of the moment Gravelaine was sent off for a challenge on Darren Williams when it appeared that the Sunderland man was more culpable.

*

As the new millennium approached the old one still had surprises in store for me. On Boxing Day 1999 I was all set to go to White Hart Lane to report on Watford's noon kick-off against Spurs. I popped into the Capital Gold Sport studio in Leicester Square to wish everyone season's greetings and pick up the press pass to get me into the game. 'Didn't anyone tell you that you're covering Southampton versus Chelsea at The Dell?' Nope, no one had told me. 'Well, you are.' Fortunately, as it was Boxing Day the roads were clear and although he hadn't been starting regularly it would hopefully be another chance to watch Matt Le Tissier play. I made it to Southampton in time for the game, which also kicked off at noon.

Just as I rushed into the press box, sat down and started to digest the team sheet Rob Wotton, who had left Capital to become one of the original presenters on Sky Sports News in 1998, came up to say hello. As he did so he casually made a crucial observation which proved extremely helpful. He said to me, 'It's the first time it's ever happened.' I didn't want to show my ignorance by asking him what it was that had happened for the first time so guessing it was something to do with selection I looked closely at the team sheet and realised that the Chelsea starting line-up didn't include a single British player, obviously a big story.

The previous week Chris Sutton and Jon Harley had started for Chelsea against Leeds United but they were both missing from the starting XI against Southampton and there was also no Graeme Le Saux, Dennis Wise, Jody Morris or John Terry. The team was Ed De Goey; Albert Ferrer, Emerson Thome, Frank Lebouef, Celestine Babayaro; Dan Petrescu, Didier Deschamps, Roberto Di Matteo, Gus Poyet; Tore André Flo, Gabriele Ambrosetti.

Chelsea played well in the first half and established a two-goal lead, both scored by Flo: the first a low, angled shot after he'd been played in by Poyet, and for the second Deschamps was the provider. Flo was inches away from a hat-trick when he hit the post in the second half.

Southampton hadn't scored in the four league games they'd played prior to Boxing Day. Manager Dave Jones hadn't included Le Tissier in the starting line-up for any of those fixtures and Le Tissier was threatening to leave the club if he wasn't selected. Le Tissier was in from the start against Chelsea and was a big influence without being able to turn the game in Saints' favour. In the 14th minute with the score 0-0 Le Tissier crashed a free kick against the post and in the second half he sparked a revival by the home side with his precise, dangerous deliveries. First a Le Tissier free kick was headed across goal by Francis Benali for Trond Egil Soltvedt to hit the post then ten minutes later another Le Tissier free kick was converted by Kevin Davies. Chelsea withstood late Southampton pressure to win.

Vialli explained after the game that he only realised his side didn't include a single British player after he'd picked it.

*

I saw Le Tissier in action again two days later at Vicarage Road as Xavier Gravelaine, available again after suspension, returned to the Watford team against Southampton. Without a win since beating Chelsea three months previously and in 19th, three places below Southampton, this looked like an opportunity for three points Watford had to take if they were going to have any chance of staying up. The match produced great drama and the outcome was in doubt right up until the final whistle. Alec Chamberlain kept the score level with a sharp early reaction save from a Davies header before Watford took the lead in the 18th minute. Neil Cox crossed and David Perpetuini won a header on the edge of the box. He knocked the ball up into the air and it fell kindly in front of him on his left foot about ten yards out with no covering defender between him and the goal. As Paul Jones came out and hesitated, Perpetuini drilled the ball past the Southampton keeper.

Watford's second goal 15 minutes later came through exactly the sort of direct, effective, decisive football Taylor wanted his team to play, which they weren't able to replicate often enough in that Premier League season. It was also Gravelaine's finest moment in a Watford shirt. Chamberlain half-volleyed a clearance long, straight on to the head of Ngonge inside the Southampton half. Ngonge nodded the ball infield into the stride of Micah Hyde who slid a beautiful first-time pass to Gravelaine just inside the box. Gravelaine took a few touches with his left foot to control the ball and evade the challenge of two Southampton defenders. He cut back on to his right foot and with Jones and four Southampton defenders between him and the goal he smashed a shot high into the net before turning and running backwards flapping his arms around in celebration like a demented pigeon.

It was 2-0 at half-time but that lead was wiped out in three second-half minutes. First Davies beat Page on the right and crossed for Luis Boa Morte to fire past Chamberlain into the corner of the goal. Then the roles were reversed as a Boa Morte cross was turned in by Davies. If Gravelaine's first goal had been a beauty his second, scored four minutes after Saints had equalised, was less photogenic but it proved to be the winner. Again a Cox cross from the right led to a goal. This time it was deep into the Southampton box and their defence could only deal with it by nodding the ball out to the edge of the penalty area where Gravelaine met it first time with a scuffed shot. As it made its way towards goal Ngonge, standing in front of Jones thus unsighting the Southampton goalkeeper, dodged out of the way and turned to see the ball end up in the net.

In a frantic finish to the game Hyde cleared off the line to deny Southampton an equaliser.

*

Watford's next game, on 3 January 2000, was a dream gig for a reporter as my preview wrote itself. Football reporters love to talk about 'firsts'. This was Watford's first trip to Pride Park; it would be Watford's and Derby County's first game of the new millennium; and Derby were looking for their first home win since October and first home goal since November. On top of that some 30 years previously the opposing managers, Graham Taylor and Jim Smith, had played together at Lincoln City. You only had to look at the positions in the Premier League of the two clubs to see the importance of the game. Watford were 19th in the table, Derby one place above them.

I always used to like it when the first goal of the day was scored in the game I was covering. The show would usually start at 2pm and then at 3pm after an hour's build-up JP would begin commentating on the match he was covering. But goals were what made the show tick and I loved it when before any goals had gone in at the games we were covering I was able to shout down the line to King Darren in the studio to let him know that there had been a goal at my match so that he could tell JP who would cross over to me straight away for a report in which I would give the score and the scorer and describe the goal. The first goal of the day was an ice-breaker and after that the show was really up and running.

Before the first matches of 2000 kicked off I was in an optimistic mood after Watford's dramatic win over Southampton, thinking that it could be the start of a climb to Premier League safety, and I was dreaming of informing the Capital Gold Sport listeners that the Hornets had scored the first Premier League goal of the new millennium. Instead I ended up telling them at about two minutes past three that they had been the first to concede.

Belgian international Branko Strupar had been bought by Derby in December 1999 for £3m from Genk, for whom he'd scored 106 times in 168 appearances, to score the goals to keep them in the Premier League. He made a pretty good start to his Rams career and was making his second start against Watford. Derby began on the front foot and in the second minute Rory Delap, full of purposeful running throughout, pulled the ball back from the byline on the right. The Watford defence failed to deal with the cross under pressure from a couple of Derby players, and the ball fell loose about ten yards out to Strupar who smashed it into the net.

While playing for Genk, Strupar had been dubbed 'the Belgian Beckham' and in the second half he got the opportunity to show why he'd been given that nickname. Watford seemed to be unnerved by their inability to get a foothold in the game and in the 72nd minute Page bundled over Marvin Robinson to concede a free kick about 25 yards from goal. Strupar bent the ball round the wall to clinch the win and hand Watford a demoralising defeat.

*

Watford's next Premier League game also ended in defeat but not as dishearteningly or unexpectedly. Twenty-year-old Michael Owen hadn't played back in August when Watford had won 1-0 at Anfield and he'd missed Liverpool's first match of

2000, away to Tottenham Hotspur, due to injury. Watford needed the points in their survival bid and it was a big game for Liverpool as well as they were already out of both domestic cups. Owen needed to get in a good run of appearances and prove his fitness and form for Euro 2000. He was back against Watford and although he didn't score he did just about everything else. His composed pass picked out Patrik Berger who gave Liverpool a tenth-minute lead after Robert Page and Steve Palmer had got in each other's way in the box and both had failed to clear the ball. Owen then brought a save out of Chamberlain with a low shot and hit the bar with another effort, all this in the first 35 minutes. I started to pen a half-time report with Liverpool 1-0 up but two goals in the last five minutes of the half caused a frantic re-write.

The 1999/2000 season was when Steven Gerrard first started to play regularly for Liverpool as a central midfielder and he lined up at Vicarage Road alongside Dietmar Hamann. Gerrard hadn't yet been given responsibility for free kicks and it was the German who took one about 30 yards from goal in the 41st minute. The shot beat the wall and a very slight deflection by David Thompson took it past Chamberlain into the net. Three minutes later Xavier Gravelaine showed his class, taking a crossfield Paul Robinson pass on his chest, evading the challenge of three Liverpool defenders and nudging the ball back into the path of Richard Johnson who side-footed the ball in from 25 yards, to give a half-time score of Watford 1 Liverpool 2. I'd hardly sat down after my interval cup of tea when I was on air describing Watford's equaliser.

At Graham Taylor's insistence Watford had continued to keep a tight rein on the purse strings in their first season in the Premier League but they did splash out a club-record £1.5m on Iceland international striker Heidar Helguson, signed from Lillestrøm SK. Helguson was making his debut against Liverpool, playing alongside Gravelaine, and in the 46th minute the Iceman cometh, scoring with the type of brave header I was to see him score from many times. David Perpetuini swung a free kick from the right with his left foot into space about eight yards from goal, tempting Sander Westerveld to come out and attempt to intercept the ball. In these situations Helguson could have had a steam train coming at him at full speed and he would still have flung himself at the ball and got his head on it, leaving the train smashed to tiny pieces.

From 2-0 down to 2-2 at home to Liverpool early in the second half, the possibility of a double over the Anfield club was on. Watford battled but Liverpool's quality started to tell. They came close when Owen received the ball in the box with his back to goal, turned and ran across the penalty area before having his shot cleared off the line. Then in the 71st minute Owen, who had drifted out to the right, made ground and found Vladimír Šmicer, who had come off the bench, just outside the penalty area. After the Czech international had fired in the winner, Owen, already suffering from repeated hamstring injuries, was taken off by Gérard Houllier as a precaution.

Watford were still 19th in the Premier League after the Liverpool game. Defeat at Bradford City the following Saturday saw them drop to rock bottom, the position the bookies had forecast they would end the season in before a ball had been kicked.

Geoffrey Richmond had taken over as Bradford chairman in 1994 and had promised top-flight football within five years. In his first full season as manager Paul Jewell, in his mid-30s, made that dream come true as in 1998/99 City finished second in Division One to win promotion and return to the top league after an absence of 77 years.

A famous final-day 1-0 win over Liverpool through a David Weatherall header would later see Bradford move into 17th place and avoid the drop but on 22 January they were just one place above Watford. The previous week they had lost 2-0 at Sheffield Wednesday and Jewell was being heavily criticised by the club's supporters. I commented in my pre-match scene-setter that as far as Watford supporters were concerned Taylor could have taken them into the Ryman League and still kept his job.

Whatever the mood in the Valley Parade stands the vibes in the press room were excellent and the pre-match hospitality included a magnificent curry with rice and naan bread, on a par with any I'd eaten in Brick Lane. The whole experience was so good that I wrote to Richmond to thank him and I received a nice acknowledgement in return from the chairman.

Bradford, who hadn't lost at home since October, were not as generous on the pitch and for the second week running Watford lost 3-2. Jewell had brought back Stuart McCall to Valley Parade to captain the side and the 35-year-old produced a dominant performance in midfield. Just one year younger than McCall, Peter Beagrie scored the opening goal in the 25th minute when a penalty was awarded for a Page challenge on Dean Windass despite huge Watford protests. Helguson and Gravelaine played a delightful one-two on the edge of the City box before Helguson crossed and Micah Hyde slid home an equaliser against the run of play in the 33rd minute. It was a tantalising glimpse of what might have been if Helguson and Gravelaine had continued together up front but the Bradford game proved to be the Frenchman's last for Watford as he disappeared as mysteriously as he had arrived, to Le Havre. For the second week running I was forced to hastily re-write my half-time report as a long range shot from Gareth Whalley, preferred by Jewell to Neil Redfearn, bobbled in front of Chamberlain and went in off the post after the Watford keeper had got an indecisive touch.

Watford began to play after Andy O'Brien had given Bradford a 3-1 lead with a header from a Beagrie corner in the opening minutes of the second half. Four minutes from the end Helguson scored for the second week running to set up a hectic finish but Bradford held on for the win.

*

Reporting on Premier League matches was a bit like appearing on *The Generation Game*, except that instead of furry toys passing by in front of my eyes on a conveyer belt it was highly talented footballers. Next up was Paul Merson, dubbed 'the Magic Man' on Capital Gold Sport during his time at Arsenal. He was now with Aston Villa, to whom I saw Watford lose 4-0 at Villa Park on 5 February 2000, all four goals scored in the second half. In scoring two of those Merson showed exactly why the nickname had been bestowed upon him. For the first he went on a diagonal run to the edge of the right-hand side of the penalty area, forced wide by a Watford defender. Chris Day, recalled in goal in place of Alec Chamberlain, was on the edge of his six-yard box and with rare skill and technique Merson floated a delicate chip over him into the far corner of the net. The shot was so gentle that it took forever to go in but as soon as the ball left Merson's foot everyone in the crowd of 27,747 knew that the ball was going to end up in the net. So too did Day but the keeper had been taken completely by surprise and the trajectory of the ball left him powerless to do anything to stop it, and he didn't even attempt an intervention. The ball floated up like a balloon and having passed over Day it gently came down and into the goal. In a game in which goals are so often the product of pace and power, this was stunning in its subtlety and delicacy.

For his second goal, Merson demonstrated a different but also very difficult technique. Alan Wright nodded a Benito Carbone cross into the box and with his back to goal Merson controlled the ball on his chest, swivelled and volleyed the ball into the corner of the goal.

Steve Stone had shot Villa into the lead and the Watford defence left Richard Walker unmarked to head in Wright's cross for the fourth. Again Watford only began to compete when the game was beyond them.

21

The Capital Gold Sport approach to broadcasting was for commentators and reporters to be bright and positive. Pete Simmons explained to us once in a pre-season meeting that listeners might not be hanging on to our every word but they wanted to hear a pleasant, harmonious sound emanating from the radio. The instruction from the studio was to be 'nice and up' when giving reports which I didn't have any trouble delivering most of the time because I loved reporting on match after match for the station and fitting in with the broadcasting style and ethos came naturally as reporting on games was intrinsically exhilarating. My role required me to convey to the listeners the excitement I was experiencing and the thrills I was witnessing at football grounds around the country, from St James Park in Exeter to St James' Park in Newcastle, from Carrow Road to Ashton Gate.

There were times though, particularly during Watford's 1999/2000 season in the Premier League as the inevitability of relegation drew closer, when it was more challenging to fulfil the remit. Being 'nice and up' when giving a report on a Watford defeat which had brought relegation a step closer wasn't easy but I had to forget my allegiance and remember that it is a reporter's duty to be objective.

When Watford travelled to The Dell on 15 April 2000 to face Southampton, who they had beaten at Vicarage Road in the final game of the old millennium, they were still rooted to the bottom of the table. I had reported two weeks previously after a 4-2 defeat at Everton that Watford 'now have the look of a side waiting for their relegation to be confirmed'. A week later, after a 0-0 draw at home to Derby County, I had said that 'Watford were playing for pride' but despite that relegation had not been confirmed mathematically.

Watford had been in the last-chance saloon so many times that season they were as drunk as lords and the trip to The Dell was just one more visit to that mythical hostelry.

It did seem like the end at Southampton when I gave my full-time report on a game which Watford lost 2-0, conceding a soft goal in each half. In just the fourth minute Wayne Bridge played a ball into Kevin Davies, no challenge came in from his marker and Davies turned and shot low past Alec Chamberlain. In the second half Watford allowed Saints substitute Marians Pahars, at 5ft 8in the smallest player on the pitch, a free header from a Matt Le Tissier corner to score the second.

I finished my considered report by saying, 'Watford can't go down this weekend but it's a case of "when" rather than "if" as far as the drop is concerned.'

*

The 'when' came the following Saturday, the day before Watford lost 3-2 at home to Arsenal. Bradford City won 1-0 at seventh-placed Sunderland to move up to 17th in the Premier League. With five games to play Watford couldn't catch Bradford or anyone else and were relegated.

On the last Saturday in April the 3-2 defeat at home to champions Manchester United was the story of much of Watford's season. They pushed a superior side all the way with their effort and commitment but lost when four minutes from the end player of the season Robert Page's back-pass failed to carry and Jordi Cruyff nipped in to score the winner.

It was the seventh game of the season that ended 3-2, with Watford losing six of them. They were entertaining and competitive matches but Watford were not quite able to come out on top.

There was a nice touch of humour and irreverence at the Riverside for Watford's last away match of the season, on 6 May. The supporters had got behind the players, encouraging them all season, and on a not-so-warm day they wore wigs and t-shirts with 'WATFORD – WE'RE OUT OF YOUR LEAGUE' printed on them, chanted for the whole game, partied and blew on kazoos, painting a colourful yellow picture to celebrate the joy of supporting a smallish football club with a big heart and demonstrating that life would go on despite relegation.

For Middlesbrough fans there was humour on the pitch as well albeit unintentional with another of the defensive errors that had proved so costly to Watford that season gifting the home side the lead just before the half-hour mark. David Perpetuini's back-pass fell short and Chris Day's attempted clearance rebounded off Robbie Stockdale and into the net. Again Watford battled and this time they came away with a point, Darren Ward turning in Heidar Helguson's low cross in the second half.

The season ended with a win, just Watford's sixth, as Helguson's overhead kick in the first half was enough to beat Coventry City who finished the season in 14th without an away win throughout 1999/2000.

*

During the campaign Graham Taylor was voted the 18th best manager of all-time in a poll of fellow bosses. It was some accolade and came from his peers who acknowledged the achievements of a man not always fully appreciated by the media and the general football public. Despite his strengths Taylor, surprised at how the gap between the top two divisions in English football had grown, could not keep Watford up and he was unable to replicate the top-flight success he had brought to the club in the 1980s.

Taylor had taken over as manager again after they'd finished the 1996/97 season 13th in Division Two. He'd won promotion in each of the following two seasons to give the club their first appearance in the Premier League. It's no wonder really that Watford finished bottom in 1999/2000; they simply didn't have the quality of player required to stay up and were unable to go out and buy them. Of the 29 players who started for Watford in that Premier League season ten had won Division Two in 1997/98. The step up was too much. Of the 29 players only six – Des Lyttle, Tommy Mooney, Tommy Smith, Paul Robinson, Alec Chamberlain and Heidar Helguson – ever played in the top division again and none of them set the world alight. So you could conclude that if it hadn't been for Taylor it's probable that the vast majority of the 29 players would never have tasted the champagne of the Premier League, never tested themselves against Alex Ferguson's Manchester United, Arsène Wenger's Arsenal, Gérard Houllier's Liverpool and the rest, never competed with Thierry Henry, Rio Ferdinand, Paul Scholes, some of the greats of the Premier League era.

For me it didn't turn out the way I wanted it to or the way I thought it would but I had been living happily in a fantasy world and I could accept relegation. Before the start of the season I'd had a bet on Watford to win the Premier League but, as I told Robert Page at the next pre-season press day, 'I bottled it, I did it each way.' I was a million miles away from being right, or to be precise 20 places. But I'd been given the chance to dream and, sitting in a Covent Garden pub in a euphoric and drunken state with Bill Leslie and Dominic Johnson after Watford's Division One play-off final win over Bolton Wanderers, anything had seemed possible.

I'd seen some amazing footballers during the season – Alan Shearer, Paul Merson, Matt Le Tissier, Michael Owen – and although they'd all been playing against Watford and had contributed to Watford's relegation the memory of the greatness of those players lives far longer than the feeling of disappointment which starts to dissipate after the final whistle has blown in a game which has ended in defeat.

*

Graham Taylor had said that Watford might have to accept being a 'yo-yo' club and at the start of the 2000/01 season it looked like they were on course to bounce back at the first attempt. They had spent relatively little in the Premier League but to try to secure an instant return in August 2000 they shelled out a combined £3.5m to bring in Allan Nielsen (£2.25m) and Espen Baardsen (£1.25m) from Tottenham Hotspur. Both were looking for regular first-team football and Taylor sold them the dream of playing in the Premier League.

With the new signings and the players they had added while in the Premier League, on paper Watford were stronger than when they had been in Division One previously and had been promoted. They started the season like they meant business, going on a 15-match unbeaten run which stretched from 12 August to 4

November and included a club record equaling run of seven wins on the bounce. The supporters were confident and before a ball was kicked in the 2-1 opening-day win at Huddersfield Town they were singing 'we are going up.'

For me a victory at Blackburn Rovers on 12 September was the highlight of the unbeaten run and extraordinary in several ways. Firstly, it was played during the height of the 'fuel crisis' of 2000. Demand for a reduction in government fuel taxes led to protests and blockades and petrol shortages at garages up and down the country. It being a midweek game, I had no option but to drive from London to Blackburn and back. When I set off I didn't have enough fuel in the tank for the return journey but it was a match I couldn't even contemplate missing, I had to get there and hope that somehow I would be able to get back. Fortunately, on the way home I found a petrol station on the M1 that was open and had supplies so I made it home OK.

By that time my head was full of thoughts of a seven-goal thriller which Watford had edged. The win was against a very good Blackburn side whose season ended in promotion and which included in its line-up Stig Inge Bjørnebye, David Dunn, Jason McAteer, Damien Duff and Henning Berg, all internationals who each played many games in the top flight in their careers. Also starting for Rovers were Craig Short, Gary Flitcroft, Nathan Blake and Matt Jansen. Blackburn had won all three of their home league games and Blake and Jansen had three goals each from five matches.

In a stunning first half Blackburn built up a two-goal lead inside 17 minutes through Dunn and Blake but Micah Hyde inspired a comeback, scoring twice with Helguson getting one as well to send Watford in 3-2 up at half-time. Tommy Mooney, captain in the absence of Robert Page, headed Watford 4-2 up from a Paul Robinson corner. Blake scored his second of the game in the 87th minute to set up a storming finish but it ended Blackburn 3 Watford 4. Blackburn manager Graeme Souness was furious in his press conference after the game that the referee had missed a foul in the build-up to one of Watford's first-half goals. He showed his annoyance by thumping the wall behind him, which adjoined the officials' changing room, with his fist.

As I shot back down the motorway, I was looking at the bigger picture. It seemed to me that if Watford could turn round a game in such thrilling fashion, at the home of an excellent previously unbeaten and highly fancied side, their prospects for the remainder of the season looked very good.

The bookies agreed with me. The following Saturday they made-free scoring Watford the Nationwide League banker of the day at home to Crewe Alexandra, who had yet to score a goal or win a single point away from home. Again, Crewe provided attractive opposition as Watford won comfortably 3-0.

But it wasn't to be that season. The 15-match unbeaten run ended with a 3-1 home defeat to Sheffield Wednesday on 7 November 2000 which was the first in a run of eight games which resulted in one draw and seven defeats and saw Watford supporters booing their side off the pitch at the end of home fixtures. In the final game of that sequence, on Boxing Day, Watford were taken apart 5-0 by a Fulham side who ended the season as Division One champions with 101 points, 32 ahead of Watford. Fulham, managed by Jean Tigana, started 2000/01 with 11 straight wins and were top of the table for virtually the whole season. Barry Hayles with a hat-trick and Louis Saha were scorers against Watford and their side also featured Steve Finnan, Rufus Brevett, Andy Melville, Chris Coleman, Bjarne Goldbæk and Lee Clark. The defeat left Watford in eighth, one place higher than where they finished the season.

While promotion was still a possibility, in March 2001 Graham Taylor announced that he would be retiring at the end of the season. Before the final day Watford announced that Taylor's successor would be Gianluca Vialli.

*

I was excited by Vialli's appointment and so was Watford chairman Elton John, who called it 'one of the most stunning coups we have pulled off.' The good vibes created by the ambitious appointment were enhanced when Vialli said at the press conference, held on 2 May 2001, to introduce him as Watford manager, 'I want to take Watford to the next level. This club wants to belong in the Premier League. I will do my best to deliver. It will be a challenge but we have an exciting time ahead.'

Vialli had been an elite player and a serial winner in Italy and he had continued in the same vein after becoming, in February 1998 aged 33, Chelsea's player-manager. When Vialli took over Chelsea were already in the semi-finals of the League Cup and the quarter-finals of the European Cup Winners' Cup and they went on to win both competitions. That season they finished fourth in the Premier League. Winning the Cup Winners' Cup qualified them to face Champions League winners Real Madrid in the 1998 UEFA Super Cup, a one-off match they won 1-0. At the end of the 1998/99 season Vialli retired as a player so that his sole focus was on management. In 1999/2000 Chelsea finished third in the Premier League and Vialli added another trophy to his CV with a 1-0 victory over Aston Villa in the FA Cup final. Vialli won his fifth trophy in charge of Chelsea when they beat Manchester United in the Charity Shield just before the start of 2000/01. Despite this success, following a poor start to the season Chelsea dispensed with Vialli's services after five games.

I will always try to be positive about my club and I found it easy to be optimistic when Vialli was appointed. His record at Chelsea was impressive and my thinking was that he was such a big and respected name in football that he would attract good players to Watford. I thought that Vialli would build a strong side well able to compete in Division One.

Capital Gold Sport sent me to the first game involving Vialli's Watford, a pre-season friendly played on 14 July 2001 away to Aylesbury United. The shaven-headed, stylish Vialli dressed in a cream suit walked across the pitch before the game and received a rapturous reception from the Watford supporters. The sun shone, the Hornets looked impressive playing a new style of passing football, and they won 2-1, Heidar Helguson and Dominic Foley scoring the goals. After the game I conducted the first radio interview with the new manager, welcoming him to Watford. In my optimistic state I allowed myself to overlook the fact that at the time Aylesbury, a good little club, were a Ryman League Division One side.

Division One of the Football League was a slightly different proposition. Watford's first fixture of the 2001/02 season was away to Manchester City who following their relegation from the Premier League had appointed Kevin Keegan as manager. It was Keegan's first job since he had resigned as England's boss, when he had acknowledged with typical and engaging honesty that the task had been beyond him. Pre-match, Manchester City v Watford was billed as a clash between two likely promotion contenders. Watford started the game with five of Vialli's new signings – full-back Patrick Blondeau who had previously had an unsuccessful spell at Sheffield Wednesday; centre-back Filippo Galli who was a top, top player and had won Serie A five times and the UEFA Champions League three times at AC Milan, but at the age of 38 was nearing the end of his career; his fellow central defender Ramon Vega; forward Marcus Gayle who had been a stalwart at Wimbledon in the Premier League but never reached the same heights at Watford; and midfielder Stephen Hughes whose time at Vicarage Road was disrupted by injury. Of the players brought in by Vialli a transfer fee was paid only for Gayle, £1m to Glasgow Rangers. The rest of Vialli's budget, which was substantial for Watford at the time, went on player wages.

City won 3-0 and went on to become Division One champions that season, scoring 108 league goals in doing so.

I went to Hillsborough, which hosted matches during the 1966 World Cup, twice in the 2001/02 season to report on matches between Sheffield Wednesday and Watford. I was astonished on both occasions but for different reasons.

The first visit was on Wednesday, 19 December 2001 for a League Cup quarter-final. It was an interesting stage of the competition and to reach the semi-finals would have been most welcome. At the time Watford were in mid-table but had won their previous two league matches and were unbeaten in five. Sheffield Wednesday were 21st in Division One with one win in their past seven matches. It was not a game in which I would have expected a manager to experiment but to my surprise Vialli changed the shape of the team and the personnel, leaving leading scorer Tommy Smith on the bench. The outcome was a disjointed, unconvincing Watford display and a resounding 4-0 win for the Owls. The half-time soup in the press room was excellent though.

My second visit was on Saturday, 16 February 2002. I reported on the game, which Sheffield Wednesday won 2-1, and then went to hear Vialli talk to the press. The main story was that a couple of days previously Watford had announced that Espen Baardsen, Marcus Gayle, Pierre Issa, Allan Nielsen and Ramon Vega had been transfer-listed. When I initially heard the news, I assumed that this step had been taken for financial reasons but Vialli explained to reporters at Hillsborough that the decision was football-related. This was a stunning revelation. Gayle, Issa and Vega had been Vialli signings only the previous summer and I had presumed were an integral part of his plan to return Watford to the top flight. To learn that after a little over six months since signing them he wanted to ditch them did not make sense to me. The decision was perplexing because it seemed to me that Vialli, having made a plan, was very quickly giving up on it. It was big news and even though I had already given my considered piece I rushed back to my point in the press box to pass this extra information on to Capital Gold Sport's listeners.

Watford finished the season 14th in the table, losing four of their last six matches, and then it all kicked off.

In June 2000 ONdigital, rebranded in July 2001 as ITV Digital, had agreed a £315m deal with the Football League to broadcast matches during the 2001/02 season. Watford factored the money they were due to receive as their share into their calculations when they decided on the budget to make available to Vialli. ITV Digital never got anywhere near the number of subscribers it needed to make a profit. By 2002 it was said to be losing £1m a day and on 27 March 2002 it went into administration, subsequently going into liquidation with debts of £1.25bn.

Football clubs, including Watford, took drastic action to compensate for the loss of budgeted income. The steps taken by Watford included, just over a year after announcing his appointment, terminating the contract of Vialli. He had signed a three-year deal and was disappointed not to be given more time. Earlier the same week first team coach Ray Wilkins and several members of the backroom staff had been axed. Filippo Galli would no longer grace the Watford side and he was released at about the same time. Shortly after that terms were agreed for the departure of Ramon Vega, one of the highest earners at the club.

*

It was left to Ray Lewington to pick up the pieces. Lewington had been reserve team manager during Vialli's tenure and following the Italian's departure and a one-month spell as caretaker manager in July 2002 he was given the job on a permanent basis.

Following the collapse of ITV Digital and the failure of the Vialli experiment the main aim was the survival of Watford as a going concern. Thoughts of promotion back to the Premier League were put on hold. Lewington's remit was, despite considerable constraints, to ensure the continuation of the club's participation in Division One. The target over a three-year period was to reduce the annual wage bill from £14m to £3m.

In August 2002 Watford sold their ground for £6m and the following month the crisis reached a point at which the club announced a share issue to raise capital and a campaign to encourage supporters to donate money. Watford were close to going into administration but were saved from that fate when in September 2002 the majority of the players and some office staff agreed to a 12 per cent wage deferral. A new found unity developed and on 28 September 2002, a few days after the deferral had been agreed, the team came from behind to win 2-1 against Sheffield United at Bramall Lane through a Neil Cox penalty and a goal from Heidar Helguson.

In 2002/03 Lewington comfortably achieved the objective of keeping Watford in Division One and indeed the 13th-placed finish was one position higher than it had been the previous season under Vialli.

The most memorable moments for me in 2002/03 came in the two domestic cup competitions.

22

The 1960s was a decade of strange contrasts in the behaviour of the youth subcultures that were around in England at that time. The hippies espoused peace, love and understanding while Mods and Rockers took part in violent clashes in seaside resorts in the southern part of the country and skinheads attached themselves to football clubs and fought their battles with each other on the terraces of grounds while matches were being played as a way of trying to assert their superiority over each other.

I became aware of football hooliganism during the first season I watched Watford, 1968/69. The following season after promotion to Division Two the fighting became more frequent and intense as bigger clubs with larger followings visited Vicarage Road. As a 13-year-old starting out on my journey as a football supporter who had yet to develop meaningful critical faculties, I found the fights between rival groups fascinating and for me for a while watching them was part of the matchday entertainment.

At first the police were taken by surprise and struggled to deal with the phenomenon. For a while there was little or no segregation and supporters of both clubs congregated in the same end. A game used to play out which involved the supporters of the away club infiltrating the home end, often quietly and unobtrusively. Once inside they would form a group before revealing their true identity and they would then try to seize territory by rushing the home supporters and kicking lumps out of them. When the charge took place, a gap would open up on the terraces and the police would intervene and try to keep the rival supporters apart. Each flurry of fighting would last no more than a few minutes and when things settled down again there would be a line of police separating the two groups and you could see whether either set had managed to gain any ground, before it all began again. The number of supporters on each side would reduce because the police would evict some of those involved in the fighting. The ultimate objective was to force the departure of the home supporters from the home end and for the away supporters to 'take' that end. If this was achieved by West Ham supporters at Arsenal, say, they would crow about it for weeks by chanting repeatedly 'we took the North Bank!'

At Watford the fighting took place in the Rookery End which was where I watched matches. I was drawn to that part of the ground because it had the most atmosphere and it was where the chanting emanated. I liked the sense of danger and excitement that standing in the Rookery End generated.

At that time my friends at school were crazy about football and we wore the same clothes – Dr Martens, red socks, Ben Sherman shirts, Harrington jacket – and listened to the same music – ska acts like Dave and Ansel Collins, the Pioneers and Desmond Dekker – as the skinheads. But we referred to the people who participated in football violence as 'boneheads' and while we observed and discussed what was happening, we didn't have any inclination to get involved. I would always watch the violence from a safe distance. I found it compelling and when the fighting started, I would often be drawn to watch it rather than the match. My interest in it was a short-lived, adolescent phase that only lasted a couple of years. Pretty soon anyway segregation was introduced inside the ground so that away supporters were no longer able to freely gain access to the home end.

I got an insight into why one particular person became a football hooligan, and what it was like to be involved, after I moved to North Kensington in 1989. Kenny was mates with members of the Six-Pack and was a well-known local character. His family had a fruit and vegetable stall on Portobello Road market. Kenny was a *bon viveur*, someone who didn't go home until everywhere was shut which meant quite a few late nights because places around Portobello didn't tend to close early. On one occasion he was out drinking and one by one his mates drifted off leaving him alone. At about 2am he found himself in a West Indian haunt, the only white person in the joint. As soon as he entered everyone stopped talking and stared at him. The previous day the West Indies had been all out for 52 in a cricket match and to break the ice Kenny shouted, 'Fifty-two all out!' Everyone in the place fell about laughing and Kenny had made a roomful of friends.

As well as being funny Kenny was articulate and self-aware and one day he sat down and told me about his days as a football hooligan.

'My mum and dad split up when I was young. I used to live with me dad. He used to like a good drink and really I brought meself up. Going to the football was my get-out. I used to really look forward to going to QPR, home or away, whoever it was. If the crew was too big we had to leave it out, but if we could half have a little shot we did have the fight.

'Years ago the old bill didn't know what to do and we did. When it was good we sorted it out. On the coach we knew what we were going to do. There was a coach, a 56-seater, 56 people knowing what they were going to do, what they had to do. In London, it was different. You'd make your own way there, meet in a pub out of the way. We'd march there and if it got too heavy we wouldn't have it. Five or ten of us out of the mob would take the decision.

'If you get done, you get done. No one runs, that was half the idea, no one runs. If anyone didn't fancy it we'd say, "Well, it's a bit heavy here." Just say for instance it's Arsenal, Tottenham, Chelsea, some of the big clubs. They've got their own boys. We used to suss it out first. If it was too heavy, we wouldn't do it. If we had half a chance, even going in their end, causing a disturbance and getting slung out then walking round the pitch, escorted, we'd do it. We did that at Bristol Rovers and Carlisle and a few other pitches. We'd be getting marched round the pitch by the touchline while the game's going on and the home fans are going, "There's QPR!" We used to say we didn't know which end we were going in. All bollocks really.'

It turned out that like me, Kenny had been part of the 27,968 crowd at Vicarage Road for the Division Two match between Watford and Queens Park Rangers on 20 August 1969. 'I remember the Watford game very well because we planned to go in their end, without a doubt. Ten or 15 of us went in their end, made out we were Watford supporters and once we got in there, as soon as QPR came on the pitch, it kicked off. We sort of half threatened a few people, I'm not being flash but we opened up a bit of space and stood there. We slapped a few people. Watford were not a lot really.'

Kenny found some sort of fulfilment through his exploits as a football hooligan.

'A lot of QPR fans used to go up to the end where they was told to. There was a few of us who'd go where we wanted to go. That was basically what we used to do. We would definitely miss out any old bill, any escort from station to ground and from ground to station. We would slip away from there and just have a row.

'To take someone's end is like scoring a goal at Wembley. You've got the wankers at one end and the fighters at the other. They're looking at you more than the team. If you took an end that was the best. To take someone's end, run someone out, kick a few on the way and stand there and hold it. That was one of the things, to try to hold it.

'There were people coming in the turnstile to try and take it back, but to stand there for 90 minutes and hold it, then walk out with no police escort was definitely one of the best feelings ever, better even than having a bunk-up. Well, almost!'

It might seem as though it was a jungle out there in the world of hooliganism but Kenny and his mates did abide by their own code of ethics.

'I want to emphasise that if there was say ten of them, 30 of us, we'd leave them alone. If there was 30 against 30 fight them. But if you used to go up north they'd kick your head in one-handed. If there were 20 of them they'd kick your head in if you were on your own. If you used to get run, get straggled along or get caught they'd kick your head in ten- or 15-handed.

'I always used to emphasise and tell the boys, "If there's two or three of them get caught say, 'You're a ****, you got caught, you can be done. Next time get your boys around and we'll have it.'"

'I've never carried a tool in me life, I always fight with me hands, although I've been cut a few times with a tool. Nowadays it gets a bit harder, you talk about people squirting people up, cutting people. People who don't go in the grounds, wait outside for people, then I don't agree with that at all. I think if you're going to have a fight, have a fight, ten on to ten, 20 on to 15, have a go.'

By the time I got to know him Kenny had moved on and his days as a football hooligan were well in the past. 'These days I take my young nephew and his mates to see Rangers and I wouldn't like to see them do what I've done.'

*

The fixture involving Watford which generated the most violence was the one against Luton Town. The animosity between the two sets of supporters increased during the 1968/69 season as both clubs went for promotion from Division Three. The game that season at Kenilworth Road, on 30 April 1969, which I didn't attend, was one of the most violent in the history of the fixture. On a night that was described by Luton manager Alec Stock as 'bloody, belligerent and brutal', players lost their heads and three – Barry Endean and Tom Walley of Watford and Luton's Alan Slough – were sent off as the Hatters won 2-1. The violence on the pitch was mirrored off it and over 100 people were injured as supporters fought in the ground and outside.

On 10 September 2002 Watford played Luton at Vicarage Road in the first round of the League Cup and I was there to cover it. By then the fixture had been dubbed the 'M1 Derby' and the rivalry between the supporters was as intense as ever. Given the history of the fixture, you didn't need to be a soothsayer to predict that there would be trouble that evening. Sure enough, as kick-off approached, not long after Capital Gold Sport had begun broadcasting at 7pm, about 50 Luton supporters left their seats in the Vicarage Road end, jumped over advertising hoardings and began to goad and threaten Watford supporters sitting in the adjacent Rous Stand. This stand was occupied by fans, including children and families, with no interest in fighting or confrontation and they were clearly intimidated and disturbed by what was happening. The situation was made worse because of the lack of police in the ground. Word had reached us in the press box that widespread fighting was taking place at various locations in Watford including the town centre and the railway station. The police had been diverted to deal with these disturbances leaving in the stadium stewards who were clearly out of their depth. Some Watford fans who found the provocation too much left their seats in the Rookery End and ran on to the perimeter of the pitch. Stewards did their best to keep the two opposing factions apart but there was some fighting on the pitch. An eerie, frightening and uncertain atmosphere developed until after a long five or so minutes police in riot gear arrived on the scene and order was eventually restored.

I had to decide how to react to the scenes unfolding before my eyes. My initial thought was, 'I'm here to report on a football match, I don't want to give these morons any publicity unless I really have to.' Then it was announced that because of the disturbance the kick-off would be delayed by 15 minutes. That made up my mind and I realised that I would have to say something. The story was sure to feature prominently in the papers the following day and if I didn't alert the studio to what was happening, they would quite rightly question why I hadn't said anything. Reluctantly I shouted down the line 'trouble at Watford' and went on air to give a report.

The game, when it did kick off, was won 2-1 by Luton, an upset because they were in the division below Watford. Matthew Spring, with a fierce 25-yard shot into the top corner of the net, and Steve Howard scored the Luton goals that won the game. Watford replied late on through Dominic Foley.

*

Watford's performance in the FA Cup that season was in stark contrast to the League Cup exit. After a 2-0 win at Macclesfield Town in the third round, on 25 January 2003 Watford played West Bromwich Albion at home in round four. At the time West Brom were 19th in the Premier League, battling relegation and low on confidence and the Hornets took full advantage.

In 1999 Jermaine Pennant had been signed by Arsenal from Notts County at the age of 15 for £2m but he couldn't establish himself in the side. He played against West Brom having returned to Watford for a second loan spell in November 2002. He'd scored one of the goals in the victory at Macclesfield and against West Brom he showed the type of form that had persuaded Arsène Wenger to invest so heavily in him. Pennant tore into the Baggies down the right-hand side and set up Heidar Helguson for the only goal of the game in the 80th minute, a beautiful outcome for Watford and by extension for me. West Brom had looked beatable from the off and Watford players and supporters immersed themselves in the game and forgot about all the off the pitch tribulations.

The income from the FA Cup run would help towards stabilising the finances and on 15 February the team advanced one stage further. For the second round in succession Watford were drawn against a side struggling in the Premier League, this time Sunderland who finished the season bottom, one place above West Brom.

Sunderland had sacked Peter Reid in October 2002 and, with Howard Wilkinson now in charge, they were a shadow of the vibrant, positive side I had seen beat Watford twice in the Premier League in 1999/2000. Only 26,916 turned up to see the fifth-round tie at the Stadium of Light. The belief was gone and Watford beat a hesitant Sunderland 1-0. Even Kevin Phillips, who'd scored in both the Premier League games between the two clubs a few years previously, could not conjure up a goal despite providing Sunderland's main attacking threat. Midway through the second half Watford benefitted from referee Mike Dean deciding to award a penalty for a challenge on Helguson and then ruling that Tommy Smith's spot-kick should be retaken when Thomas Sørensen moved off his line before making a save. Smith held his nerve and this time fired the ball home off the post.

Ray Lewington was beaming when I interviewed him after the game. I asked what meant more, the money the club would earn by extending the cup run or the win itself. He answered, 'I'm sure that the chairman would say the money but for me it's the win that's most important.'

Another Smith goal and a wonderful 20-yard Stephen Glass free kick gave Watford a 2-0 quarter-final win over Burnley on Sunday, 9 March. Lewington's demeanour afterwards was incredulous. I was delighted to be able to say to him, 'Ray, it's your first season as Watford manager and you're in the semi-finals of the FA Cup!' A big smile spread across his face and in a manner that suggested he was struggling to believe it was really happening he said, 'I know!' It was great to be able to share these moments of triumph with the Watford manager. At around this time a remix of 'Can You Dig It?' by the Mock Turtles, a catchy little ditty, was released. Hearing it being played at the ground after the win over Burnley I thought to myself, 'I sure can.'

I felt that Lewington was more suited to working at a moderately sized club in Division One than his predecessor Gianluca Vialli, who had previously always dwelled in the upper echelons of the game and for me did not really 'get' Watford.

Ray was working in very different circumstances to Vialli and his financial remit was to save money rather than spend it. He was a real down-to-earth football man and he earned respect for the way he rolled up his sleeves and went about the job. He reminded me of Glenn Roeder and was a pleasure to interview. The FA Cup run was a fitting reward for his efforts.

The week before the semi-final against Southampton I drove up the M1 and across the Pennines to cover Burnley v Watford in Division One. Before the game Watford had drawn three and lost six of their previous nine league matches. Michael Chopra, signed on loan from Newcastle United in March 2003, made five appearances in the league for Watford, four starts and one from the bench, and he scored five goals. The first four of the goals came in a wonderfully insane 7-4 win at Turf Moor, Chopra's second appearance in a Watford shirt. The Hornets were 5-4 up at half-time before Chopra added two more to the brace he had already scored in the first half. Gareth Taylor hit a first-half hat-trick and ended up on the losing side.

Watford had reached the semi-final of the FA Cup, for the fourth time in their history, without conceding a goal. Southampton were, however, a different proposition to the two Premier League sides Watford had already beaten in the run. The Saints were having a good season and they finished eighth in the top flight. In James Beattie, who scored 23 league goals, they had a prolific striker who was on form. At Villa Park Southampton were particularly dangerous down the left flank through full-back Wayne Bridge and midfielder Chris Marsden. It was Marsden who set up the opening goal just before half-time with a cross clipped on to the head of Brett Ormerod. Southampton had more quality in and around the box but Watford displayed the spirit and resolve typical of them under Lewington. Glass came desperately close to an equaliser in the second half before Southampton doubled their lead when Ormerod sent the ball into the six-yard box and Paul Robinson, under pressure from Beattie, bundled it into his own net. Watford kept going and right near the end Marcus Gayle, by now converted to a centre-back from his regular position as a striker, pulled a goal with a looping header inside the far post from a corner.

Despite Watford performing admirably the defeat hit me hard. They had previously only competed in Europe once in their entire history, in the UEFA Cup in 1983/84 under Graham Taylor, but I'd already started dreaming of heading off to exotic locations the following season to report on the club's second European adventure. I felt deflated, empty and bereft following the FA Cup exit.

It was a good lesson in the futility of expectation.

*

Those feelings were well behind me as 2003/04 approached. Pre-season cleanses the soul washes away the tribulations of the previous campaign. Watford had performed commendably in 2002/03 given the financial circumstances. The FA Cup run had added spice to a solid 13th-placed finish in Division One, although even after the worst of seasons I could always find reasons why the next one would be better.

One reason for looking forward to Watford's 2003/04 campaign was Jimmy Davis. Jimmy had been at Manchester United as a professional since August 1999. He played four games on loan at Royal Antwerp in Belgium in 2001 and later the same year, on Monday, 5 November, he started for United alongside his mate Danny Webber in a 4-0 defeat at Arsenal in the third round of the League Cup, his only senior appearance for the club. He played for England at under-16, under-18 and under-20 levels and in August 2002 he joined Division Two side Swindon Town on a three-month loan. He made a big impression in his time at the County Ground, scoring three goals in 15 appearances. Swindon were keen to extend the loan but Alex Ferguson insisted that he return to Old Trafford. Town manager Andy King described Davis as 'an inspiration on and off the field', saying, 'Jimmy's attitude, enthusiasm and desire on the training ground has been wonderful.'

Jimmy had enjoyed playing first-team football and wanted more and on 8 July 2003, after signing a three-year contract with United, he joined Watford on a season-long loan. The move was made even sweeter because Webber, having previously played for Watford on loan, joined permanently from United in the summer of 2003. Lewington was delighted to have acquired the services of Davis and he gave him a game at the first opportunity. On 9 July Jimmy scored as Watford beat JJK Jyväskylä of Finland in a pre-season friendly. Jimmy played in four more friendlies, scoring once more, in a 3-0 win over Aldershot Town. In the last of those games, against Queens Park Rangers, Jimmy injured his groin which ruled him out of Watford's opening Division One fixture at home to Coventry City, scheduled for Saturday, 9 August.

I hadn't seen Jimmy play myself but I was well aware of the buzz surrounding his arrival and I made sure that he was one of the players I interviewed at the pre-season press day. Every player relishes the prospect of a new season and before a ball has been kicked anything is possible. The loan move to Watford was just right for Jimmy at that stage in his career. He was 21 years old, he had made a big impression in Watford's pre-season and he now had the opportunity to play regular first-team football in Division One. He had everything going for him; he couldn't wait to get started and I couldn't wait to see him play. When I interviewed him sitting in the Rous Stand on a glorious summer's day his enthusiasm and sense of anticipation left me with a big smile on my face.

I turned up at Vicarage Road for the Coventry game at about midday. It was another gorgeous day, I would be reporting on a Watford match for the first time in a few months and I felt good. Then as I made my way to the ground my phone rang. It was my mate Nick London who by this time was working for Sky Sports, who had sources which meant that they often obtained information before other outlets. Nick's voice was grave. At that stage details were sketchy but a Watford player had been involved in some sort of accident. As I walked down Occupation Road carrying my bag of broadcasting equipment, I passed a door which led down to club offices. I would normally walk past the door without a second thought on my way to the media entrance where I would have a jovial chat with the stewards – which today would have been longer than usual because we had a whole summer to catch up on and a new season to look forward to – and then make my way to the press room. But as I walked towards the door leading to the offices a club official emerged and asked me to follow her down the steps. Something was clearly very wrong. This was unprecedented, nothing like it had ever happened before and it was disturbing. I was utterly stunned when I was informed that the Coventry game had been postponed.

I made my way to the press box, set up my equipment and told the Capital Gold Sport studio as much as I knew. A written club statement was circulated to the press which explained that the match had been postponed due to tragic circumstances beyond their control. Just before 3pm it was revealed that Jimmy had died. Instead of spending the afternoon giving reports on a game of football it was my duty to inform the listeners of the passing of a promising young player with an exuberant personality. Up until then reporting on matches had been pure fun for me; now I was dealing with a human tragedy.

Fuller details of what had happened emerged gradually. As his injury had made him unavailable Jimmy had asked Ray Lewington if he could return to his home in Redditch before the Coventry game, a request the manager had granted. Driving back to Watford down the M40 in the early hours of Saturday Jimmy's BMW hit the back of a lorry. He was driving over the speed limit and was over the drink-drive limit and he died instantly.

The first game I reported on that season was played the following Tuesday evening, 12 August, at Vicarage Road, a first round League Cup tie against Bournemouth from the division below Watford. Arriving at the ground there were wreaths and tributes to Jimmy everywhere. The sense of sadness was overwhelming and I thought to myself, 'That's it, you can write this season off, it's going to take a long time for the club to recover from this and to heal properly.'

For his initiation ceremony after joining Watford, Jimmy had enthusiastically sung 'Gangsta's Paradise' by Coolio. The track was played as the players walked out for the Bournemouth game and before every home match that season. Both Watford and Bournemouth wore black armbands and there was a minute's silence before kick-off.

Scott Fitzgerald scored the only goal of the game in extra time to send Watford through but they lost their first three league fixtures of the season without scoring a goal to sit rock bottom of Division One.

23

I had always assumed that Capital Gold Sport would continue forever and that I had a job for life. Eventually I would report on Watford's Champions League final victory over Real Madrid even if I needed a Zimmer frame to get to the press box. Then one day in November 2003 I received a phone call from King Darren. The news was fresh and Darren had done me the service of making me one of the first people to hear it. The 2003/04 season would be the last one in which the programme would air.

Really it was inevitable. The band had been broken up and all the original members had departed. The stoic Julian Waters on bass guitar had joined Sky Sports in 1994. Ian Crocker, who'd hit the high notes on his trumpet, moved to Sky Sports in 1997. Steve Wilson, who'd played some incredible solos on lead guitar, made the move to Radio 5 Live in the summer of 1998. Also in 1998 Rob Wotton, whose drumming had kept a steady beat which held the whole thing together, became part of the team that began Sky Sports News. Dave Clark had left with his wailing saxophone in 1998 to be part of the same project. Finally, Jonathan Pearce, who had written the songs and had been the lead singer, left for Radio 5 Live in May 2002.

A host of other really good broadcasters had passed through and gone on to have soaring careers after they left, such as Sam Matterface (Talksport and ITV), Jim Proudfoot (Talksport and Sky Sports), Phil Parry (BBC Radio London), Adam Leventhal (Sky Sports News and The Athletic), Vinny O'Connor and Phil Blacker (both Sky Sports). Even Angus Loughran aka Statto on David Baddiel and Frank Skinner's Fantasy Football show had done a stint. My old mucker Mick Conway had left in the late 1990s, going on to appear many times on Jeff Stelling's Soccer Saturday. Backing singers like Tony Incenzo, Deano Standing, Jamie Hill and me were still there but the stardust had disappeared and the only course of action was to stop the music altogether. We'd become a tribute band and lost our authenticity.

That's showbiz, I guess.

*

As this was to be my last season I would have to pack in as much as I could before the curtain finally came down, and around the time I received the fateful phone call I covered a game which had more twists and turns than a road through the Himalayas. It was the game of the day in Division One and was played on 8 November 2003 at Upton Park between West Ham United and West Bromwich Albion, both relegated from the Premier League the previous season and among the favourites for promotion in 2003/04. In the 2002/03 season West Ham had gone down with 42 points, with players like Les Ferdinand, Joe Cole and Paolo Di Canio in the side. The season before that they had finished seventh in the Premier League.

Five draws in their five league games before facing West Brom made West Ham hard to beat but it wasn't exactly promotion form. The Baggies under Gary Megson had already won four times away from home in the league and were second in the table. A tricky fixture for Alan Pardew, appointed West Ham manager on 18 October and still looking for his first win since taking over.

The first half was electric, Jermain Defoe scoring a solo goal in the first minute to put West Ham one up. They were three up inside 20 minutes with Brian Deane, whose signing had received a mixed reception from Hammers fans, scoring twice on his home debut. In my preview before the game, I had talked about the way West Ham were widely perceived throughout football as a club that produced sides capable of playing mesmeric, off-the-cuff football but lacked the ruthlessness to win trophies. They provided entertainment for the neutral and their own fans who seemed to have just about got used to and accepted the frustration following them sometimes caused.

All of that was evident in abundance in the way the West Brom game played out. A mix-up involving David James and Christian Dailly let in Rob Hulse to pull one back, then the striker fired an excellent left-footed shot into the top corner from long range for his second goal before, just as half-time approached, Defoe was sent off for a lunge on Sean Gregan. With West Ham 3-2 up and down to ten men, I said in my half-time report, 'Anything can happen here.'

Even though they were leading, West Ham's belief that they could win the game seemed to disappear in the second half and they conceded the initiative. Deane sliced the ball into his own net from a corner for the equaliser, then the winning goal summed up West Ham's afternoon. In the 77th minute a Jason Koumas shot from just outside the box was deflected up in the air. James came out of his goal to round about the penalty spot but with bodies in the way he could only punch the ball a couple of yards into the air. Second-half sub Lee Hughes, with his goalscorer's instinct, was in exactly the right place to volley home to win the game to the disbelief of just about everyone in the stadium.

In the press room afterwards, Pardew was subdued and as stunned as anyone as we all tried to make sense of what we had just seen. It was difficult to comprehend how a team could have been so brilliant and commanding for the first 20 minutes and then collapse so completely. The only explanation I could offer was that this was West Ham, an intrinsically bewitching and beguiling club. It's West Ham innit. Pardew insisted that lessons had to be learned and West Ham did go on to reach the play-off final that season where they lost 1-0 to Crystal Palace.

The win at Upton Park took West Brom to the top of Division One and they boing-boinged back to the Premier League that season, going up automatically behind Norwich City, to continue their period as a 'yo-yo club'.

*

The 2003/04 season was a nervy one for Watford as they were in a relegation battle for most of it. They moved out of the bottom three in mid-October 2003 but hovered just outside most of the time until April 2004. Then they managed to find some form and pick up points at just the right time. Two huge wins in three days at Easter, 2-1 at home to Crewe Alexandra and 3-2 away at Burnley, moved them on to 50 points, at the time generally considered to be about the required number for safety, although at the end of the season Walsall actually went down with 51 points.

The week after the Burnley game I rocked up at Rotherham to cover one of my last Watford away matches for Capital Gold Sport. There was a poignant moment before kick-off which meant a lot to me. I had been to Millmoor before and, in common with every ground I visited to report on matches, I had always received a warm and friendly welcome. Millmoor had its quirks and eccentricities, one of which had been that previously the press box had been located in a Portakabin on top of one of the stands. The seats with the best views were reserved for local reporters. Visitors like me were allocated a seat from which the pitch was partially obscured by a wall in the Portakabin. If the ball went down the far end, I would have to lean forward to see what was happening which was fine, to me it only added to the charm of the experience.

By the time I turned up for Rotherham v Watford on 17 April 2004 the press box had been moved to the stand, affording me an unobscured view of the whole pitch, which was great. It was what happened as I sat in the press box waiting for kick-off which made such an impression on me.

When I was at a ground to report on a game there was not much time to think about eating or drinking, particularly before kick-off. There would nearly always be some refreshment at half-time, squeezed in between giving my report and the start of the second half. Soup was my favourite because it was both a drink and a meal but a strong, hot cup of tea was always very welcome and if there was a sandwich as well then that was a feast.

What happened at Millmoor was on another level and blew my mind. Once I was in my seat and the show had started on Capital Gold Sport at 2pm I wasn't going anywhere until half-time. I didn't entertain any thoughts of receiving sustenance of any kind before then. In a development which took me completely by surprise, seemingly out of nowhere at about 2.15pm piping-hot steak and kidney pies suddenly appeared and were passed along the row of reporters so that I didn't have to move a muscle to receive and enjoy the succulent delicacy. It was a supreme gesture and, as I was nearing the end of my time working for Capital Gold Sport, I interpreted it as some sort of ceremony to signify that I had at last been accepted into its midst by the unofficial body of football commentators and reporters.

The game ended in a 1-1 draw, a Bruce Dyer header cancelling out Martin Butler's early opener, to extend Watford's unbeaten run to four. In midweek Lee

Cook was the match-winner as Watford came from behind to win 2-1 at Millwall. Danny Dichio gave the Lions, who had a forthcoming FA Cup final against Manchester United on their minds and were chasing a play-off place which ultimately proved to be beyond their grasp, the lead in the 16th minute. Millwall gave Watford a football lesson in the first half, with Dennis Wise dominant in midfield, Darren Ward solid at the back and wide players Peter Sweeney and Paul Ifill regularly skinning their full-backs Paul Mayo and Chris Baird. There was a complete turnaround in the second half with left-winger Lee Cook inspired. Cook sent in a cross which Paul Devlin headed on for Bruce Dyer to equalise and then hit the winner with a scintillating 18-yard shot. The win moved Watford on to 54 points, not yet mathematically safe but almost.

The game at Vicarage Road the following Saturday was a carnival and evoked memories for me of one played nearly 32 years previously almost to the day.

On Saturday, 29 April 1972 Norwich had played at Vicarage Road, and I'd attended as a 16-year-old Watford supporter. It was the final game of the 1971/72 season for both clubs. Founded in 1902, Norwich joined the Football League in 1920. A 2-1 win at Leyton Orient on 24 April 1972 had earned Norwich, managed by Ron Saunders, their first promotion to the top flight. They needed a point at Watford to clinch the title. Thousands of Norwich supporters congregated in the Vicarage Road end hoping to see their team make history. As I was standing with friends in the Rookery End waiting for kick off many of the away fans decided to leave the Vicarage Road end and try to take the Rookery. As soon as I saw them swarming across the pitch towards me my instinctive reaction – which was how I always reacted when faced with trouble at a match – was to turn and run. It was never a popular move with the hardnuts who wanted people to stay and try to fight off invaders but my main motive was self-preservation, and I didn't stop running until I reached Watford town centre. When we felt it was safe to do so we returned and paid to get into the ground again, this time at the Vicarage Road end which by now had empty spaces vacated by the Norwich supporters who had gone down the other end.

Norwich got the point they needed to go up as champions in a 1-1 draw. Dave Stringer headed a first-half opener past Andy Rankin from a Ken Foggo free kick, which was cancelled out by Ron Wigg in the second half.

There was a strong sense of déjà vu on 24 April 2004 when Norwich visited Watford in a similar position to the one they had been in 32 years previously. It wasn't the final game of the season but there were only a few left to play. As in 1972 Norwich had already been promoted, which meant a return to the Premier League after an absence of nine seasons. They were top of Division One, a position they had occupied since December 2003, and were again closing in on the title. Norwich had won their previous five league games and nearly 5,000 of their supporters in the Vicarage Road end were ready to celebrate in the spring sunshine. This time they were content to remain in their allocated positions and there was no pre-match pitch invasion.

One of the beauties of a football league is that it's generally acknowledged that at the end of a season the best team finishes top. I'd seen a lot of Division One football in 2003/04 and Norwich looked to me the best of the bunch. They were a good team, with Darren Huckerby the outstanding individual. They played controlled and measured possession football and were 2-0 up just after half-time. Damien Francis finished off a good move for the first, then Leon McKenzie deflected in a Kevin Cooper free kick. Seemingly thinking that they had the game won Norwich relaxed a little. Dominic Blizzard, on as a substitute for his first taste of first-team action, pulled a goal back and Sean Dyche and Bruce Dyer both had shots that cracked the woodwork without going in. Norwich went on to win the Division One title.

*

By the time I took my place in the press box to report on a Watford game for the final time for Capital Gold Sport, the Hornets had achieved their objective for the season and were safe from the threat of relegation. It was at home to Reading, who needed a win to have a chance of finishing in a play-off place, and was played on Saturday, 9 May 2004. Reading were motivated but well beaten. Ray Lewington spent much of the second half applauding his side's attacking play as Watford carved out a bucket load of chances, and the only goal of the game was scored by a player who promised much for the future. Ashley Young, who had come up through the academy, had made his first start for the club in a 1-0 second round

League Cup defeat at Bristol City on 23 September 2003. He had yet to make a league start and against Reading he came on as a first-half substitute for Lee Cook after 19 minutes. Just before half-time Young's low shot through a crowded penalty area deceived Reading goalkeeper Jamie Ashdown and bobbled off the post into the net.

*

Capital Gold Sport had one more Saturday to broadcast and I was given a peach of a game to cover which took me full circle back to the first professional side I'd ever seen play. In 1960, six years before I saw them trounce a Singapore XI 6-0, Fulham, inspired by Johnny Haynes, had finished tenth in Division One, their highest top-flight finish. On Saturday, 15 May 2004, the final day of the 2003/04 Premier League season, Fulham visited the Reebok Stadium knowing that a win over Bolton Wanderers would guarantee that they would better that achievement. Plenty for me to think about as I drove to the game, on the way paying to sit in a traffic jam on the M6 toll road. When I recounted this experience to Gary O'Reilly in the press room before kick-off he told me that I was being a grumpy old man.

Both Bolton and Fulham had been tipped for relegation before the start of the season and both had dramatically overachieved. Bolton went into the game on the back of five straight league wins, making them the form side in the Premier League, knowing there was the possibility of a top-six finish.

Fulham had a lot going for them at the time. They were poised to return to a refurbished Craven Cottage the following season, having shared Queens Park Rangers' Loftus Road, and Chris Coleman's first full year as a manager had been a big success. Meanwhile, Sam Allardyce was manager of a Bolton side which finished in the top eight in the Premier League for four successive seasons beginning in 2003/04. Neither Bolton nor Fulham were fashionable clubs but both starting line-ups that day featured quality players, many of whom achieved great things elsewhere.

For Bolton, Spanish defensive midfielder Iván Campo had played in the Real Madrid team that had beaten Valencia 3-0 in the 1999/2000 Champions League final; attacking midfielder Jay-Jay Okocha played 73 times for Nigeria including in the World Cup finals; and the attacker Youri Djorkaeff's 82 France caps included a start in the 1998 World Cup final when his corner was headed in by Zinedine Zidane for the second goal in the 3-0 win over Brazil. Aiding these exotic foreign players, Kevin Nolan scored nine Premier League goals from midfield in 2003/04 and Kevin Davies the same number as a striker.

For Fulham, the previous season Edwin van der Sar had caught my eye with a commanding display in a 3-0 win over an admittedly poor Sunderland side at the Stadium of Light; Steed Malbranque had contributed creativity and six goals to help the club arrive in the position they were in on the final day of the season; and Portugal international Luís Boa Morte was somewhat inconsistent but in 2003/04 had his best season for Fulham, scoring nine times in the Premier League.

With so much creative talent on the pitch the omens were good for an entertaining game and it didn't disappoint. Fulham soaked up pressure, with Davies missing a trio of good chances and Okocha hitting the bar with a free kick, and caught Bolton on the break. In an inspired selection decision Chris Coleman had recalled Brian McBride for only his fifth Premier League start of the season. It was a move which proved decisive as McBride turned out to be the match-winner. Just before half-time he headed in a far-post Boa Morte cross and late in the second half the American slotted in a ball from Malbranque.

It was 2-0 to Fulham, game over and so almost was my time as a Capital Gold Sport football reporter.

The win for Fulham meant that they had achieved their highest top-flight finish, ninth in the Premier League, with Bolton finishing one place higher. All that was left for me to do was give presenter Andy Burton and the listeners the news, which delighted regular Capital Gold Sport pundit Tony Gale, who played nearly 300 games for Fulham as a defender between 1977 and 1984 and was also working that day.

24

After hanging up my microphone I didn't find it easy to transition back to being a football supporter.

There had been so much to enjoy about being a reporter for Capital Gold Sport for 13 years and for Charing Cross Hospital Radio and Sportsvox for two years before that. All I had to do was turn up at the ground a few hours before kick-off and a press pass would be waiting for me. I would receive a free matchday programme and hospitality before the game, at half-time and after the final whistle. There would be the opportunity to engage and swap information with local reporters who followed their club closely and were keen to find out about developments at whatever club I was reporting on. There was usually a good view from the press box and reporting on a match meant that I watched it in a different way, more intently, knowing that I would have to describe the action and provide context at various points in the show. It was essential to make sure I didn't miss anything crucial, and a game can turn on an incident which takes place in a split second. At Capital Gold Sport it was great being part of a team of football-lovers dedicated to providing the best possible coverage of London football and to have the honour of providing information about my Watford to a wide audience.

Of course, I did my preparation but for me one of the great joys about watching football is that it is inherently unpredictable and you never know what is going to happen, and when you're reporting you have to be ready for anything and respond immediately. People would drink in what they heard on Capital Gold Sport and I used to love the idea that the programme would boom out in barber shops, taxis and across markets all over the south-east of England, keeping people up to date with what was taking place around the country in real time.

The adrenaline rush was intense. After I had finished reporting for the day and was making my way home, I would experience a feeling of extreme wellbeing. The endorphins and dopamine must have been flying around in my brain like crazy to give me such a natural high. When the show had gone well and I had played my part I slipped into a paradisiacal state. The world was still out there with all its suffering, war, disease, famine, violence, lies and deception but for a while, until I came down and returned to reality, none of it touched me. There was still evil in the world when I was in that elevated, unreal state but for a couple of blissful hours until reality returned, I entered a different realm and floated in a bubble above and beyond it.

After I'd finished working as a reporter, I started going to the occasional Watford game, usually sitting in the Lower Rous Stand at Vicarage Road with a view of the side of the pitch. The experience was often depressing because it seemed to me that the main aim of quite a few supporters was to hurl abuse at the assistant referee when they disagreed with their offside decision and for a while, I felt detached.

Gradually though I rediscovered the joy of being a Watford supporter. An ongoing debate I have with myself which I haven't resolved is whether I am a football follower first and a Watford fan second or the other way round. Logically football should come first because without football there would be no Watford, whereas without Watford there would still be football. Football is the form and Watford FC is a manifestation of the form.

I am not sure my relationship with football and Watford is as simple and clear-cut as that though and I don't know if I want to explain it away logically and dispassionately. If I was to do so it might lose some of its magic and mystery.

On one level I see supporting a football club as being a bit like doing a PhD in that specialising in a particular club and following developments closely on a day-to-day basis enables me to go deeper and get into its life and heartbeat. For me supporting a club greatly enriches the football experience. There inevitably comes an emotional attachment which over the years has caused ecstasy and fulfilment and pain and suffering, and everything in between. Following a club is irrational in one sense because as a supporter I have no control over its destiny. I abandon myself to it and accept the consequences.

With time I have realised that while I want them to win there is more to watching Watford than just their results. If the result is all that matters, I may as well stay at home and wait for the end of the game to check the score. For me each match is a passage in a story that began in 1881 and every season is a chapter in that story. I choose to attend matches because I like to witness for myself first-hand what happens. Bearing in mind the level at which I played the game myself, I will always find something to admire in the performance of the team. If Watford do not win because they have not played well enough, I will give due credit to the opposition. I consider myself fortunate to be able to attend matches on a regular basis and watch the story unfold.

The Pozzo family buying Watford in 2012 saved the day for me. Shortly after they became involved, I bought a season ticket to sit with friends in my spiritual home, the Rookery End. We were treated to an unbroken run of five seasons in the Premier League and an FA Cup final.

Of course, I still retained my capacity to delude myself about Watford's prospects. After two seasons in the Premier League under Quique Sánchez Flores and Walter Mazzarri, in May 2017 the club appointed Marco Silva as head coach. It was an exciting move. Having a head coach for a season at a time was OK and Watford had enjoyed two decent seasons in the Premier League doing just that but I was hoping that someone might be found to do the job on a longer-term basis. When he was appointed, it appeared that Silva could be the man. His star was on the rise at the time. He was 39 years old and had made a promising start to his career as a coach. In his first job at Estoril, he won the Portuguese Second Division which was followed by a fifth-placed finish in the top division, which brought with it qualification for the Europa League. After leaving Estoril he moved to Sporting Lisbon and in his one season there, 2014/15, they finished third in the top flight and won the Taça de Portugal, the country's FA Cup equivalent. In July 2015 Silva departed his homeland for Olympiacos. In Silva's single season in Greece, Olympiacos secured the championship with six games left, winning a record 17 consecutive matches on the way, and they won 3-2 at Arsenal in the Champions League group phase.

Silva first came to the attention of the English public when in January 2017 he took over at Hull City, who were bottom of the Premier League. Hull's bid to avoid relegation was ultimately unsuccessful but they finished two places higher than when Silva had taken over as he oversaw a transformation in performances and results. Hull took their survival push to the penultimate day of the season and won six and drew three of the 18 Premier League matches played after Silva's appointment. One of the successes was a 2-0 home win over Watford on 22 April 2017 and his appointment at Vicarage Road just over a month later seemed something of a coup. Watford chairman and chief executive Scott Duxbury called Silva 'one of the most sought-after head coaches in the Premier League' and stated, 'His pedigree and promise speaks for itself with his achievements in top divisions elsewhere in Europe, as well as with Hull City last season.'

Watford had finished 2016/17 in 17th with 40 points, six points clear of Hull in 18th, and despite losing their last six Premier League matches they were never in danger of being relegated. The final game, a 5-0 home defeat to Manchester City in Pep Guardiola's first season as head coach, was shambolic though and supporters were keen to see whether Silva would bring about an improvement.

He provided an instant answer. With Jürgen Klopp still finding his feet at Anfield the opening fixture of the 2017/18 season was a pulsating 3-3 draw at home to Liverpool. It was clear from the start that under Silva, Watford were going to try to play on the front foot and attack teams, particularly those of roughly the same ability as themselves.

One player who was ideally suited to the type of game Silva wanted to play was Richarlison. Silva had been instrumental in bringing the highly promising 20-year-old to Vicarage Road from Fluminense just before the start of the season for £11.5m. With Richarlison as yet unable to speak English, the manager was able to communicate with him in Portuguese and convince the Brazilian youngster to turn down other offers in favour of Watford.

Richarlison had an immediate impact, making a huge contribution in the dramatic opener against Liverpool. He came on as a 49th-minute substitute for Roberto Pereyra and, with the Reds leading 3-2, from a corner in time added on at the end of the game his header was pushed on to the bar by Simon Mignolet for Miguel Britos to nod in an equaliser.

Richarlison's performance against Liverpool earned him a start in Watford's next Premier League game, away to Bournemouth. In the five seasons Watford and

Bournemouth spent together in the top division the sides were evenly matched and the most common result was a draw. The meeting on Saturday 19 August 2017 was an exception and Richarlison was the main difference. Silva was delighted with his man-of-the-match performance, describing him after Watford's win as a 'great talent'. Richarlison opened the scoring in the 73rd minute, knocking home an Andre Gray cross at the second attempt, before 13 minutes later Étienne Capoue sealed the win with a fine long-range strike.

Richarlison was providing pace, he had an ability to create chances, he was able to beat opponents, he was strong and good in the air and he offered a goal threat. He quickly became an automatic starter wide on the left in an advanced position, although in Watford's next game, at home to newly promoted Brighton & Hove Albion, he had little opportunity to shine. With Britos sent off in the 24th minute for an outrageous challenge on Anthony Knockaert, Brighton had the greater share of possession and Watford didn't manage an attempt on target as the teams played out a goalless draw.

Watford were back on the south coast for their third Premier League fixture of the season and, playing with assurance and belief, they beat Southampton 2-0. In each half Abdoulaye Doucouré and Kiko Femenía both had the confidence to try long-range strikes and both had the ability to hit the jackpot. The defensive organisation Silva had also brought restricted Saints to one attempt on target, which came in added time at the end of the game.

It wasn't good for very long under Silva at Watford but when it was good it was very good. After his first four Premier League games the team were unbeaten with two wins and two draws. They sat fourth in the Premier League on eight points, with Manchester United (ten points), Manchester City (also ten) and Chelsea (nine) the only teams above them.

Then along came Manchester City for a 3pm kick-off at Vicarage Road on Saturday, 16 September 2017. City were also unbeaten after four Premier League matches with three wins and one draw. Their most recent Premier League game had been a 5-0 annihilation of Liverpool at the Etihad Stadium. I was relishing the prospect of seeing Silva's Watford take on Pep's City. With United and Chelsea not playing that day a Watford win would have taken them to the top of the Premier League which would have been a big deal for the club. In their 136-year history

Watford had been top of the top division for one week only. That had been under Graham Taylor after a 3-0 win over West Brom (Luther Blissett with two and Les Taylor) at Vicarage Road on 11 September 1982.

To have been top of the Premier League for just one day would have been cause for celebration and discussing the possibility in row T in the Rookery End before kick-off, we convinced ourselves that Watford, rejuvenated by Silva, could beat City.

Then reality struck like a velvet hammer. The previous season Watford had beaten Manchester United and Arsenal at home but they got nowhere near doing the same to a majestic Manchester City that Saturday. The game ended in a 6-0 victory for City, who went on to win the Premier League for the first time under Guardiola. It was a complete performance; City were good in and out of possession. Every player was comfortable on the ball and everyone, even creative players like David Silva, worked their socks off to regain possession when it had been lost. City were unrelenting, at 3-0 up at half-time they had the game won but they continued to go for goals until the end and Raheem Sterling scored their sixth in the 89th minute from the penalty spot.

In keeping with their early season performances Watford didn't play badly. With the game still goalless Christian Kabasele made a brilliantly timed tackle in the penalty box to rob Sterling as he closed in on goal, found by a precise Kevin De Bruyne pass, and Richarlison headed a curling José Holebas free kick narrowly wide.

The outstanding individual performance came from Sergio Agüero, who scored a hat-trick. My sense was that Agüero scored his treble for the team and not for himself. His first goal came in the 27th minute and not for the only time against Watford I marvelled at how the 5ft 8in striker evaded much taller defenders and scored with a header, this one glanced in from eight yards out at the near post from yet another perceptive De Bruyne free kick. Time and again City got behind the Watford defence to the byline and from a Silva cut-back in the 31st minute Agüero put City 2-0 up. Agüero's cute pass in between two Watford defenders found the diagonal run of Gabriel Jesus who shot past Heurelho Gomes for City's third.

With Watford threatening to get back into the game, Nicolás Otamendi powered in a header from a Silva cross after a short City corner, then Agüero completed his hat-trick with a goal of mesmeric beauty. Kyle Walker carried the ball down the right-hand side of the pitch from inside his own half and laid it inside to the Argentinian who was some 25 yards out with plenty of well-positioned Watford defenders between him and the goal. Agüero ran at the defence and weaved in and out of four players like they were traffic cones on a training pitch then slotted an angled shot across goal which hit the far post and went in despite Adrian Mariappa's desperate attempt to keep the ball out.

Manchester City's first and third goals should have been disallowed for offside but that didn't detract from the experience of watching a team in such consummate form.

It was a sophisticated, polished, tactically aware City performance but above all it was a team performance and for me it was a metaphor for how the human race would be if it lived up to its potential. Everyone working together, striving to achieve a common objective, all mindful of each other's needs, abilities and limitations, each contributing positively, no one seeking individual glory, the ego subjugated in favour of the collective.

Whether the human race will ever fulfil that potential is open to conjecture.

If it does, I suspect it ain't gonna be any time soon.

ACKNOWLEDGEMENTS

A big thank you to Charing Cross Hospital Radio, Sportsvox and Capital Gold Sport for giving me the opportunity.

ND - #0269 - 270225 - C0 - 234/156/15 - PB - 9781780916491 - Gloss Lamination